What Do New Teachers Need to Know?

What knowledge will make you most effective as a teacher? New teachers are often bombarded with information about the concepts they should understand and the topics they should master. This indispensable book will help you navigate the research on curriculum, cognitive science, student data and more, providing clarity and key takeaways for those looking to grow their teaching expertise.

What Do New Teachers Need to Know? explores the fundamentals of teacher expertise and draws upon contemporary research to offer the knowledge that will be most useful, the methods to retain that knowledge, and the ways expert teachers use it to solve problems. Written by an educator with extensive experience and understanding, each chapter answers a key question about teacher knowledge, including:

- Does anyone agree on what makes great teaching?
- How should I use evidence in my planning?
- Why isn't subject knowledge enough?
- What should I know about my students?
- How do experts make and break habits?
- How can teachers think creatively whilst automating good habits?
- What do we need to know about the curriculum?
- How should Cognitive Load Theory affect our pedagogical decisions?

Packed with case studies and interviews with new and training teachers alongside key takeaways for the classroom, this book is essential reading for early career teachers, those undertaking initial teacher training and current teachers looking to develop their expertise.

Peter Foster is a teacher and school leader. He has worked in state comprehensives since qualifying as an English teacher in 2010. Peter currently works to support and develop teachers across a multi-academy trust in the South-West of England. His interests include teacher development and evidence-informed practice.

'If only this book had been there for me as a new teacher twenty-something years ago. But it is here now, and I commend it to you. Peter writes so engagingly. He has a deep knowledge of teaching and a love of the profession. This is a book you'll keep coming back to throughout your career'.

> Matthew Evans, secondary school Head Teacher, author of *Leaders with Substance* and co-author of *The Next Big Thing in School Improvement*

'Starting out in teaching can be daunting; it's a steep learning curve with so many ideas to absorb that it can be overwhelming. With this book Peter Foster has used his experience to produce a superb guide through the big issues that new teachers face including cognitive science, behaviour management, curriculum development and the process of teacher development itself. Written in a punchy style with excellent summaries, great signposting to key research and further reading, and lots of grounded-in-reality case studies from practising teachers, I can see this being incredibly reassuring and useful as a reference for any new teacher – and plenty of more experienced colleagues too'.

> Tom Sherrington, author of *Teaching Walkthrus*

'This book should be owned by every trainee and early career teacher, their mentors and senior leaders responsible for CPD, although teachers at any career stage will find content of both interest and practical value. It's an incredibly rich and comprehensive text, covering a wide range of areas from behaviour, to pedagogy, to curriculum and assessment, with an evidence-informed approach and engaging, accessible style. What makes this book so unique and valuable is its approach to knowledge building – the reader is taken through not just a list of the knowledge we need as teachers, but a description of what the development of this knowledge looks like in practice. How does "how we learn" affect "how we should learn to be great teachers?" – Foster has the answers. If you read one book on education this year, make it this one'.

> Ruth Ashbee, Senior Deputy Head Teacher, Holly Lodge High School, author of *Curriculum*

'In *What Do New Teachers Need to Know?* Peter provides an evidence-informed overview of key aspects of knowledge that teachers develop. Rooted in reflections of his own experience, Peter highlights how teachers develop expertise in specific domains, from managing behaviour in a class, to knowledge of the curriculum. A practical user-friendly guide, this book is a must for teachers entering, or starting out in the profession'.

> Nimish Lad, Curriculum and Research Lead

'If you're a trainee teacher, an ECT or you work with new teachers, this book is a fantastic resource. It demystifies the process of improving as a teacher and is full of crystal clear advice. I only wish that I'd had this at the beginning of my career!'

> Nick Hart, Executive Headteacher, The Alwyn and Courthouse Federation

'This superb book sets out with remarkable clarity and credibility what any new teacher would need to know to hit the ground running in the first few years of their career. Full of evidence-informed wisdom, Foster's writing pulls no punches in challenging some of the less effective but deeply ingrained practices that exist in schools. Like any good mentor, this book takes the reader under its wing and supports them to acquire the knowledge they need to flourish, not flounder, in the classroom'.

Andrew Percival, Deputy Headteacher, Stanley Road Primary School

'In his introduction, Peter Foster explains that this book is a manual for improvement, based on the knowledge we need as teachers to improve. This theme is woven throughout the book, and Peter explores themes such as memory, expectations of students and subject knowledge, sharing research in an accessible way to help teachers understand the "why". The practical strategies and case studies which are embedded in every chapter are incredibly helpful – everything from how to manage your time, to approaching development through problems is explored. I found this book inspiring, relevant and full of knowledge that I wish I'd had access to in my first few years as a teacher. This is a highly recommended read for anyone who wants to become a better teacher'.

Rachel Ball, Assistant Principal, Co-op Academy Walkden

'Peter Foster has created a playbook for new teachers. Rather than suffering a baptism of fire in their early years of teaching, informed predominantly by trial and error, colleagues can feel equipped by the core mechanisms that underpin highly effective teaching. This book is the wise colleague in the staffroom, sharing not just what works, but the rationale behind it. I highly recommend a copy for any teacher seeking to understand the fundamental components of classroom preparation and practice better'.

Kat Howard, DRET Teaching School Hub Director, author of *Stop Talking about Wellbeing* and co-author of *Symbiosis: The Curriculum and the Classroom*

'This is a terrific book which both summarises and preserves the essence of some key elements of our work. It draws on the current findings from research, making it clear that these are insights, rather than three-line whips. Some excellent examples of what the implementation of strategies look like in practice together with accounts of Peter Foster's own experiences makes this a compelling read. *What Do New Teachers Need to Know?* is an elegant book which will be a boon to all teachers new to the profession and an aide-memoire for their mentors'.

Mary Myatt, curriculum writer and speaker, Curator of Myatt & Co.

What Do New Teachers Need to Know?

A Roadmap to Expertise

Peter Foster

Routledge
Taylor & Francis Group

LONDON AND NEW YORK

Designed cover image: © Getty Images

First published 2023
by Routledge
4 Park Square, Milton Park, Abingdon, Oxon, OX14 4RN

and by Routledge
605 Third Avenue, New York, NY 10158

Routledge is an imprint of the Taylor & Francis Group, an informa business

British Library Cataloguing-in-Publication Data
A catalogue record for this book is available from the British Library

ISBN: 978-1-032-25047-2 (hbk)
ISBN: 978-1-032-25048-9 (pbk)
ISBN: 978-1-003-28130-6 (ebk)

DOI: 10.4324/9781003281306

Typeset in Melior
by KnowledgeWorks Global Ltd.

Contents

Part 5: Subject knowledge

Part 6: Knowledge of students

Introduction

I didn't enjoy teaching to start with.

I had enjoyed training at university. Teaching as a cyclical process where you go into school and then retreat into a kind of group therapy with other trainees, that was fine. Returning to university to swap horror stories or compare scars, we'd only be vaguely aware of why we'd returned at all. Days like these extended into the evening, with a large group of us on a large table at the back of the nearest pub. For a moment, the dread of teaching *that* class receded. For a moment, it felt like Monday morning wouldn't be so bad.

My dread of Monday morning stemmed from this feeling that teaching was something you just had to figure out, a blisteringly frustrating game of Snakes and Ladders where every triumph was followed by setback. The idea that teaching is something you basically explore on your own (or with a group of other novices in the pub) and not a domain you can study, practise and refine is incredibly unhelpful. For so long, I was striding forwards before falling back without any real knowledge of *how* I was improving or could improve, or what I was getting so wrong. My brain was embarrassingly disengaged from the path I was taking and the improvement I was making.

At the start of your career, I want to make it clear that whilst it won't be easy, it can be easier. Starting to teach is difficult. Becoming a good teacher takes work. How then do you go from novice to expert teacher? The purpose of this book is to offer an answer to that question. But it's important you know what this book will and won't do and what it can and can't do. It isn't a survival guide. It isn't full of tips and tricks. The knowledge this book points to isn't the bland contents of policy documents or basic staffroom trivia. This book doesn't try to do or be those things because something else is far more valuable. Teacher expertise isn't based on and doesn't emerge from those things. What, then, is it based on?

DOI: 10.4324/9781003281306-1

At the risk of giving away my main points before you've left the introduction, teacher expertise is founded on the following principles:

- Expertise requires vast webs of interconnected knowledge.

- This knowledge includes *know-that* (of substantive concepts and ideas) and *know-how* (of processes and skills).

- New teachers should focus on the retention of knowledge and the automation of process to rapidly develop proficiency.

- Developing vast quantities of knowledge and automating processes reduces the strain on our mental capacities.

- In turn, we can reinvest these capacities in solving new problems or tackling more complex versions of existing problems.

Ultimately, *expertise is the application and creative use of knowledge to solve complex problems.* That might sound like a basic definition. It might sound like it's missing something. Whilst there is much to unpack, knowledge is what drives our journey towards expertise. An investment in knowledge is an investment in the teacher you are becoming. Every time we develop knowledge of curriculum or students or classroom craft, we are making life for future-us a little bit easier. But importantly, we are also making ourselves more effective teachers; we are upgrading our capacity to cope with new challenges.

To clear the fog engulfing your development, we're going to map the thinking teachers do from expert to novice. I hope, more than that, this book will guide and prompt thought, making clearer a future where expertise, whilst elusive, is within reach. That said, it is not possible in a single volume to bullet point, list or explain everything teachers need to know. *Cop out*, you cry. *That's literally the name of the book!* Bear with me. You won't find lists of subject content to memorise, nor will you have every pedagogical concept explained to you. Instead, each section of the book will offer a framework within which to build your knowledge as a new teacher. At times, the following chapters will provide useful things for new teachers to know and understand. More often, you will be directed to consider your development in light of research into and experience of different facets of teacher knowledge.

I've tried to write in a logical order but the parts of the book can be dipped into depending on what you're thinking about and working on in any given week. Teacher development is not linear. Much like those books I read as a child, you can choose your own adventure. Just don't, as I did, flick forwards and back without committing. And, if you're not sure where to start, start at the beginning.

Part 1 argues the case for a knowledge-based view of expertise. We'll go on a whistle-stop tour of expertise research, consider memory and practice before looking at what all this knowledge is for.

In Part 2, how teachers improve and learn is the focus. Before we look at types of knowledge, we must understand how an individual travels from novice to expert. We'll focus our attention on how what we know and can do are retained in long-term memory.

That ever-present concern of the new teacher – behaviour – is our focus in Part 3. From planning to policy, from classroom to consequences, building a foundation of solid behaviour is our goal.

Pedagogy is the thinking behind teacher behaviour and action in the classroom. Rather than unpack every possible strategy, Part 4 gives principles, based on the available evidence, for how to make pedagogical decisions.

Part 5 gets to the heart of *what* we teach: our subject or subjects. To many, this is the most important aspect of teacher knowledge. Part 5 explores different kinds of subject knowledge and what we need to know about our subjects to be effective. Beyond the background knowledge, Part 5 explains how we identify and refine our subject knowledge for classroom explanations, models, questions and tasks.

If you're concerned we've left them out, students are the focus of Part 6. In particular, Part 6 provides tools to navigate a tension between what we can know about students and what we can't.

Although I wrote lots of this book alone in a frenzy in my kitchen, I had someone – like you – in mind. You might be looking ahead with excitement or trepidation to your first teaching placement. Your first lessons might have been a great success or already fallen flat. You might be anxious about the lessons for the coming week. Whatever your starting position, it's important to remember that teaching is something we never stop working at.

I didn't enjoy teaching to start with. It's a shame it took me so long. What changed it for me was the gradual realisation that teaching was something I could work on and get better at, something I could learn. My classroom, my practice, were things I could take charge of and had control over. My hope, as you read this, is that it doesn't take you as long as it took me.

PART I
The reason for knowledge

Think for a moment about knowledge teachers call on in an ordinary day: knowledge of students, of learning, of subjects, of policies and systems, of training and experience. What then do the best teachers know? Or what does their knowledge look like? To some, these might feel like strange questions. What do the best teachers *do?* seems more worthy of attention.

We spend countless hours mapping out the route for students to acquire knowledge, but rarely do the same for teachers. Maybe there isn't one route. Each teacher sets out from a different starting point; we all teach different things; we all teach different students. In offering an answer to the question *What do teachers need to know?* I'm not talking about what teachers should be 'taught' in training sessions. The intellectual life of the teacher extends beyond the relatively short periods spent in training and continuing professional development (CPD). We develop knowledge in the classroom, when we read through a set of books, when we speak to students, when we read the latest policy, when we plan a lesson or write a new scheme of work. The beating heart of teaching is understanding and applying knowledge.

Teaching is, therefore, intellectually demanding, but also intellectually rewarding. Few jobs require such creativity of thought; few require the daily adaptations and tweaks it takes to be a great teacher. A career in teaching is a career spent learning. I don't mean that in a shallow *I learn as much from them as they do from me* way. To be a great teacher, you need to refine your knowledge constantly.

I don't think anyone is angrily disputing this. You'd be hard-pressed to find an argument against knowledgeable teachers. But, frustratingly, it isn't often clear which knowledge levers to pull. Different types of knowledge vie for our attention. Whether it's subject knowledge, cognitive science or knowledge of assessment, teachers are sold different types of knowledge as solutions to the problems they are facing. Professional development also tries to change teacher knowledge, perhaps knowledge about classroom strategies or evidence-informed practice, but there is plenty of evidence that this does little to improve teacher quality.

DOI: 10.4324/9781003281306-2

Better teachers know more. They know more about what they're teaching. They know more about their classes: what the students do and don't know, what they can and can't do. They know which classroom strategies to deploy at which moment for maximum effect. If you asked them about this, they might not be able to articulate what they know. Surprisingly, being good at something often makes it harder to help someone else understand it. Novices need implicit expert knowledge made explicit if they want to improve rapidly at the start of their careers. In reading this book, my aim is that you understand the intellectual journey of the individual teacher. My hope is that the path from novice to expert, whilst not an easy one, becomes clearer for you.

If you don't buy what I'm saying – that teaching is about knowledge, that being a better teacher is about expanding your knowledge – I'm keen to persuade you. What follows is the case for knowledge. In Part 1, we'll examine the following questions:

- What is expertise and how does it develop?

- What is all that knowledge for?

- What are our knowledge best bets?

What is expertise and how does it develop?

I used to play chess with my dad. We'd take a set on holiday and sit in the sun outside our tent sending pieces back and forth. I never got particularly good at it. I'd spend anxious moments before my turn, weighing up the least-bad move, fixating on the largely negative consequences of all my options. Often, I'd knock over my king (or maybe half the board) in frustration when I realised too late the mistake I'd made. If I pause to think about it now, I can't remember my strategies in those games. I can't picture the boards. If you put a chess board in front of me now, I'd know what the pieces do but I'd be moving them, like a monkey, in a frustrating process of trial and error. Berating myself for a lack of strategic thinking, I should have been more concerned about a lack of knowledge.

This chapter is going to make three points in our case for knowledge:

1. Expertise requires the combination of two things: vast stores of relevant knowledge *and* automated processes.

2. Knowledge development overcomes the limits of working memory.

3. Practice reduces the constraints of working memory by making processes automatic.

These points are the foundation on which we build any understanding of expertise. Let's look at them in turn.

Expertise requires the combination of two things: Vast stores of relevant knowledge *and* automated processes

The path between chess and our understanding of expertise is well-worn. A couple of investigations into chess masters in the mid-twentieth century originate the idea that expertise is knowledge-based. In 1973, two researchers found that chess masters were able to reconstruct mid-game chess boards from memory in impressively short spaces of time.[1] If you put a mid-game chess board in front of them for

DOI: 10.4324/9781003281306-3

a moment, perhaps from a classic game or typical position, they'd have no trouble arranging the board from memory. Yet this result couldn't be 'attributed to the masters' generally superior memory ability' because they couldn't do the same for pieces placed randomly on the board. Chess masters weren't cognitively superior in general terms; they had the specific knowledge they needed to tackle the problem: a long-term memory full of game positions from their own experience and from classic games. If chess feels too niche, similar results have been replicated successfully in sport – where experts make a more accurate assessment of a match after a brief glimpse – and music – where experts remember melodies more successfully than non-experts.[2]

Teaching is not chess. Students, unfortunately, don't respond in predictable ways. But, if you put me in front of a secondary English class, I'd have a host of experiences and knowledge to draw upon. I'd have opening moves and possible responses. Certain processes in the lesson would be performed automatically, which would help free up space in my head to deal with whatever was thrown (hopefully not literally) at me during the lesson.

Experts and novice teachers have been extensively compared and studied. Sometimes experts and novices are made to watch videos or read descriptions of lessons taught by others. Sometimes they debrief on lessons they have taught themselves. Expert teachers tend to *see the whole board*: they notice things happening around the room, the kind of things novices often miss. Like the chess masters, after a short glimpse of a lesson, expert teachers were better able to diagnose the problems with it. Novices needed longer and made less detailed judgements after being given the same glimpse.[3] Like chess masters, expert classroom teachers have a wealth of experienced situations to draw upon both to prompt and inform their understanding and action.

Kate, a secondary Maths trainee, describes starting a school-based training route.

I definitely walked in in September thinking, *Oh, I can do it. I'm doing great.* And then about October, November time, I thought, *Actually, hang on a minute. There's a lot here, I don't know.* So I got a little bit overwhelmed. For a while I was surviving but not thriving. I'm now aware of what I don't know and I'm aware of how I can action it. I'm aware of *some* of the things I don't know.

A four-step process described as Cognitive Load Theory shows us the potential differences (and similarities) between experts and novices here:

1. **Working memory – what is held within our conscious thought – is limited.** We can keep a handful of things in our conscious thought at one time. This is true of novices *and* experts. The novice teacher struggles to manage the class and explain a difficult concept because their conscious thought struggles to hold

on to the complexity of both those things at once. Why, if *everyone* is affected by the limits of working memory, doesn't the expert struggle in the same way?

2. **Long-term memory – what we've retained – is effectively limitless.** The expert teacher has a wealth of subject knowledge, knowledge of students and strategies they draw on in lessons. This knowledge might expand and change but it doesn't have to be made anew each lesson.

3. **Expertise develops as relevant knowledge is embedded in long-term memory.** This knowledge bypasses the limits of working memory because it can be recalled as a chunk. To the expert, this knowledge isn't an array of different things. It is connected. An expert teacher doesn't have to pause to consider the causes of World War I; their long-term memory contains webs of knowledge, called schema, about World War I that can be recalled in one go.

4. **Expertise develops as we develop 'high degrees of automaticity'.** When processes become automatic – embedded in long-term memory – we find another way to work around the working-memory problem. An expert teacher has automated a process for getting the students into the room, starting an activity and taking in homework; a novice may find this combination of processes overwhelming.[4]

If complex processes, like a chess game, require a significant commitment of content to memory, teachers should consider how best to retain knowledge, understanding and skill. In any given moment, a teacher might be trying to explain a topic – the water cycle, say – as well as carefully managing a teenage drama, calling on understanding of cognitive science, all whilst trying not to draw attention to the bee that just flew in at the back of the room. The cognitive demands of teaching are demands to know more and automate more. We know students need knowledge because working memory is limited, because overloading working memory stalls learning and because knowledge in long-term memory overcomes these problems. The same is true of teachers.

Some might not like this idea of expertise (knowing more, automating more). Isn't it about creativity? Or critical thinking? Or solving complex problems? It's true that knowing more and automating more don't make you a better teacher *on their own*. Knowing and automating the right things are essential when working towards expertise. Let's turn to look at those two things in turn.

Knowledge development overcomes the limits of working memory

My wife is a doctor. Once, when having dinner with some of her colleagues, they asked me, an English graduate, if a poem was *just some words on a page* or if I immediately saw *the meaning and what the writer was doing*. They were – momentarily – fascinated by the alien concept of looking at this irrational thing on a piece of paper and understanding it. Facetiously, I responded with a question about what they saw when they looked at the human body.

If we take what we know about expertise, the doctors' surprise at my ability to understand *some* poetry is really a recognition of a small amount of knowledge I have that they don't. Doctors are an interesting comparison to teachers, not because the jobs are similar – of course they are not – but because they both must develop and apply knowledge. In both teaching and medicine, the knowledge you start with in training and study is far from the knowledge you use in practice. One medical journal describes medical expertise as the process of *restructuring* knowledge, not just *expanding it*.[5] The journal describes the 'effortful and error-prone process' of taking the scientific knowledge gained in lectures and translating it – restructuring it – into case knowledge and diagnoses.

Medical students remember more about specific cases than expert doctors. Because they don't recognise patterns of symptoms to reach a quick diagnosis – like experts do – they have to recall similar cases. Medical students also think more about specific scientific knowledge than experts because experts see patterns that go beyond the information from their lectures. As they reach expertise, this knowledge changes into a series of scripts prompted by information received from patients. Teachers undergo a similar process.

Expertise is hard to see in others because it appears effortless and, at times, quite simple. Everyone knows what it's like to be in the classroom and so it's hard to recognise the process of *restructure* and *encapsulation*, an impressive alchemy that happens every lesson. Lee Shulman, a great thinker in teacher education, described it like this:

> A teacher knows something not understood by others, presumably the students. The teacher can transform understanding, performance skills, or desired attitudes or values into pedagogical representations and actions.[6]

But the teacher doesn't just *know* what students have to know or be able to do. The effective teacher uses that knowledge to shape their interaction with their students. A teacher plans, Shulman goes on:

> Ways of talking, showing, enacting, or otherwise representing ideas so that the unknowing can come to know, those without understanding can comprehend and discern... Thus, teaching necessarily begins with a teacher's understanding of what is to be learned and how it is to be taught.[7]

Practice reduces the constraints of working memory by making processes automatic

David Berliner, an expert in teacher expertise, describes two classrooms to illustrate the problems of being a novice.[8] In both classrooms, the same thing is happening:

students are coming into the room at the start of a lesson and the teacher is collecting homework. The experienced teacher moves quickly through this process, keeping track of the opening task and the homework as it's handed in. The novice struggles. Everything is effortful – taking the register, keeping track of homework, getting the lesson started without distraction. The expert had automated the process, had knowledge of it and of the class; the novice, understandably, hadn't got there yet. For new teachers, the feeling of being overwhelmed is common; it happens when 'processing demands' exceed available resources.[9]

The first time I met my first tutor group I laid out books on the desk. I checked the technology was working (it was). I carefully placed the seating plan where I could see it and use it. Two minutes before the day started, I got a message that the room had changed and I had to move to a science lab two floors down. I scooped up the books, unplugged the laptop and ran to the new room with wires, bag and paper flailing in my wake. The lesson was a disaster. The seating plan didn't work. I didn't know who anyone was. In the precious time it took to set up my laptop, a boisterous conversation had settled and was hard to shift.

Automating process takes time; you need to repeat and tweak practice regularly, preferably after receiving some feedback. Automation is about the creation of positive habits. Of course, we can also ingrain habits which make our time in the classroom harder or less effective. That journey of practice and refinement is one that happens best in supportive relationships. In those relationships, someone, often a coach, can get to know your teaching; they get to know your good and bad habits; they can help you determine the best next steps when it comes to breaking bad habits and making good ones.

In summary

A lot of attention in education is paid to those giving the feedback and those doing the coaching. This is fine; supporting new teachers is a vital task, an important responsibility. But this isn't something done *to* you. A book can't replace those coaching relationships. What it can do is show you what the intellectual life of the expert is like, how it might be different to what you'd expect and what individuals can do to develop it. As you read this book, my hope is that you are more able to engage in those conversations, in coaching relationship, and in the practice and refinement of your teaching.

We have seen how expertise is based on the accumulation of knowledge and the automation of process. Each part of this book will examine knowledge that will be useful for the teacher to know. This might be *know-that*, knowledge of concepts and ideas that will support your classroom practice. But, at times, this book will delve into what could be called *skill* or *practice* or *know-how*. Initially, you might feel that grates with the concept of *knowledge* but, as we'll see, those things are so connected in the expert's understanding of the classroom that it is impossible to separate them. Together they shape the way we perceive and then act in the classroom. That interaction of knowledge and practice is the subject of our next chapter.

Possible next steps

Each chapter will include a set of next steps. It is not the intention that you do every one of these steps. In fact, trying to do all the steps would cause the outcome we're trying to avoid: cognitive overload. The next steps should instead offer potential solutions to the problems you're facing. They offer ways to grow or apply your knowledge as you face those problems. Reading them, it might be clear what you should do or clear that, for the moment, none of these steps is right for you. Either outcome is fine as long as thought has gone into what your current priorities are and how these steps either do or don't support those priorities.

In this first section, the next steps will focus more on developing a mindset suited to teacher development. As we work through the sections, they will become more concrete.

Know your limits. Your limits are like everyone else's because everybody has to come to terms with the challenge of working memory. Hopefully, this is encouraging for new teachers setting out and trying to be better. It will be difficult. Awareness of the challenge isn't the same as knowing how to improve but understanding this challenge does define the ways you can develop. Thankfully, this also means you have a clear aim.

Notes

1 Chase, W.G., and Simon, H.A. (1973). Perception in chess. *Cognitive Psychology*, 4(1), 55–81.
2 Bereiter, C. and Scardamalia, M. (1993). *Surpassing Ourselves*. Open Court Publishing.
3 Hogan, T., Rabinowitz, M., and Crave, J. (2003). Problem representation in teaching: Inferences from research of expert and novice teachers. *Educational Psychologist*, 38(4), 235–247.
4 Sweller, J., van Merrienboer, J.J., and Paas, F.G. (1998). Cognitive architecture and instructional design. *Educational Psychology Review*, 10(3), 251–296.
5 Schmidt, H. and Rikers, R. (2007). How expertise develops in medicine: Knowledge encapsulation and illness script formation. *Medical Education*, 41(12), 1133–1139.
6 Shulman, L. (1987). Knowledge and teaching: The foundations of new reform. *Harvard Educational Review*, 57(1), 1–23.
7 Ibid.
8 Berliner, D.C. (1986). In pursuit of the expert pedagogue. *Educational Researcher*, 15(7), 5–13.
9 Feldon, D. (2007). Cognitive load and classroom teaching: The double-edged sword of automaticity. *Educational Psychologist*, 42(3), 123–137.

2 What is all that knowledge for?

Imagine you're cooking a paella for the first time. You've not done it before so you don't know the steps. You just have a kitchen full of chicken, prawns, rice and, the surprisingly expensive, saffron. Depending on your disposition, your approach will vary. You might have read the recipe through a few times and have all those ingredients measured into their own little bowls ready to be tipped into the pan. You might only realise the garlic was meant to be finely sliced when you arrive at that line of the recipe.

If you cook paella once a week for a year, you learn the steps to the point where you no longer need the recipe. You know it. The knowledge has become a series of actions you execute with ease. Your experience and knowledge also mean you can solve the problems cooking paella might pose: making sure meat and shellfish are cooked, managing the amount of stock in the pan, adjusting seasoning to the feedback from your taste buds. The phrase *I know how to cook paella* becomes interchangeable with the phrase *I can (or I am able) to cook paella*. You could conduct the same thought experiment in countless fields, with countless processes: when we say we *know* how to do anything, we're referencing – consciously or otherwise – the merging of theory and practice. Our knowledge realised for the real world becomes something else, something we'll call a mental model.

The previous chapter explained that expertise is based on the presence of knowledge in long-term memory and the automation of process. Attaining a critical mass in these two areas makes teaching a whole lot easier. Mental capacity is released because recall and execution of certain behaviour have become automatic. At this point, it would be reasonable to ask *So what?* Teaching becomes easier. This is undeniably good news but an expert isn't simply someone who finds their job easy. Our aim is not to attain a robotic journey through the school day.

What have we made teaching easier *for?* This chapter will address that question by looking at two connected concepts:

1. Mental models.

2. Progressive problem solving.

DOI: 10.4324/9781003281306-4

The two sides of the teacher development coin are mental models and progressive problem solving. Mental models are organised knowledge to support action in specific circumstances. Progressive problem solving is the method by which we continually seek to find more effective solutions to the challenges of the classroom. The mission of this book is to create mental models to enable progressive problem solving.

Mental models

What are mental models?

What do I do when...? and *What do I do if...?* are common questions for the new teacher. Understandably, there are myriad situations where the answers aren't clear. Faced with infinite possible situations, you might endlessly ask experienced teachers about every possible student behaviour. Or maybe you'll silently brood over these possibilities, painstakingly thinking through what you might do in every single one of them. Unsurprisingly, neither of these approaches will yield spectacular results. And unsurprisingly, given what you've read so far, lack of appropriate knowledge and automation are the reasons for this faltering start. Even when you 'know' the answers to some of these questions, applying the answers can be harder than it seems. What's called the knowing/doing gap means we can theoretically *understand* how we should act but the constraints of cognitive load make it difficult to do so.

Are knowledge and automation then ends in themselves? It would be reasonable to ask what we're developing towards or what we're missing when we pose those *What do I do...?* questions. The answer is a mental model or mental models of classroom practice. Mental models are 'internal representations of external reality that people use to interact with the world around them'.[1] Or, more simply, mental models are 'what someone knows and how that knowledge is organised to guide decision and action in a specialist context'.[2]

If you drive, your mental model of driving is made up of experience, knowing the rules of the road and understanding how a car works. We can have a deficient mental model – of driving or anything else – where our automated habits aren't great. We don't check our mirrors or our clutch control is poor. Perhaps we get a speeding ticket because we misunderstand the restrictions on a particular route. If you don't drive at all, your mental model of driving is built from watching others and will, understandably, be full of gaps and misconceptions.

How do we build mental models?

As a new teacher, whether you like it or not, you are building mental models of classroom practice. We create models for getting students into the room, for explanations, for questioning and class discussion, for practical demonstrations. We use these pre-constructed (or under construction) mental models to understand, plan and act in familiar situations. And these models act like knowledge we've stored in our long-term memory. New teachers struggle because they face a host of unfamiliar situations with few or no models to reference. As you experience the classroom, your knowledge of subject and theory meets your experience of teaching. In this way, a mental model is the most useful kind of knowledge a teacher can have.

In my mind, the biggest objection you might have to the *expertise is about knowledge argument* is that it appears to force you into intellectual activity which is distinct from the classroom. It could be misconstrued as a call to learn to teach by reading about it in a book. That would be like saying you learn to cook by memorising recipes or you learn to drive by passing your theory test. Recipes and theory are useful, essential even, but mainly in their application to real situations. And a book about teaching is only useful if it shapes and upgrades your mental models to help you act appropriately in the classroom.

Mental models are going to emerge with time whether we're conscious of them or not. Your job is to ensure effective models emerge. Investment in knowledge of the recipe or the theory is a good place to start if there is a clear link to practice in the classroom. Part 2 will look at how we create these models by embedding knowledge in long-term memory and automating processes. Ultimately, we build that necessary knowledge out of the classroom – subject, pedagogy, policy, principles – and marry it with our growing knowledge of practice in the classroom. A coach or mentor helps to drive this initially, offering regular direction, whilst training and study help to build knowledge.

How are mental models important for this book?

Daniel Willingham has done more than most academics to unpick how evidence should interact with the practice of being a teacher. You'll see that he crops up at various points in this book. As a cognitive scientist, much of his work deals with how the mind learns – what helps and hinders the learning process.

Given his expertise, Willingham has written on how teachers can and should develop a mental model of learning. Willingham describes a tension you will be familiar with as a new teacher: the tension between theory and practice. Teachers, particularly new teachers, want practical strategies. But, as Willingham points out when talking about learning, 'the teacher who understand the psychological principles undergirding the recommended strategies will presumably find them more sensible and will see ties between seemingly disparate strategies'.[3]

I wasn't the most studious trainee teacher during my PGCE. Looking back, I sort of thought I'd soak up understanding along the way. I wasn't seeking out the knowledge but rather waiting for it to find me. But a lot of theory existed at such a disconnect from practice that it felt difficult to understand what I had to understand. I attended a lecture on adolescence and vividly remember the one and only question asked at the end – *How should this affect what I do in the classroom?* The question was pointed because the lecture had been empty of the practical. The lecturer paused before responding, 'I'm honestly not sure'. The theory was interesting and not irrelevant but unapplicable, at least in the short term.

Mental models: From theory to practice

There's another problem with knowledge. You might feel that a book about what teachers 'need to know' sounds elitist or arrogant. Knowledge changes, is refuted and upturned. What use then is knowledge? But power lies in mental models when they speak to the truth of a practice, situation or concept *as we understand it now.* We hold these things lightly because our understanding will inevitably change, develop and expand and we should hope that it does all these things. Your mental model joins the dots from theory to practice. If those dots need re-routing because you've learned something new, that's exactly what should happen.

Your mental model of managing behaviour might include:

- Principles like *Clarity and consistency are important* or *Give take-up or wait time after giving a consequence.*
- Growing knowledge of your school's behaviour policy.
- Observations of effective (and ineffective practice).
- Initial experience in the classroom managing activities or lessons.

You need this model when:

- You're planning a lesson to ensure positive behaviour.
- You have to give a consequence to a student.
- A student responds poorly to a warning or consequence.
- A student describes an incident that happened at lunchtime.
- You're not sure whether to send a student out of the classroom for their behaviour.

You develop this mental model for and in the classroom by:

- Learning the behaviour policy inside-out.
- Watching teachers manage difficult behaviour.
- Practising the language used to give warnings and consequences in your school.
- Using the behaviour policy in lessons.
- Receiving feedback on your management of a specific aspect of behaviour (e.g. routines or giving warnings).

- Getting to know the students you teach and how they respond to your action or inaction on their behaviour.

- Gradually, figuring out what works for you through a process of focused trial and error.

The principles and theoretical knowledge are important. Faulty understanding of theory might lead you to believe that managing behaviour is about being a strict, unwavering authoritarian or a friendly counsellor. The policy also gives you theoretical understanding of *how things work here*. But principles and theory aren't enough on their own. Your mental model is honed by the application of these things. A theory that fails to get you results is not a helpful theory. Mental model creation is the testing of, as well as application of, theory.

When it comes to learning about learning, Willingham makes clear that teachers don't need a broad understanding of the academic discipline of cognitive psychology. We need to 'understand, coordinate and remember' the generalisations and observations that 'capture an important aspect of the domain' of cognitive psychology. Generalisations Willingham offers include:

- 'Practice is crucial to gaining expertise'.

- 'Probing memory improves retention'.

- 'The attended aspect of an experience will be learned'.[4]

Whilst understanding the thinking and evidence behind these generalisations will be useful, they form part of a mental model of learning that helps us when:

- Students are finding learning difficult.

- Students don't remember what we expect them to.

Again, the principles aren't enough. Such principles should work with your understanding of subject and the needs of your class to plan your lessons. You might, therefore, start to develop this mental model through your own flourishing knowledge of research on how students learn. Observation of strategies for practice and retention bring this research to life. Then, your application of principles from research is worked out practically: you try and refine something until it works for you, in your classroom and with your students. More on this in Part 4.

Speaking of a mental model of your subject or subjects is probably a little ambitious. If you're a primary teacher, the sheer quantity of knowledge, the number of mental models you have to build, is staggering. Slow and methodical work to build knowledge of the curriculum will be essential. As will a patient, long-term perspective. A secondary teacher, with subject specialism, still has work to do, as all teachers will, in shaping their knowledge for the classroom.

The role this book plays in the development of your mental models is simple. In the realms of your development, subject, pedagogy and students, it aims to get you to know, think and act to build these models. The gap between theory and practice must be bridged. Trainers, lecturers and reading all present you with ideas – theory. Coaches and mentors help you to sift it into something applicable. You consciously engage. You act and then reflect. You seek to understand and then apply. You pose questions and test answers. Be that in the realm of behaviour, learning or subject knowledge, you are developing a mental model. Don't, like me, wait to soak up that knowledge.

Progressive problem solving

What should we do with any additional mental capacity?

The more you teach, the easier and easier it gets. At a certain point, you're going to reach a plateau where it seems like there are no new problems left to solve. Reaching this plateau is not the same as reaching expertise, as if expertise is a state we reach and then stop. But we do emerge into a space where more of the job is manageable. Whilst liberating at first, this plateau becomes a groove which is hard to escape.

Taking what we know about expertise, teaching becomes easier because more of it has become automatic. Previously stretched resources now find there is a little extra capacity. In their excellent guide to expertise, *Surpassing Ourselves*, Carl Bereiter and Marlene Scardamalia offer a useful perspective on this concept of mental capacity: reinvestment.[5] For new teachers to make progress, resources gained have to be put back to use to solve new and more difficult problems. It's true that you don't really know when mental capacity has gained some space. You don't have a live gauge telling you how much space your mind has left. Reinvestment then becomes an attitude or perspective rather than a definite calculation.

What is progressive problem solving?

Bereiter and Scardamalia describe reaching the point where the novice has 'mental resources to spare'. *Surpassing Ourselves* offers two routes onwards from increased mental capacity:

● Problem reduction.

● Progressive problem solving.

Problem reduction is settling for wherever you end up when teaching has become a little bit easier. It could be captured in the thought *I don't have to worry about X anymore.* For the new teacher, this might be planning or behaviour management or giving feedback or any other problem faced so far. My argument isn't that you *should* worry about those things nor is it that you should continue to spend hours of your weekend planning even after you feel you don't need to. The problem with problem reduction is the tendency to rest in this state.

For much of my career, I made teaching easier without necessarily solving any problems. Or at least, without improving my approach to the problems of my classroom. I made marking books quicker but not necessarily more effective. I taught myself to plan my lessons using other people's resources but without scripting the most significant moments of those lessons. My point is not that we should *always* work harder or that we should feel guilty for finding a way to go home earlier. In the previous chapter, we saw how automation is a key ingredient in achieving expertise. Before we feel proud of such automation, we should make sure we haven't just settled for problem reduction.

In contrast, progressive problem solving starts with using new and additional mental capacity to pay attention 'to other aspects of the problem that previously had to be ignored'.[6] Teaching has no ceiling limiting your development. Teaching is enjoyable and frustrating because we're just peeling back layers of complexity from an infinite problem. You might have reduced the time it takes to plan lessons. Now, focus on improving your explanations. You might have sorted the entry routine so that the class comes in calmly and gets started. Now, make sure that what they're getting started on is the best use of their time. You might have got into the good habit of asking questions to the whole class (not just those with their hands up). Now, work on the habit of listening carefully to what is said and responding accordingly.

Bereiter and Scardamalia's concept of investment is useful here. Progressive problem solving is about both reinvesting mental resources into new problems you've not worked on before *and* on searching out more complex versions of problems you've already been working on. Learning to teach is beset with *new* problems: you have assessments to mark and respond to for the first time, you're introducing a new topic, you're taking on the responsibilities of a tutor.

What does progressive problem solving look like?

More complex versions of existing problems are sometimes harder to spot. Behaviour is an area with ever-increasing complexity if you look for it. It's also at the top of the list when it comes to concerns for new teachers. The progression in problem solving might look something like this:

- A new teacher might start by working on getting the attention of the class, setting activities and making sure students are focused on the task through monitoring and reminders.

- A more complex version of the previous problem involves managing a class's behaviour whilst navigating trickier processes like modelling under a visualiser, explaining a new concept or leading a discussion. Behaviour was less of a problem when students were busy but when expectations of them are raised and they have to focus on what the teacher or a peer is saying, a host of new problems emerge.

● Having made progress at managing behaviour through more complex aspects of teaching, a new problem rears its head. Students are generally well-behaved, but they don't seem motivated. The problems of managing misbehaviour have given way to the problems of promoting positive behaviour.

● Whilst all this is going on, the teacher has had their first run-ins with a couple of the more difficult students in the class. The school's behaviour system has helped and the teacher has practised using the language of choice: *If you continue to talk when I'm talking, you'll be choosing a demerit.*

● The class is settled; routines are in place. In the event that a child misbehaves, the teacher has a process they use… But there's one child none of this seems to work for. They are sent out every lesson. The school's behaviour policy allows for this but the teacher wants to figure out why it is happening and what can be done about it.

You could outline a similar progression for planning or giving feedback or for modelling an explanation as discrete components of your teaching.

How do we progressively problem solve?

Progressive problem solving can only work where you're able to identify and work on a small number of problems at any given time. Sometimes next steps are obvious; sometimes they are far from it. I want to be clear from the start that this is something you do, at least initially, with the help of those responsible for helping you: coaches and mentors, university tutors, training staff, middle and senior leaders. Usually, there will be, at least for a time, a single person who is providing you with support. What follows is not a guide to leaving those pillars of support behind. Instead, this process reflects how you interact with those people and your own development.

1. Problems with clear solutions.
   Sometimes we struggle despite knowing the solution. It might sound strange in a book about knowledge, but knowing the answer in and of itself is not enough. Whatever the answer, it needs to become embedded and automatic. Many teachers *know* they need to do something but struggle to change it. Ingrained habits, even in very new teachers, make change difficult.
   What are you trying to achieve? Maybe it's about the atmosphere of work in your classroom. Silence for short periods in the lesson could be a massive

victory you've been working to achieve. Spoiling that silence by talking over it is incredibly common. You know when you start to talk over a fragile silence or get drawn into a conversation – even a productive one – with a student too quickly, you'll lose it. You know – and you've also received feedback – that you need to shut up for a minute and just scan the class from the front. A post-it note on your desk that just says 'Be quiet' can help; a colleague at the back holding up a hand for a moment by way of reminder is also useful.

The gap between knowing and doing is traversed by automating and embedding solutions you know exist. Chapters 4 and 5 will help focus on how you can do this.

2. Problems without clear solutions.

What is a struggle for you right now? What seems like an uphill battle? These will be problems without immediately obvious solutions, or at least not ones you feel capable of implementing currently. No-one expects you to be able to solve every situation in the classroom right away. You are coached and taught and trained because you need help to understand the problems you're facing but you also need help to understand and implement the solutions.

Tension exists, therefore, between the independence of a new teacher devoting time to solving problems with unclear solutions and the direction they receive from mentors and trainers. It's true that new teachers struggling to fit in planning, assignments and rest should not devote additional time to finding and solving new problems. The struggles you're facing *are* the problems you should seek to solve first. Progressive problem solving is still a useful lens through which to view early teaching practice.

It's likely you'll be receiving coaching regularly. This coaching is designed to help you arrive at actionable next steps to help you improve. In a way, coaching gives you solutions to problems you may have been unaware of. You could feasibly wait for feedback and improve by responding to this as you receive it. But *just* seeing your development this way is likely to lead to a complacent fatalism where improvement is dependent on waiting for feedback.

In summary

Whether we're accumulating knowledge in the lecture theatre, the classroom or the staffroom, we're building mental models. These mental models are frameworks of knowledge to support and guide our actions in the real world. Understanding mental models helps us understand why knowledge is important (and begin to understand *which* knowledge is important). We build knowledge that faces the problems of the classroom. We build knowledge to solve those problems but also to make it easy to solve new problems or more complex versions of the ones we've already tackled.

Equipping a new teacher, or any teacher, with the tools to progressively problem solve is about giving them ownership over their progress. Know your job as a developing teacher: develop mental models and search for solutions to the problems you face. You aren't simply a receiver of teacher training and development. Other people can't develop *your* knowledge. The best coach in the world can't automate processes for you. Tracking the problems you're facing, however small, will give a sense of progress and control over your development.

> **Kate, a secondary Maths trainee, describes how she tried to solve some initial problems in her classroom.**
>
> I don't think I would have got anywhere if I just sat in my own little bubble because I have a tendency to be really self-critical. So I just knew, *I have to talk to other people and use their expertise.* Particularly, to ask them questions. *What am I doing well? What could I do better? How would you teach that group? How would you teach that topic?* That's helped the journey, talking to people around me.

Possible next steps

Know your aim. The aim of experts-in-training is knowledge and automation. Through these things, we overcome the limits of working memory. Knowing lots or automating a lot doesn't necessarily make you an expert. You can know irrelevant things or automate processes poorly. Expertise requires these things to flourish. Part of our challenge in the sections that follow is to define the expert knowledge of the teacher and look at ways we can develop it.

Notes

1 Jones, N.A., Ross, H., Lynam, T., Perez, P., and Leitch, A. (2011). Mental models: An interdisciplinary synthesis of theory and methods. *Ecology and Society*, 16(1), 46.
2 Mcrea, P. (2017). What do expert teachers need to know? Ambition Institute. www.ambition.org.uk/blog/what-do-expert-teachers-need-to-know/ (accessed 16/02/2022).
3 Willingham, D. (2017). A mental model of the learner: Teaching the basic science of educational psychology to future teachers. *Mind, Brain and Education*, 11(5). doi:10.1111/mbe.12155.
4 Ibid.
5 Bereiter, C., and Scardamalia, M. (1993). *Surpassing Ourselves*. Open Court Publishing.
6 Ibid.

3 What are our knowledge best bets?

I've visited the opticians for pretty much as long as I can remember. The optician's favourite question tends to be, 'Is your eyesight better like *this* or like *this?*' as they change the lenses in the mechanical monstrosity they've sat on your head. I always found this question difficult to answer. Sometimes the changes between the lenses are almost imperceptible but, as you work through them, gradually you reach a surprising level of clarity. As you develop knowledge as a new teacher, you reach a level of clarity that felt unattainable just a short time previously. But, with all this talk of knowledge, it would be reasonable to ask *Which knowledge?*

To consider 'best bets' when it comes to knowledge, this chapter is going to make four points:

1. Teaching doesn't change as much as you think.

2. Knowledge helps us to navigate the tension between theory and practice.

3. It is useful to codify *some* of this knowledge into categories or problems.

4. Categories and problems help us to focus our development.

Teaching doesn't change as much as you'd think

Not that long ago, a manual for new teachers predicted how technological advances would reshape schooling by 2015. The author asked us to 'imagine' turning up at a 'newly built school, sponsored by a local software company, on a Monday morning'. How would the dizzy technological heights of 2015 shape the teacher's day? The author suggests several changes to the average teacher's morning:

> The first thing you do is to download the homework that has been emailed to you over the weekend, along with one or two excuse messages. You check over your slide presentation that has been put together for you from your notes by the department's ICT assistant.[1]

DOI: 10.4324/9781003281306-5

Technological advances haven't simply improved the admin tasks of the teacher. The ways students learn and interact with their teachers and with each other are also irrevocably altered:

> [You] set off to greet your Year 10 tutor group who have been working on their personalised learning programme. Six of your group have registered remotely from the industrial unit where they are on a work-based learning placement. The rest of the group are busy checking the e-conference noticeboard...[2]

It's not so much that the predictions are wrong – some are close – but underlying this vision is the belief that technology would revolutionise school rather than just bring new complications. Whilst homework is now often handed in online, the idea that your department has an ICT assistant to make a PowerPoint presentation is fanciful. The writer also reveals his beliefs about what a child's education should involve and it isn't a curriculum set by a school or teacher. Students are engaged in 'personalised' and 'work-based' learning. Here, the teacher's knowledge is of technology and its uses, and perhaps the skills students need to enter the technological workplace. Knowledge of subject or pedagogy has become less important in this imagined scenario, where the teacher is more of a supervisor than educator.

School has the habit of changing a lot whilst, simultaneously, not really changing that much at all. Is this a problem? Many will bemoan the old-fashioned, ingrained approaches. Hand-wringers make easy comparisons to the Victorian's love of desks in rows and rote learning content devoid of relevance. Why aren't schools modern, like the ones described? If you think about it though, the lack of change in schooling is encouraging for the new teacher. You're entering a relatively stable environment.

When we think about the cutting-edge technology responsible for enriching our lives, we're likely to think about our newest purchases. Shiny devices we're proud to own. Economist Nassim Nicholas Taleb offers an alternative view.[3] The technology we treasure will soon be out of date, in need of an upgrade, and new and shiny ideas will soon be replaced by newer and shinier ones. Anti-fragility, Taleb explains, is the concept by which disorder and pressure strengthen a system, idea or person. Fragile things break under pressure. Robust things cope under pressure. Anti-fragile things become stronger as pressure is applied. A knife and fork, or the wheel, are anti-fragile technologies, particularly when compared to the technology we use which will be soon out of date. They have endured the pressures of time and remain useful. In some cases, we've found new uses for them or designs have improved with age. In contrast, the laptop you used five years ago is probably rage-inducingly slow and liable to turn itself off if you expect too much from it.

What does this have to do with our best bets for teacher knowledge? Ideas are like technology. Taleb contends that 'the old is superior to the new', at least in its power to work long after newer ideas are dropped. Subject distinctions, sitting children at desks, explaining things to a class, having students answer questions and complete tasks, rules and order can all feel outdated, a landscape ripe for revolution. But we erase what already exists in teaching at our peril. Teaching does change but the core tasks and activities of the teacher remain largely static. The aim of teaching is naturally progressive – social mobility, changed minds, broadened horizons – but the activities of teaching are largely conservative (with a small c) – the passing on of knowledge, inducting students in the traditions and norms of a society, defining and exploring subject domains, preparing students for the world of work. These activities imply the jobs and tasks that make up the daily life of the teacher:

- Planning lessons and activities.
- Managing class behaviour so that they can complete these activities.
- Explaining concepts, tasks or examples.
- Asking questions and leading discussion.
- Helping students who are stuck or don't understand.
- Giving feedback.

And so on. Now, you might disagree with the *conservative* view of teaching. The progressive seam of education has produced some excellent thinkers who would unpick what I have said already. You might agree with Romantic philosopher Jean Jacques Rousseau that teachers should give children 'no verbal lessons' and that students should be 'taught by experience alone'.[4] Or, like giant of educational philosophy John Dewey, you might think teachers should 'never educate directly, but indirectly by means of the environment'.[5] Or you might, like anti-authoritarian Paolo Freire, be struggling with the belief that 'There's no such thing as neutral education. Education either functions as an instrument to bring about conformity or freedom'.[6]

These thinkers are worthy of our attention. They can open our minds to alternative views of teaching but generally don't offer practical advice. They offer a perspective but not the reality of day-to-day life as a teacher. They offer a revolution, describing how education *could* be, without the roadmap of how we get there. It's not that their ideas haven't shaped education. Each thinker has been influential. In some cases significantly so, but the fragility of their ideas means they are often picked up, attempted and then dropped when we realise they don't work in practice. Few schools are teaching by 'experience alone'. Lots of teachers have attempted to teach 'indirectly' – allowing students to discover content for themselves – and found it close to impossible.

Because the core activities of teaching don't change rapidly, we can alight on the knowledge best bets for new teachers. New teachers need the knowledge that helps them to carry out the role and responsibilities outlined above. You won't find any predictions about the future in this book. I'm too embarrassed about the certainty of getting them wrong. In reality, though, I'm not doing anything that different. In asking

What Do New Teachers Need to Know? we're looking at what will stand some of those tests of time.

Knowledge helps us to navigate the tension between theory and practice

It's not that you can't expect revolution from your career in teaching. Teaching might feel at odds with this apparently conservative sentiment to stick to *how things are.* You may well witness, or be an instigator of, revolution in education through your career. More likely, however, is evolution, a graduated development of what works well already and what doesn't. Therefore, because it gradually evolves, the knowledge teachers need is not ever-changing, but broadly consistent. Teachers, and especially new teachers, need to develop knowledge of their subject, of pedagogy and of behaviour management and more.

Theory is all the new teacher has to go on when starting out. By theory, I mean both the lofty ideas and evidence you're taught – a *theory* of learning – and the strategies you're pondering – how to get that reluctant but winnable Year 5 boy onside. Ideas for the new teacher are all theories to begin with. Suggestions and training about how you plan lessons or manage behaviour or lead class discussion are all theory until you practice them. Sometimes these ideas, these theories, are useful. Sometimes they aren't. But your job, in the early days at least, is to accumulate and test the theories. This is a complicated process because the classroom is a complex environment.

A theory you might be encouraged to try is *Start each lesson with an engaging 'hook' for the content.* A colleague might tell you this in passing or a lecturer might dwell on the methods of doing this. If you take this theory to mean, *do something extravagant and surprising at the start of each lesson,* you'll find the theory exhausting and unsustainable in practice. When you enter the class dressed in a toga to introduce a topic on the Romans, you notice unhappily that whilst the children find this funny, it doesn't seem to prepare them for learning. They remember the lesson when *Sir wore a dress!* but they don't remember much about the topic. You drop the theory. But perhaps your theory of *'engaging' hooks* is grounded in planning a question to intrigue students, prompting thought at the start of each lesson. You try it, noticing that these questions do help to start lessons, preparing the way for deeper thinking.

At the start of your career, it's worth focusing on knowledge building. Knowledge building includes knowledge of the theory – from lectures, training, reading and advice – as well as the practice of how these things are implemented – from observation, teaching episodes, first lessons and coaching. Preferable to going it alone, accumulating theories and testing them in practice is a valuable way of seeing your job as a new teacher. When a theory – an idea prompting a strategy to use in a lesson – doesn't work, we can go back to the source, if we have them available, and ask for clarification or support or coaching. We can reflect and refine.

Taleb describes how knowledge 'feeds on attempts to harm it'. For example, if you use a behaviour management strategy you've been taught and it doesn't work, you've gained knowledge. Perhaps, you've been told to give take-up time, a brief period for students to follow your instructions without losing face by having to do something the second you asked. You try this with a particular student but it makes things worse – they're more disruptive in the take-up time. It's easy to feel sensitive or like a failure in these moments – *I had a strategy and it failed* – but what you've experienced strengthens your understanding of that theory in practice. Take-up time could still work for you but with clearer expectations and timeframe, or it might not work with *that* student in the way it works with others. You go back to your mentor to discuss when take-up time will and won't work.

We shouldn't drop a theory, idea or strategy because it hasn't worked once. But we shouldn't work ourselves into the ground to make something untenable work. Some theories must be dropped. The purpose of developing knowledge is to find knowledge that works in practice. Too often, we're encouraged to *keep trying* to put a theory into practice, when – as Taleb notes – theories come from practice. Successful teachers are better able to recognise the balance between the two – where theory meets practice, and how they interact.

It is useful to codify *some* of this knowledge into categories or problems

If knowledge is important, which knowledge? Whose knowledge? The debate this question prompts is not new. When I was a trainee, a lecturer asked us if we wanted to teach subjects or children. To me, the question implied further questions. Do you want to be a great teacher *of children*, with a knowledge of what makes them tick, how to engage them and how to build relationships? Or do you want academic, perhaps dry, and deep knowledge of your subject or subjects? The knowingly unfair either-or entirely misses what a teacher does. A teacher takes a subject, or in many cases *subjects*, and makes it accessible and understandable *for* students.

No one is really asking you to choose and to commit to your choice. But the existence of the question troubles me. Hannah Arendt was troubled too; in her 1954 essay 'The crisis in education', Arendt worried that teaching had become 'emancipated from the actual material to be taught'. To her, teachers had come to be seen as *teachers of anything* rather than *teachers of something*, complaining that it often 'happens that [the teacher] is just one hour ahead of his class in knowledge'.

Subject knowledge

Knowledge, then, hovers in the background of teacher development – necessary but often misunderstood or maligned. Various educationalists have attempted definitions or categories of teacher knowledge, trying to make overt what is often hidden. In the late eighties, Lee Shulman[7] argued that the link between knowledge of effective pedagogy, our thinking about classroom behaviour, and subject knowledge was the 'missing paradigm' of teacher education. Lee Shulman chose to categorise teacher subject knowledge as follows:

- Content knowledge: The domain-specific subject knowledge of the teacher.

- Pedagogical content knowledge: A combination of subject knowledge and the ways to apply it in the classroom.

- Curricular knowledge: Understanding of the content and the materials of the curriculum.

In 2020, the *Great Teaching Toolkit*[8] referenced Shulman's categories of knowledge, highlighting their enduring relevance, whilst increasing the focus on the knowledge of the curriculum and knowledge of how students understand (and often misunderstand) what they are being taught. Between Shulman and the *Great Teaching Toolkit*, there are a host of studies looking at these categories: some looking at the impact of what teachers know, others examining how changing teacher knowledge changes (or doesn't change) teacher effectiveness. As we look at different categories of teacher knowledge, we'll delve into some of these studies and what they can tell us about effective and impactful teacher knowledge.

Knowledge of practice

All this talk of knowledge can feel incomplete. Content knowledge alone, you might feel, is not a priority. More concerning is *what to do* in the classroom. This knowledge of classroom craft is a type of knowledge too. Increasingly, this craft is being informed by evidence – evidence from studies in school and from the field of cognitive psychology. This knowledge of pedagogy and classroom behaviour can be broken down and sequenced; it can be taught and then practised. Evidence of this is seen in the various ways teacher behaviour has been codified.

Barak Rosenshine wrote a seminal paper, 'The principles of instruction', on the classroom actions of the most effective teachers. The *Making Every Lesson Count* series of books defines the six teacher behaviours that lead to expert teaching. Doug Lemov's *Teach Like a Champion* goes further, slicing teaching into a large set of concrete techniques whilst offering video content to emulate. A perennial criticism of these texts is that they state the obvious to the point that they aren't helpful. But this criticism fails to recognise:

- The power of getting simple things right all day, every day.

- Getting the basics right frees up cognitive capacity and enables you to tackle more complex classroom challenges.

- As Stephen Covey has said, 'common sense isn't always common practice'. Lots of teachers could benefit from attending to the simple and straightforward.

Knowledge of pedagogy or classroom craft reminds us that much of what new teachers need is a set of strategies for the classroom and a growing understanding of how to act in the classroom. These strategies form a central part of the mental models that we looked at in the previous chapter.

Lee Shulman had a novel idea for how to ensure teacher knowledge moved from the theoretical to the practical. Much like our mental models, Lee Shulman describes 'case knowledge': 'knowledge of specific, well-documented and well-described events'.[9] Shulman envisioned case knowledge being constructed out of written descriptions or videoed sections of lessons. Case knowledge would be categorised and organised into a curriculum for new teachers, giving them concrete examples of various situations that they might encounter in the classroom, and guidance on how to manage them. Unfortunately, you're unlikely to arrive at teacher training to find a library of cases to work through.

Case knowledge points at a gap that can exist in teacher training. When we train to teach, we do a lot of background work on subject and planning and theory. Sometimes, the foreground – what actually happens in the classroom – is left to take shape over time. Whilst we might not have access to a catalogue of cases, we can build them with a proactive approach to our relationship with colleagues.

Behaviour management is a good example here. Starting out, your mental model is an almost empty space, sparsely populated with principles, ideas and a school policy or system for managing behaviour. Experienced and expert teachers have a fuller picture of behaviour management, including a richer understanding of strategies to deploy as well as nuanced understanding of how to deal with specific students. A novice mental model recognises the need to work through the school's behaviour system with a difficult Year 6 student whilst maintaining high expectations. Doing this works: the deputy head arrives to support and the student spends some time out of the lesson. An expert knows and does all this too but also knows the student. The expert knows, perhaps, that *this student* will calm down and re-enter the classroom if they are given a job to do. The teacher sends them to collect some resources from another classroom. A mental model is never finished. We add to it with our own cases and nuance based on the knowledge we are always accumulating.

The limitations of categories

Of course, the types of knowledge discussed so far can be expanded on or rewritten. They aren't definitive. There are other types of knowledge that are also important to the wider role of teacher. Some might add knowledge of students, or child development, or education policy. And the best teachers clearly aren't those with more facts in their heads than everyone else. It would be misreading the research to claim that expert teachers are those who have mastered all the information in their domains. We've all encountered a teacher who knows a subject or pedagogical theory better than everyone else but is still a bad teacher. Expert knowledge is not a set of facts but more an indelibly fused web of content, theory and experience – a mental model – all working together to construct useful models for each aspect of classroom practice.

Categories of knowledge, however, come with a health warning. Professor of Education Mary Kennedy describes how, as a profession, we have 'never reached agreement on any partitions'[10] of knowledge. Furthermore, the more we seek to cut up and categorise teacher knowledge, the more likely we are to 'reach a stage where so many bodies of knowledge are relevant to teaching that the curriculum of teacher education becomes unwieldy'. This doesn't mean we can't usefully think about subject knowledge or pedagogy or cognitive science. However, illusions of a curriculum you can work your way through are tempting. *If I've just studied all the right modules, I'll be an expert teacher.*

Kennedy explores the various attempts to categorise even part of what a teacher does. One attempted list of teacher activities includes over 1000 items and even then doesn't manage to 'distinguish what *good teachers* do, as opposed to poor teachers'. Where will this book succeed as others have failed? It won't try so hard. I cannot, nor do I claim to, offer you everything when it comes to knowledge or solutions. This isn't a taxonomy or full classification of teacher knowledge. The sections on types of teacher knowledge are a starting point. A map is a good analogy for what this book can do insofar as it offers a route but there are always choices and detours, obstructions and possibilities.

You might wonder why it is important for you to know how teacher trainers have considered the categorisation of teacher knowledge. Does a new teacher need to worry about such things? Picture yourself, for a moment, in the landscape of your development. Depending on your present circumstances, that landscape might be a pleasant meadow or a volcanic dystopia. In either case, my goal is to give you the toolkit to navigate that landscape. Knowledge is your map insomuch as it helps you to face and overcome challenges.

Categories are a useful reflection point. What do I know and what don't I know? But awareness of categories is not our destination. We need to go further. Knowledge building needs to be directed at our development as new teachers.

Categories and problems help us to focus our development

What do these categories mean for teacher development? Each section of this book examines a type of teacher knowledge. Each type of knowledge is useful insomuch as it is a lens with which to view our burgeoning practice. A lens is another way of viewing a mental model, with knowledge providing a new mode of 'seeing' your classroom. In this way, this book doesn't guide you through the tasks of a new teacher: planning a lesson, completing an assignment, creating a seating plan, calling a parent for the first time. These are useful things to know about but the lenses of knowledge make up our narrow focus: creating mental models to face the persistent challenges of the classroom. Whilst real-life lenses aren't anti-fragile – they crack and break under pressure – a knowledge lens will grow and last. Lasting change and improvement are our aim. A commitment to knowledge is a commitment to anti-fragile growth.

From categories to problems

As with our discussion of progressive problem solving, Mary Kennedy sees learning to teach as learning to solve 'persistent challenges'. Kennedy argues 'that most observed teaching behaviours can be understood if they are characterized as addressing one of these challenges'. Framing learning to teach through the lens of challenges leads to a focus on solutions and strategies that teachers learn to apply in a range of settings.

Kennedy's challenges are:

- **Portraying the curriculum.** Teachers must find ways to make content 'comprehensible to naïve minds'.

- **Enlisting student participation.** Kennedy frames student participation around the paradox that 'education is mandatory but learning is not'. How, then, do we ensure participation that will lead to learning?

- **Exposing student thinking.** Teachers must find out whether 'students understand, don't understand, or misunderstand'. Each day, in every lesson.

- **Containing student behaviour.** Teachers must manage this behaviour 'not only as a matter of public safety but also to ensure that students are not distracting each other, or distracting the teacher, from the lesson'.

- **Accommodating personal needs.** For teachers, new teachers in particular, solving these problems doesn't mean you need to become someone else. All teachers must find 'a way to address the first four problems in a way that is consistent with their own personalities and personal needs'.

Knowledge is not accumulated for its own sake, though, but as a problem solving, direction providing resource. As we examine subject knowledge, we'll begin to consider how we use it in planning to solve the problems of portraying the curriculum or exposing student thinking. Evidence from cognitive science will offer strategies to enlist the right kinds of student participation. Best bets are those areas of knowledge that will help us in our early forays to solve these problems. Your knowledge, therefore, is not accumulating in a linear fashion.

The problem solving knowledge we require will vary:

- **Pre-emptive knowledge**, developed for problems you know you will face. You can prepare to solve these problems by pre-emptively developing knowledge of the curriculum or banking some classroom management strategies.

- **Reactive knowledge**, developed in response to problems surfacing from day to day and week to week. Because teaching is so complex, it's not definite which challenges you will face initially. There is some logic in starting with the knowledge that will support positive behaviour and implementing routines. You can't get much done if your classroom is chaos. Beyond that, certain classes or topics or teaching techniques might be causing you difficulties.

Teaching, therefore, involves solving persistent challenges. These challenges are unlikely to change. In turn, the knowledge of how to solve them is likely to expand but not drastically change. New teachers develop this knowledge. The knowledge becomes a theory The theory is applied and tested. Anti-fragility comes back into play. For Taleb, our knowledge grows and strengthens under pressure if, and only if, we learn from our errors. In classroom problem solving, trial and error is 'not really random' but based on the rational application of knowledge, ultimately 'what we think is wrong' (or right).[11] Our successful solutions to Kennedy's problems, however we come by them, are anti-fragile. We can only learn from their application.

In summary

Teaching is both simple and complex. It is a series of problems and a wealth of solutions. You can spend your working life unpicking and refining and practising your way through those problems and solutions. None of that should hold us back from now stepping into the classroom and doing our best for the children in front of us with what we know now. That is the simplicity of it. Deep oceans of complexity swell beneath you and still, even as your knowledge of the route is in its infancy, you can chart a course.

Expertise is built on the accumulation of knowledge in long-term memory and the automation of process. In themselves, these things aren't expertise but they intertwine to create mental models – ways of seeing situations and understanding possible courses of action. Mental models help to reduce cognitive load on us and, in turn, we can reinvest our freed capacities to continue to solve the problems and face the challenges of the classroom. When it comes to which knowledge we should prioritise for our mental models, those categories of enduring use – subject, pedagogy, practice, behaviour, knowledge of students themselves – provide a wealth of classroom solutions for us.

Possible next steps

Make aims specific. General aims are hard to achieve and can be unhelpful. The aim to be better at questioning is unlikely to yield results because there's little there other than a vague intention. A narrow focus – on putting students' names at the end of your questions – can be practised and a bit of self-awareness, a video or audio recording, or someone in your lesson can give some immediate feedback on how successful you've been. The same is true of knowledge about our subjects. Feeling your teaching would improve if you knew more about human geography doesn't have the same focus as the desire to better understand a culture or case study you are going to teach later in the year.

Notes

1 Abbott, I. (2007). Government policy. In V. Brooks, I. Abbott and L. Bills (eds), *Preparing to Teach in Secondary School* (pp. 335–344). McGraw Hill Education Press.
2 Ibid.
3 Taleb, N.N. (2012). *Anti-Fragile*. Penguin.
4 Rousseau, J. (1763). *Emile*. Penguin Classics.
5 Dewey, J. (2006). *The Collected Works of John Dewey*. Southern Illinois University Press.
6 Friere, P. (2017). *The Pedagogy of the Oppressed*. Penguin Modern Classics.
7 Shulman, L. (1986). Those who understand: Knowledge growth in teaching. *Educational Research*, 15(2), 4–14.
8 Coe, R., Rauch, C.J., Kime, S., and Singleton, D. (2020). *Great Teaching Toolkit Evidence Review*. Cambridge Assessment International Education.
9 Shulman, L. (1986). Those who understand: Knowledge growth in teaching. *Educational Research*, 15(2), 4–14.
10 Kennedy, M. (2016). Parsing the practice of teaching. *Journal of Teacher Education*, 67(1), 6–17.
11 Taleb, N.N. (2012). *Anti-Fragile*. Penguin.

Further reading

Bereiter, C., and Scardamalia, M. (1993). *Surpassing Ourselves*. Open Court Publishing.
Coe, R., Rauch, C.J., Kime, S., and Singleton, D. (2020). *Great Teaching Toolkit Evidence Review*. Cambridge Assessment International Education.

PART 2
Developing teacher knowledge

My favourite teachers taught my favourite subjects. Mr Baker, an English teacher, was ex-army. Occasionally, he teased us with fragments of stories from life in the military but mainly he just worked us hard. And as you'd expect, he was strict but we didn't mind. I saw him once over a decade after I'd left school but such was my reverence for him that I couldn't bring myself to say anything.

Mr Doran, a history teacher, was kind and warm and full of knowledge. My enduring memories of his lessons are the discussions and debates about history and interpretation – his regular invitation to hear what we thought and only gentle rebuke when we came close to error. His monologues about a moment in time or a book he'd read fascinated me. As a teacher, I'm not much like Mr Baker or Mr Doran but I'm grateful for the experience of their classrooms.

Your image of a good teacher will not only be shaped by your training or your tentative first moments in the classroom. Like me, you might call to mind a particular teacher. Even when we have no positive examples, we draw on a wealth of experience. As Mary Kennedy points out, 'Learning about teaching is different from learning about any other occupation, in that our learning begins when we are children'. We have all, Kennedy goes on, 'spent roughly 12,000 hours watching teachers through our child-eyes, developing our own conceptions about what the job entails and what makes some teachers better than others'.[1]

The journey to teacher expertise is clearly not a given just because you have, at one time, been taught. Action and activity – yours and those training you – drive that journey. Yet it would be foolish to ignore or suppress what you already think and believe about teaching. Knowledge you acquire through training isn't written on a blank slate. At times, this knowledge will support the construction of your image of an ideal teacher. At others, you might be challenged to re-evaluate this image based on new understanding or fresh experience. Bear that in mind, as we look at ways to develop knowledge here.

Although you are a novice, I am certain that you know lots already that will help you to reach expertise. Your part in that development is to be clear on what you know already and how you will use what you know. Even if you do have a

DOI: 10.4324/9781003281306-6

clear mental picture of what good teaching is, you need to start at the beginning. Your favourite teachers probably didn't become the ones you really loved by just stepping over the threshold of the classroom. In Part 2, we're going to examine the foundations of how teachers learn.

In Part 1, we saw that the essential ingredients for expertise development were large quantities of knowledge in long-term memory and automation of effective processes. Together, knowledge and automaticity help to create our mental models of effective classroom practice. These mental models help us to progressively problem solve and to tackle those persistent challenges of the classroom.

This part answers the questions:

- How do we retain knowledge in our long-term memory?

- How do we automate effective processes?

Note

1 Kennedy, M. (2019). How we learn about teacher learning. *Review of Research in Education*, 43, 138–162.

4 How do we retain knowledge in our long-term memory?

A student asks you a question and you don't know the answer. How do you respond? Talk about something else. Talk around the question. Tell them, *I could tell you but I want you to work it out for yourself.* It's up to you but *I don't know* is not a bad option. When we can't answer a student's question – from the definition of a word to the motivations of a historical figure – it's quite clear we're lacking in knowledge. The same is also true, however, when we struggle to mark assessments because the mark scheme appears to be written in another language. It is true when we hesitate to give a consequence because the behaviour policy hasn't fully crystallised in our minds. It is true when we struggle to articulate an answer to *How does this relate to what we were doing before?* In each situation, our minds reach for knowledge that is absent or undeveloped.

If experts have large quantities of knowledge in long-term memory, our first task must be to understand how to retain such knowledge. The mental models we develop shouldn't just consist of what we teach or how we act in certain situations. A mental model of how *we* learn as new teachers offers a valuable insight into how we can spur on the improvements we are making. We are, therefore, looking at any activity where your aim is the retention of the knowledge that will help you to become an effective teacher. This is not so much about 'studying' for an exam that isn't coming; instead, it's about awareness of what you know, how you use it and whether you've retained it.

I hope, therefore, in talking about knowledge development it's clear that we're not just talking about an optional extra. This book is not just for those who are happy to give up evenings and weekends to extra-curricular study activities. Knowledge activity is everyday activity for teachers. But there is a problem. You don't have unlimited time or resources – you're already teaching or training to teach. Waiting might not seem practical but spending your evenings deep in study isn't sustainable either. Our aim then is to find manageable things you can do to focus your energies early in your career.

DOI: 10.4324/9781003281306-7

Examples of such knowledge activity might include:

- Reading up on the background of the topics you are about to teach.

- Examining curriculum materials to make sure you understand what must be taught.

- Training or reading on effective or evidence-informed classroom practices.

- Getting to know students generally (understanding of student needs or how students learn) or specifically (the students you will be teaching).

- Applying knowledge of specification or statutory assessment to planning and curriculum materials.

- Planning with the information you've gained in the above activities.

To 'build knowledge', the Education Endowment Foundation's guidance report on Effective Professional Development emphasises the need to manage cognitive load and revisit prior learning.[1] The principles underlying the strategies in this chapter are:

- Managing cognitive load makes learning more likely.

- Revisiting what you've learned makes retention more likely.

Cognitive Load Theory describes how conscious thought can only hold a small number (around four) of new items in your mind at any given time.[2] Cognitive load increases when the number of items required for a task exceeds your ability to manage them. Learning to teach feels like a constant and unrealistic expectation has been placed on your cognitive capacities. In many ways, it has.

Managing cognitive load is about ensuring we can cope with all the new information coming our way. As we'll see, the ways we 'revisit prior learning' will determine if we retain or forget what we have learned. Although we might think of study techniques as things we teach our students, they can be invaluable for retaining the massive quantities of new information we take on as new teachers.

Why are we developing knowledge?

Before we begin, it's important to remember what this knowledge is for. A new teacher is forming a variety of mental models: a mental model for classroom routines, a mental model for teaching the Vikings, a mental model for the application of evidence to classroom activity. These models are networks of knowledge we call on to act in complex situations. New teachers also face a whole host of problems or challenges: the problem of getting students thinking, of getting them to behave, of making content understandable and memorable, of checking what they do understand. The idea that teachers should *develop knowledge* or *retain knowledge* can feel overwhelming. *Where do I start?* With a coach, or on your own if you're able, work out which knowledge will help solve the most pressing problems now.

Annalise, a Science trainee, describes the different type of knowledge she had to develop.

Learning names was a point of which I saw great importance as every student feels seen when their name is used. It also empowers me in the classroom as when trying to sanction or correct behaviour. It leaves space for ambiguity when a name isn't used. Or you have to resort to the very accusatory, depersonalised 'you over there', which I don't feel goes down too well, understandably.

Otherwise, as someone re-entering my subject discipline the subject material has been an ongoing point of development for me. I have been thinking back to demonstrations and ideas which I had remembered since my time in school and tried to expand on them. This is alongside following the suggested textbook material to ensure that the correct terminology and detail are covered in my lessons.

How do we develop knowledge?

Let's look at practically how we can retain knowledge in long-term memory.

Narrow your focus

A sense that you *could* know something better or do something better is unhelpful. We narrow our focus so that we can move beyond good intentions and into genuine improvement. That improvement is won incrementally. Cognitive overload can be expected for the teacher who decides to improve their questioning in multiplication lessons whilst writing new resources and attempting to gauge student understanding. If all of those require improvement, focusing on one at a time is essential to avoid floundering.

We also narrow our focus to prioritise immediate needs. Initially, to prioritise effectively, help will be essential. A standing item in conversations with your mentor or coach should be devoted to what you are prioritising and what you are, for now at least, ignoring. If you aren't teaching an exam class immediately, the necessary job of getting to grips with the specification can be delayed in favour of your background reading on an upcoming scheme of work. If a class isn't behaving, it's no use trying to nail a new questioning technique that would require impeccable behaviour.

Your training programme or the Early Careers Framework will dictate some priorities by setting assignments and requiring reading or study. Compare your priorities with these requirements. Ask your mentor what should take precedence.

You might want to get to grips with the world of research and cognitive science, but your mentor could tell you a more urgent priority is knowing the policies and procedures at your school.

Perhaps you decide to devote several mornings next week before school to a tricky class you're teaching right now. A class with complex needs and characters. The content itself doesn't trouble you; there are prepared resources and you're happy they'll work for you. Focusing energy and time on learning names, needs and, perhaps from a more experienced colleague, how to approach some of the difficult students is likely to reap rewards.

Narrowing your focus means wilfully, if temporarily, ignoring some things. Selecting priorities demands we ask the question *What am I leaving out?* Learning to teach is intense; developing expertise will extend beyond the training or early careers years. At times, all your time and energy will afford you is the ability to get done what must get done. Play the long game. We narrow now to develop breadth for the future. Be patient as you plan future priorities.

Ask yourself:

- Is this my priority, the thing that will have the biggest impact in tackling my most urgent problems?

- Is there any way to cut this task down further?

- What other tasks or goals are competing for my attention?

Amy, a new Year 6 teacher, has been working on honing her Reading and Maths knowledge. She is beginning to feel like she's getting to grips with the mammoth expectations of the National Curriculum, at least in her year group. But there's a problem. She has to teach music for the first time next week. She doesn't know the curriculum or the school's resources. More to the point, she doesn't know music. She doesn't have rhythm. Even clapping in time poses pretty serious problems for her. Thinking about it though, she realises her feelings of musical inadequacy are getting in the way of prioritising properly. To narrow her focus, she doesn't need to be become a musician by next week. No, Amy needs to understand the materials and aims of the first lesson, plan it and then teach it. Maths and English won't be left entirely – Amy will still need to teach these lessons. But music will become the planning priority in the next week.

Ask your coach:

- I think X is my priority. Does that sound right?

- Is there anything I can stop doing or do less of to make X my priority?

- What else should I not ignore or remember whilst working on this priority?

Dan, a secondary Art teacher, is concerned about his new class's behaviour. He goes to his coach after a particularly difficult lesson to try to figure out what to do next. Dan knows *behaviour* is his priority but this doesn't feel helpful or narrow. The coach asks Dan about the lesson and, after a bit of back and forth, Dan realises he never really got them settled when they came in from lunch. They work together to plan a new routine to manage the post-lunch entry.

Break it down

> **Georgia, a PE trainee, describes how she manages her time.**
>
> It was trial and error to begin and it took me a year realistically to find the work/life balance but now find I am stricter with myself. I tried leaving at certain times, not working from home, doing some work over a half term, adapting the use of time during my PPA etc.
>
> Now I find that I pencil everything in my planner [and] I stay until no later than 5 pm. I don't take any work home unless absolutely vital that it is done that day. I have a designated morning [or] day of work during half term and sometimes I use this; sometimes it's not needed. I then prioritise my time during PPA slots to include the more important or when sandwiched between duties like mine. Then I do all of the quick jobs as I find it hard to get really involved with a task if I need to stop to go to a duty.

A strategy to manage both time and cognitive load, a granular list of the things you want to know better can be incredibly helpful. Include everything. Break everything down into component parts. Don't write down *Electricity unit* if this is a topic you are concerned about teaching. Write down each component part: include the specific things you need to do to improve your knowledge.

If you've written *Learn about the Industrial Revolution* at the top of your list because that's Year 6's next history unit, you might be no closer to adding knowledge to your long-term memory. Spending a precious PPA trying to immerse yourself in the Industrial Revolution by frantically Googling 'Year 6 Industrial Revolution lessons' is time badly spent. Instead, you might write *Read scheme of work*, *Check available resources on the shared drive*, *List questions* (for your mentor), *Read the article Jen shared*. Once you've broken the process down, you need to make sure you devote time to them.

Blocking is the time management process where you divide your day into blocks and schedule activities for those times. Like lots of time management strategies, blocking can feel galling to teachers. So much of your day is not yours to direct. For a primary teacher, blocks might only be available at the beginning and end of each day and during your limited PPA.

Primary or secondary, blocking won't create more time for you but it remains a useful way of making sure your week or your PPA doesn't get swallowed up with just a couple of activities. Jobs have a habit of filling the time we allow for them. If you have one hour on a Tuesday afternoon, devote half to admin and deliberately move on halfway through. That second half can be devoted to the background reading for your next topic. Or give the admin the small amount of time you have at the beginning or end of the day and devote the entire PPA to knowledge building.

> **Kate, a Maths trainee, discusses how she used her time to plan.**
>
> I had heard from a lot of experienced teachers that your first year training can be one of the hardest years of your life and completely consume your social calendar. I simply refused to let this happen as I knew my mental health would suffer as a result. Knowing this, I faced the realisation that lesson planning will take as long as you allow it to. This meant I could happily sit and scroll through resources for three hours or allocate a 20 minute time to be efficient and still produce (what I thought was) a great lesson.

Think hard

As cognitive scientist Daniel Willingham says, 'memory is the residue of thought'.[3] That we remember what we think about sounds obvious but it's easy to think superficially about what you want to remember. It's also easy to confuse activity with productivity. Or getting things done with intellectual engagement.

Thinking hard only works if you've narrowed your focus onto some useful content. It's also not possible to think hard about everything at once; you need to have broken down the content into something manageable. Once we've done that, we can start to think about the kind of thought we devote to the content.

All teachers need deep understanding of the content to be taught. It's easy to confuse thinking about content with thinking about resources or activities. If teachers think hard about the resources they're designing, they might arrive in the classroom with only superficial understanding of how to explain the subject content. Of course, activities need to be planned. This is not an argument against careful thought about what students will do.

Mary teaches Politics A-Level in a sixth form but her degree is in International Relations. This works for most of the A-Level course but the minutiae of local government is not something that excites her. More pressingly, she doesn't know anything about local government and lessons are coming up on that very topic. She's starting to feel anxious about *filling the time*. What will students do? And what can they do that won't reveal this is a massive gap in her knowledge? She breaks down the process and separates reading and preparation from planning the lessons. She spends an afternoon after school reading through a textbook, a revision guide and a couple of articles recommended by another teacher. Her sole purpose is understanding the content well. In this way, she thinks hard about the content rather than what needs to happen next Wednesday morning when she next sees her group.

To engage with the knowledge we want to understand, we need to devote attention to it. But we also need to know what *it* is.

Distribute practice

Distributed practice, sometimes called spacing, is 'a schedule of practice that spreads out study activities over time'.[4] Putting increasingly long gaps between study of a particular topic or process will lead to better retention. Opposite to distributed practice is massed practice or cramming. Cramming the week before you teach a new topic is only going to lead to deficient knowledge. You'll only realise the extent of the gaps when you're in front of the class.

Your aim is to return to content again in order to remember it. Student names, SEND support plans, spellings and definitions you struggle with. It's unlikely any of these will be mastered in one go. Even the plot of stories you know well can feel elusive when in front of a class, managing behaviour and preparing students for the next activity.

Research isn't definitive on how long the gaps should be between study sessions. Instead, the evidence about distributed practice is an important reminder to plan ahead when you need to learn something new. Fortunately, the school year offers pre-determined deadlines. You can always be working towards something. Spaced reading and re-reading can be scheduled throughout a term and will do more to keep knowledge in your head than massed or crammed reading. In this way, teaching is naturally distributed. Each time you plan in a learning sequence you can return to (and retrieve) what you did last time.

Jamie is an early careers D&T teacher. He teaches half of Year 9 – 90 students across four classes. The students are making bird-houses to go up around the school site. Jamie has broken the task down into its component parts. The first thing he wants to do is explain and model the measuring and marking wood for cutting – his first major practical with a class. He is going to do this four times over a fortnight. He writes out the explanation and practises it twice to himself. He does it for the first time with a nice group. He gets the technician to watch carefully and jump in when necessary. Jamie knows he can do better and practises it again before the next class (and every class after that). By the fourth and final time, he has practised outside lesson time over ten times and done it three times in front of a class. The final explanation is the best – fluent and easy but also built on the learning and tweaks Jamie has made from his first tries.

Georgia, a PE trainee, describes how she tried to learn about her students and content early on.

I learnt student names from repetition of seeing the group, the use of class photos on SIMs, and having set teams and groups so that I could form rapport with groups or individuals alongside in the classroom having a set seating plan.

Subject content was really important from a theoretical point of view where I looked through the course textbook, asked lots of questions to colleagues who have experience in teaching this course and then further by using past years' work as examples.

Retrieve

Trying to recall a piece of information (something you've just been taught, read or already know) is called retrieval or retrieval practice. Retrieval practice describes 'the fact that information retrieved from memory leads to better performance on a later test'.[5] In other words, 'retrieval can slow forgetting'.[6]

If you want to remember something for a lesson or for future planning, trying to recall it without prompts or aids is likely to help you retain that information. You could explain a topic out loud to yourself without looking at notes (as you'll have to in the classroom) and then check you included everything you wanted to. Making flashcards or a self-quizzing sheet[7] for a scheme of work with a lot of content which is new to you can be a useful resource to return to.

Here, the line between studying like your students and preparing to be their teacher might feel blurred. Many new teachers, however, get to the board and realise they're not sure of a spelling of an essential term. Or you forget the name of a student who is talking constantly at the back and your strategy for addressing this crumbles. Or a student question stumps you, the answer on the curriculum documents you printed off and left in the office. None of these are things to feel ashamed of. Cognitive load presses heavily on your ability to do *everything* required of you in a lesson. Retrieval, as well as distributed practice, both supports your memory and boosts your confidence because of a growing sense that *you know this*.

Carrie has always struggled with spelling. She now teaches Year 5 and it feels like they are constantly asking how to spell something. It's not that she doesn't know how to spell anything they ask her for. It's just that, put on the spot, she's likely to freeze. Carrie finds it easier to write things out but she wants to be confident helping children as she moves around her classroom. Her school's curriculum has a vocabulary list of words students need to learn, both spellings and definitions. She turns the vocab list into a quizzing sheet. She practises the spellings for ten minutes a couple of mornings a week before school. Carrie wants to be able to say and spell the words; she mixes practising saying the spelling out loud with writing out the spellings from memory. With time, she begins to feel confident and notices an improvement when asked for spellings from students.

Self-explain

Self-explanation involves 'explaining how new information is related to known information, or explaining steps taken during problem solving'.[8] When novices lacking in the necessary domain-specific knowledge attempt self-explanation it can lead to cognitive overload[9] so it's unlikely to help in a situation where you don't have the prerequisite knowledge. Where the new knowledge you're learning fills a gap in or adds a layer to a topic you're already aware of, it's likely self-explanation could help. If you can narrate the links between the new topic and existing knowledge, if you can pose questions about it and answer them, it's likely you're working to retain this new information.

A physicist teaching photosynthesis for the first time can explain the concept as they work through lesson resources or a rehearsed explanation. A geographer teaching an unfamiliar case study can talk through it systematically. A Year 6 teacher teaching D&T when their confidence lies elsewhere can work through the concepts they will have to explain. In all these circumstances, you are still the expert. Undoubtedly, you already know more about the topic than the students you will be teaching. You aren't checking you understand it by simply 'thinking it through', a recipe for a wandering mind. Instead, you're checking for fluency, for gaps in understanding and for your ability to simplify and distil what is necessary for students to understand.

Accept (and seek out) support

Initially, some new teachers are desperate to put in the work in *every* area themselves. Resources exist but you want to put your spin on them. A system of online homework makes setting and checking homework simple but you want to design your own tasks. A textbook gives you a base level of what students should know and do but you're concerned using it is a cop out. The school's behaviour policy gives clear guidelines of how teachers should manage difficult behaviour but you want to spend time writing your own rules with a class.

The mental resources required to engage in all these activities are a drain and despite your best intentions the quality in these areas will suffer if you try to focus on all of them. More importantly, you won't develop knowledge in the same way. You'll likely struggle to retain what you're working on because you're trying to work on everything. To manage cognitive load, and your time, you need to recognise early that perfection is not attainable. This does not mean we don't work hard or do a good job. It does mean that we outsource thinking where possible to those who have already put in the time.

In summary

You could ask *Do I really need strategies for remembering? Don't I need strategies for understanding?* Daniel Willingham explains that when it comes to our cognitive architecture, 'understanding is remembering in disguise'.[10] In order to deeply understand, we will have to commit some of what we learn to memory. Committing this to memory will also reduce our cognitive load, giving us an easier route to understanding new knowledge.

Why is learning to teach so difficult? The rapid rate of growth expected in subject knowledge, education theory, pedagogy, policy, classroom craft and more make for massive cognitive overload. To make study effective, you must manage this load. Often, you'll have to reduce it. Embrace help and support available to you as you learn to prioritise.

Once teaching, it feels like there is very little time for study. Studying feels like something that happens before you become a teacher. But you can't escape at least a kind of study. You can only do it well or badly. You can focus your thinking. You can practice retrieving knowledge (like nuggets of subject knowledge or student names). You can space out practice on a particular topic and return to it to make retention more likely. As we examine different areas of teacher knowledge, we'll look at how to do all this as you go.

Possible next steps

1. **Break down a bigger task into its component parts.** If you have a big planning task in front of you, an assignment to complete, or a new subject to get to grips with, just thinking about the process can be overwhelming. List the components in as granular a way as you can. You're more likely to focus and retain what you're thinking about if you've broken it down. Make a real list – physical, in a Word document, in a fancy app that lets you tick off items as you go. Work through the list.

2. **Focus your thinking.** Once you have a list, make sure any activity you carry out focuses your thinking on what you want to remember. Separating out tasks and directing your thought is challenging to begin with. It feels like it makes sense to do everything at once: plan lessons, learn content, get to know a class.

3. **Practise retrieving.** Retrieval helps us and, as we'll see, our students to remember. Choose something you want to remember in the classroom. Student names, spellings, processes, formula – all can benefit from retrieval. Remember, retrieval isn't just reading through a list of terms or poring over pictures of students. Cover the content you want to remember and then say the content out loud or write it down. Check your answers and repeat the ones you get wrong.

Notes

1 Collin, J., and Smith E. (2021). *Effective Professional Development* (Guidance Report). EEF. https://educationendowmentfoundation.org.uk/education-evidence/guidance-reports/effective-professional-development#nav-downloads (accessed 25/10/2021).
2 Sweller, J., Merrienboer, J., and Paas, F. (2019). Cognitive architecture and instructional design: 20 years later. *Educational Psychology Review*, 31, 261–292.
3 Willingham, D. (2009). *Why Don't Students Like School?* Jossey-Bass.
4 Dunlosky, J., Rawson, K., Marsh, E., Nathan, M., and Willingham, D. (2013). Improving students' learning with effective learning techniques: Promising directions from cognitive and educational psychology. *Psychological Science in the Public Interest*, 14(1), 4–58.
5 Roediger, H., Putnam, A., and Smith, M. (2011). Ten benefits of testing and their application to education practice. *Psychology of Learning and Motivation*, 55, 1–36.

6 Dunlosky, J., Rawson, K., Marsh, E., Nathan, M., and Willingham, D. (2013). Improving students' learning with effective learning techniques: Promising directions from cognitive and educational psychology. *Psychological Science in the Public Interest*, 14(1), 4–58.

7 A sheet with prompts on one side and answers on the other (for example, key words on one side and definitions on the other) – almost like a condensed set of flashcards.

8 Dunlosky, J., Rawson, K., Marsh, E., Nathan, M., and Willingham, D. (2013). Improving students' learning with effective learning techniques: Promising directions from cognitive and educational psychology. *Psychological Science in the Public Interest*, 14(1), 4–58.

9 Perry, T., Lea, R., Jørgensen, C.R., Cordingley, P., Shapiro, K., and Youdell, D. (2021). *Cognitive Science in the Classroom*. Education Endowment Foundation (EEF). https://educationendowmentfoundation.org.uk/education-evidence/evidence-reviews/cognitive-science-approaches-in-the-classroom/ (accessed 18/11/2022).

10 Willingham, D. (2009). *Why Don't Students Like School?* Jossey-Bass.

5 How do we automate effective processes?

Ashley, a secondary Maths teacher in his first year, describes getting through his training year.

When I first went into school, it was Inset Day. I knew nobody so I sat in the back of the room. They were all talking about all these things I didn't understand. It felt like we were going through *everything* that was going to happen in the whole year. You listen to it and you have no idea about some of what's being said and no idea where some of these things are going to end up.

You start out thinking, 'This is going to be so much work' but then by the end of the year it actually feels like it's doable. I feel more confident now compared to starting out last year. You can see where the finish line is.

Teaching is all about relationships. Your day is made up of human interactions. You aren't simply delivering knowledge and skill to the young people; it isn't transmitted from your mind to theirs. Planning is preparing to communicate something – a topic, a process, a concept – *to students*. Primarily, this planning deals with the explanations, examples and activities that will help students to understand what they are learning. Part of the excitement of teaching is discovering how planning plays out in the classroom with real-life human children. The warmth and the humour of teaching emerge as we spend each day with these people.

Where does automation fit into this view of teaching? Surely automating the processes of the classroom is a cold way to view your interaction with students? There is another problem with automation: how can it work with the infinite interactions, situations and problems posed by the classroom. Can we really automate anything useful for an environment which is constantly changing? Before we look at the practical ways to automate processes, it's worth addressing these concerns.

DOI: 10.4324/9781003281306-8

Is automation a cold way to view teaching?

It's difficult to imagine a good teacher who doesn't *care for* their students. That said, *caring* is often misunderstood. *Caring* is not the same as *being friends* with, nor do we have to care by going beyond the boundaries of the teacher–student relationship. To care, we have to want the best for our students but we also have to do our best for our students. *Doing our best* can be confused with working harder than it is reasonable or healthy to expect a teacher to work. Caring for students doesn't have to mean that all weekends and evenings are devoted to work. In part, caring for our students should be about doing what has a good chance of working in the classroom.

Picture two classrooms. In the first, a Year 7 Science class, as the students come into the room the teacher asks them about their weekends, jokes with a couple of boys about their football team's recent failure and congratulates one student on their performance in a recent concert. Once the lesson begins, the teacher fumbles through the explanation of a new topic. When the class move to practical work, the teacher hasn't thought through the transition and, on top of being a little too lively, students have no idea what they are doing: the explanation was lost in the clatter of movement.

A similar lesson is happening in a second Year 7 Science class down the corridor. This time the class aren't greeted in the same way; they enter quietly as is routine and get started on an initial task. The teacher has practised an explanation of a new topic at her desk whilst planning by saying it out loud before making some final edits. The fruit of that planning is a short list of words, an aide-memoir, written in her planner but also the familiarity won from practising the explanation. Not only did this teacher practise the explanation, she thought hard about how to move from desks to practical. She wrote out the steps and practised going through those instructions, again out loud in the room by herself. Explanation and practical both go well but, looking at her notes, the teacher notices a couple of things to tweak for next time based on how the class responded.

Which teacher cares more for their class? Of course, it's an unfair question. You can be a bit of both teachers. My point in posing the question is not really to force a choice but to be clear that caring as a teacher means more than the stereotype. If your classroom is more like the first, you can care more deeply for your students by automating some elements of your lessons. And yes, if your classroom is more like the second, you can show you care for your students by taking an interest in them.

Is automation possible in a changing environment?

Nowhere in the world is quite like a classroom. The atmosphere ranges from exuberant debate to knife-edge tension to studious silence, often in the space of a single lesson. It's true that students are individuals but classes also have a personality of their own. Even teachers who repeat similar lessons across a year group find that these lessons branch off in different directions with different classes. How then does automation meet the needs of this varied environment?

Some events in the classroom are hard to predict. I hope I can't be blamed for not expecting two boys to continue their snowball fight right into my lesson. But more can be prepared for than we might think: explanations, examples, models, classroom routines are all good places to start. Students will enter your room each day. You can automate your position in the room, perhaps by the door, what you say and what you expect of students in that moment.

Behaviour management is an understandable concern for new teachers and one where automation seems difficult. It isn't possible to practise for every potential student behaviour but we can rehearse for different situations. If you're speaking to a class from the front of the room, you can automate moving to a position where you can see the whole class and you can automate looking at each chair as you speak. For giving consequences when students don't meet your expectations, a scripted response can help alleviate anxiety. A good behaviour management system often gives you the steps or language to rehearse until automatic.

Recognising that the classroom is a changing environment is not an argument against automation. Because the classroom is a complex environment, we make automatic those processes that will allow us to manage the complexity. We don't automate processes to the extent that we sleepwalk through each day. We automate processes so we can respond more effectively to the routine as well as the tangential or unexpected. Automation frees up mental capacity to attend to the problems of the classroom and apply our burgeoning solutions.

The mental models we create of the classroom are not *just* made up of content knowledge or theoretical knowledge. These models include the strategies we deploy in the classroom, and how we react to expected and unexpected moments. A mental model is not reality; it exists inside our head. But the fuller our model of the classroom – of the Year 5 classroom, the English classroom, the D&T workshop – the easier we find it to react in the moment.

Let's turn to look at the practical ways we automate processes.

Observe

Working closely with more experienced, knowledgeable or effective teachers is likely to make you better at your job.[1] Early in your career, you are more susceptible to the benefits of having expert colleagues around you. But what do we learn from colleagues? Some of that learning is focused on how to navigate the inner workings of schools: the politics and practicalities of the day to day. If, however, all we learn from our colleagues is how to unjam the photocopier, we're missing out on an incredible resource.

Teaching staff at your school are a cavernous library of accumulated wisdom and practice. Classroom craft, subject knowledge and pedagogical understanding don't *just* – and don't mainly – exist in what we read; these domains are alive in those we work with. A small number of new teachers see experienced teachers as out of touch or unaware of recent developments. This belief always totally misunderstands what we can gain from our colleagues.

One study goes as far as to say that 'learning from colleagues is at least as valuable as formal training'.[2] In this study, teachers were placed in 'skills-matched' pairs: one teacher needed to work on a particular aspect of classroom practice, the other teacher had been identified as proficient in this area. Pairs discussed practice and observed one another. Teachers who needed to improve were accountable to their partners for the improvements made. Long after the study had ended, the improvements made in these relationships were still being felt.

If you let it, being a new teacher can become a chain of these 'skills-matched' pairs. You start out understandably deficient in a host of classroom activities. Your resources are the teachers around you. A mentor or leader at your school can point you in the right direction, towards the teachers with those strategies for behaviour management or questioning or explanations. Whatever it is you need.

How do we make sure this kind of observation is useful?

Go for something specific

It's foolish to observe a teacher just because they are seen as excellent at everything. Beware of being told in hushed tones *You should definitely observe Mark* without any clear direction as to why.

Narrow down what you're looking at with your mentor, coach or the person you're observing. Ideally, this will be based on what you're working on, the feedback you've received recently or the problems for which you're currently searching for solutions. Often we go to someone (or get sent to someone) who has everything sorted. Behaviour isn't a problem; beautiful work is produced daily. We leave deflated because learning from what looks like perfection isn't easy. Go and see someone managing a difficult class, someone in the process of changing their classroom routines, someone teaching some content for the first time.

Looking at something specific helps you in two important ways:

- **It helps to manage your cognitive load.** Trying to learn everything from a teacher in one go is too much.

- **It saves you time.** You don't need to come for the whole lesson. Ask roughly when the teacher will be doing what you want to see and turn up at that point.

Watch the teacher *and* the students

It's hard to know what you're looking for when first observing teachers. Achievements that could be a triumph for you appear ordinary in other classrooms.

Depending on what you're looking for, consider making a note of:

- What the students do without being asked.

- The apparent routines or habits of the classroom (students and teacher).

- What the teacher specifies about how students complete tasks; what is left for them to decide.

- What happens in books (or wherever/however the work is being produced).

- Anything the teacher does that doesn't chime with your experience – something you wouldn't do or find difficult to.

As you observe, collect questions about anything that doesn't make sense to you in the moment. Base these on the notes you made using the prompts above. Watching the start of a lesson, you notice the teacher says almost nothing to the class and yet students come into the room, hand out resources and get started silently. The act of watching the lesson isn't helpful on its own; the story of how the teacher arrived at that point can be.

To build knowledge of classroom craft, you need to ask questions of what you observe. Ask for those stories and you'll begin to piece together the journey you might take from where you are to where you could be. You need someone to take the implicit and ongoing aspects of classroom behaviour and make them explicit.

Note taking is a good idea but it's difficult at first to unpick what you're seeing. If you've been directed to watch another teacher manage whole class discussion, it's worth going with the person doing the directing. They can provide useful commentary. As questions arise, ask them or debrief afterwards.

Know the limits of observation

Observation is a useful way of building up a mental model of effective classroom behaviour. Until the observation, a particular strategy had felt too theoretical. Now, it feels both tangible and achievable. Observing teachers builds a sense of what your future might look like. Unfortunately, it can also make you feel inadequate as you struggle to understand how the teacher has arrived at an apparently effortless level of classroom practice. As Anders Ericsson has said of sporting expertise, 'extensive watching is not the same as extensive playing'.[3] Mental models don't develop simply through watching because you aren't trying to become an expert watcher-of-lessons.

Practice

David Feldon, education researcher, reassures new teachers that 'feeling overwhelmed by the amount of simultaneous activity in a classroom is a common experience'.[4] We all experience cognitive overload when 'the total processing demands… exceed available attentional resources'. We can only pay attention to so much; when we reach the limit, we stop being able to 'adapt effectively to complex classroom dynamics'. Why don't experienced teachers struggle to adapt? Why don't they reach the limits of the ability they're able to process? Experienced and expert teachers have broader knowledge and effective automated processes. To break through the limits of our cognitive architecture, Feldon recommends that we focus on making effective behaviour automatic whilst minimising ineffective behaviours. Practice is what promotes effective behaviour whilst also ridding us of ineffective behaviour.

For a new teacher, thinking about practice is helpful because it makes explicit the often-implicit routines and habits of your classroom. If you're already able to think of your classroom behaviour, 'I do *that* a lot and I don't like it', you're on the road to a level of self-knowledge the best teachers need. Your own simple but annoying behaviours like saying 'Perfect' after everything every student says start to grate on you. Or harder to shift habits like screaming to regain control from a boisterous, noisy class. The solution to both problems is practice.

In a way, we're always practising. If you're in the classroom, you can't escape practice. Each day, habits are being ingrained; processes refine and stagnate. As we repeat, we embed. This is an absolute necessity for a teacher. Practice leads to automation. Automation brings a process closer to effortless. Pockets of effortlessness make your day more manageable but this is not necessarily the same as getting better.

Anders Ericsson, the undisputed king of practice, describes a very particular kind of practice:

> Deliberate practice presents performers with tasks that are initially outside their current realm of reliable performance, yet can be mastered within hours of practice by concentrating on critical aspects and by gradually refining performance through repetitions after feedback.[5]

Practice is not simply about making more of your day automatic. Practice is also about fighting against the sub-par things that are already automatic. We practice away those bad habits. For Ericson, the main challenge in 'attaining expert level performance is to induce stable specific changes that allow the performance to be incrementally improved'. The challenge for the lone new teacher is twofold: identify what needs to change and know when it has changed sufficiently to be able to move on.

Deliberate practice includes the following.

Selecting a narrow behaviour

Initially, your mentor or coach – preferably in conversation with you – will direct the behaviours to practice. Don't be afraid or disheartened to practice the narrowest and apparently most basic of skills. Small changes make a big difference. Practice in the following areas can collectively make a massive difference:

- Where you stand during a particular activity.
- How you phrase a question.
- The order of your instructions.
- What you look for when you walk around the room.
- How you praise students for doing the right thing.

Don't baulk at being encouraged to master a specific behaviour before moving onto something more complex. Teaching well is the sum of specific, narrow behaviours, implemented well.

In various classrooms, students have to move from their seats to another area in the room. In D&T, the students move from the benches to a demonstration at one piece of equipment. In Music, students move from desks to keyboards. In some primary classrooms, students move from tables to the carpet. In one sense, these are things that students must practice, that students must automate. As teachers, however, we can practice the preparation and management of that process.

Decide on a process; be clear with students about what will happen. For example:

In a moment, we're going to move to a demonstration on the front bench. You will stand in one wide circle round the bench. No one will be standing in front or behind of anyone else. If there isn't room, you will move to find a space.

Write out the specific instructions:

Everyone stand silently behind your chairs... Good. Table 1, in silence walk and find a space around the front bench... Okay, good... Table 2 do the same.

Because classes are unlikely to get it right first time, it's worth practising what will happen when they don't:

Table 3, you aren't walking in silence. Go back. We'll come back to you in a moment. *Or,* I asked for one line around the bench and we've got a rabble so we're all going to go back to our seats and try again.

Practise these steps in your classroom, on your own. Or in your car on the way to school. Or, perhaps most helpfully, to another teacher who can help you tease out any ambiguities or problems. Clarity won from practice makes the early attempts to manage these transitions easier.

Defining success

When working with a specific, narrow behaviour it should be clear what you and your classroom will look like when it is successful. Be careful not to receive the success criteria from a coach or observer without seeking to understand it. Ask questions of it. *Why do I need to X?* Ask about alternative scenarios. *What happens if Y?* Your job is to make sure you understand *why* you need to achieve this success criteria and *how* to be successful. At the defining success stage, observe colleagues who are already successful to build your understanding of success.

In the transitioning around the room example from above, success is a smooth, orderly transition from one part of the room to another. You can practise the wording and the clarity without the children in the room but ultimately success is only achieved in the classroom when students follow your instructions (or are corrected when they don't).

Practice

Once the behaviour is defined, we can start to think about how to practise it. Sometimes, this can be done in an empty classroom: in front of your mentor or at your desk as you plan a lesson. An explanation of a very specific set of steps, for example, might benefit from a rehearsal outside of the lesson. Be careful of confusing practice with overthinking. You can overthink a set of instructions, dwell and stew in them. If you aren't active – writing, saying, getting feedback – you likely aren't really practising.

Certain elements of your teaching are one off – like the introduction of a new topic – and therefore quite high stakes. To allay concerns about getting this right, you could write a script with a more experienced colleague. You could rehearse it in front of them until it becomes close to automatic. We begin to make a process automatic when we practise it outside the lesson. Just make sure the practice matches what you'll be doing in the lesson. I used to write copious notes for my explanations or instructions in early lessons but, when the lessons arrived, I'd struggle to use them – too much was going on. I should have practised before the lesson and not worried so much about relying on the notes.

It is possible to overstate what can be achieved before a lesson. Practice is not simply this period outside of the lesson; it isn't just a rehearsal. It includes what happens when you take your focus back into the complex environment of the classroom. Here, your responsibility for practice becomes even more important. Some of the following reminders might feel silly but they may help you keep practising when you're on your own:

- Write a note in your planner or on a post-it and leave it on your desk or where you'll see.

- Say to yourself out loud just before the lesson, *I am working on X* or *Today, I'm going to try to...*

- Tell the children what you're working on. *Today, I'm going to try to ask more questions with hands down, Year 7. If I ask three questions with hands up, remind me to ask with hands down.* WARNING: I'd only do this with a class you already feel comfortable with and only with specific behaviours that students can observe. I'd also avoid talking about how you're working on improving your behaviour management – *Today, Year 7, I'm working on using the language of choice with Ben because he can be a real pain.* If in doubt, ask your mentor, a coach or line manager. Anything you want *students* to get better at is a good bet for this one. *Today, we're going to try to nail our transitions from the desks to the keyboards so we can spend as much time there as possible* gives a short explanation of what you want them to work on as well as a reason why.

- A coach (see below) can also help you in a lesson. For example, I know a new teacher who was working on achieving silence before he begins speaking to a class. His coach kept her hand raised at the back of the room whilst students weren't yet silent as a reminder to him to wait and look. Ask for this if you think it would help.

Feedback

Ashley, a secondary Maths teacher, describes his first experience reflecting on his lessons and receiving feedback.

The first time you ever teach you're still in a bit of shock. I'm actually in front of 30 kids, teaching. When I started, it was easy to think I'm doing something wrong instead of I can do better. I'm quite hard on myself. I would go home and say *This was awful, that was awful. I didn't do my starter right. Timings were really wrong.*

Gradually, I realised feedback wasn't someone personally attacking me. It's more that there's this person with the experience to tell you how to improve on it. In my first lesson observation feedback, I was thinking *This person just doesn't like me.* But actually they're just trying to make you a better teacher.

Feedback in deliberate practice should be directly tied to the narrow behaviour you've been practising and the success criteria defined at the outset. If you feel your observer is straying beyond the boundaries of what you've been practising, do let them know. It's not that what they have to say won't be useful. To focus practice on rapid improvement, you need to hear specifically about what you were practising. You could ask to hear specifically about what you've been practising first and leave the rest for any spare time at the end.

Whilst difficult to achieve in isolation, some forms of practice are possible on your own. Perhaps you've left training and early careers status behind and no longer are being observed as often. You can still home in on a specific skill.

Imagine you've become aware that classes are slow to settle when you want to transition between activities. Asking repeatedly for quiet and raising your voice hasn't helped. Having talked to colleagues and observed another teacher, you've decided to practice narrating your countdown. You write what you want to say on a post-it, mainly aiming to reiterate simple instructions as you countdown. This isn't high stakes: you're going to aim to narrate the countdown at least three times each lesson. You audio record your narrated countdown and notice, in your first try, your pauses are too short. The narration isn't getting through. You try again, focusing on the pause. The class settle. Developing a rhythm of ongoing practice is important for the individual teacher. Stepping out of yourself, analysing your behaviour and finding ways to alter it are essential activities for all successful teachers. Doing this on your own is sometimes possible but not ideal.

Whilst some forms of feedback work in isolation – video or student response, say – it's unlikely these things will work indefinitely, particularly as a very new teacher. Practice is an effective strategy for making a change in the classroom but we don't always know what needs to change. We don't always see every corner of our classroom. We don't hear every whispered misconception. This is why it's vital someone is supporting you to see beyond what is easily visible. This is why we need a coach.

Annalise, a Science teacher, describes her perception of receiving feedback before she started teaching.

The way [our training provider] had prepared us, they'd really prepared us to almost be hung, drawn and quartered at the end of every observation. They warned us that it would be like assassination of your personality and really torn to pieces every time that you went through it. So I was pleasantly surprised when it was no such thing. It felt much more supportive than I was expecting.

Coaching

Any comments about coaching or mentoring should be an extension of the comments about practice. Initially, a significant role of the coach or mentor is to help you practise. Learning to teach is difficult because you are just developing awareness of what is happening in your classroom. A coach helps to solve this problem.

Instructional coaching, a form of responsive and, at times, directive coaching, like practice, attempts to increase awareness of your classroom actions and behaviour before offering specific ways to change. One definition describes coaching like this:

a one-to-one conversation focused on the enhancement of learning and development through increasing self-awareness and a sense of personal responsibility, where the coach facilitates the self-directed learning of the coachee through questioning, active listening, and appropriate challenge in a supportive and encouraging climate.[6]

Whilst generic forms of coaching exist in education, instructional coaching is at the core of current thinking about how teachers improve. But definitions – and your experience – of instructional coaching will vary. Most debates about instructional coaching centre on how directive it should be. Jim Knight describes how 'instructional coaches teach others how to learn very specific, evidence-based teaching practices'.[7] For Knight, instructional coaches add this more directive element to more traditional coaching techniques like 'dialogic questioning' and 'effective listening'.

Paul Bambrick-Santoyo, a prominent voice for a more directive version of instructional coaching, emphasises the need for an 'action step', a clear, well-defined next step for the teacher.[8] In Bambrick-Santoyo's model, this action step is given by the coach, modelled by the coach and then practised, often in an empty classroom, by the coachee in preparation for the real event. It's likely you'll swing between a directive model and a responsive one as you bring ideas to the coaching relationship at times and, at others, go to your coach desperate for any solution.

It might seem strange to talk about coaching when it feels like it is something done to you. Too often, the focus in education and CPD is on what the coach will do. To maximise your understanding of what good teaching is – your knowledge of classroom craft – you need to know how to act in that coach/coachee relationship. With this in mind, it is worth going into a coaching relationship knowing what you're getting.

Beyond understanding the coaching process, you participate in it by receiving feedback. No one really tells you how to do this, which is strange because receiving and responding to feedback well is the main way you will get better. You often don't know how you're going to take feedback until you're receiving it, and in training and early careers, you receive a lot. Depending on how you've arrived in teaching, you may have only received generally positive feedback in your academic and extra-curricular pursuits. How you receive feedback also depends on your sense of yourself. If you've dreamed of being a teacher since your first day of school, being criticised for your first lessons can be incredibly demoralising.

I don't know what kind of feedback you're going to receive. However that feedback is given, even if it could be better, kinder or more productive, you can make the most of it. In their excellent book, *Thanks for the Feedback*, Sheila Heen and Douglas Stone offer three feedback triggers – three ways we can reject feedback – and what we can do about them.

The triggers are:

1. Truth Triggers – We feel 'indignant, wronged and exasperated' because the feedback is 'somehow off, unhelpful or simply untrue'.

2. Relationship Triggers – Our reaction to feedback is 'based on what we believe about the giver'.

3. Identity Triggers – The feedback makes us 'feel overwhelmed, threatened, ashamed' because we're 'suddenly unsure what to think about ourselves'.[9]

Identifying our feedback triggers, which may vary depending on who is giving the feedback and what it is, is the first step to learning as much from feedback as possible. You might recognise yourself in one or all of those triggers. Just knowing our triggers is not the same as being able to deal with them.

Some strategies for making the most of feedback include:

Kate, a secondary Maths trainee, describes her perspective on lesson observation feedback.

It's really hard to mess everything up. There is something that's going to go well. Then, I think it's also just remembering there are always things people can improve on. Someone could walk into a teacher who's been teaching for 20 years and pick apart their lesson. It's about that understanding that you're not a bad teacher because there are improvements to make and that you have done something right.

- **Pause.** Don't immediately jump to the defence of whatever behaviour is the target of the feedback. Don't immediately explain away what has been noticed even if it feels like there is an explanation.

- **Ask questions.** It's important to pause before questioning so that we don't just attack the feedback or be seen to. Ask your observer to explain it again. Ask them to give examples. Ask them to give you a reason why what they're talking about is so important.

- **Separate the feedback giver from the feedback.** When you start out, it's likely that you'll be receiving feedback on your lessons from a very small number of people. If, for whatever reason, you find one of these people difficult to receive feedback from, there is a real danger this difficulty slows your progress as a new teacher. If there's someone you dread getting feedback from, imagine the feedback from that person is coming from someone you really respect. How would your response be different?

- **Acknowledge how the feedback is making you feel.** In the moment, your heart can start to race; you can feel your face turn red with frustration or disappointment or anger. Recognise how you physically respond to feedback. Recognise that physical reaction is momentary. Perhaps thoughts about the amount of work you've put in or the progress you know you've made enter your mind. It doesn't feel like your coach gets that. Separate the feeling from the feedback where you can. Make notes if you need to so you can return to the feedback when you've had time to process the physical and emotional reaction to it.

● **Remind yourself feedback happens to help you get better.** You're not meant to feel under attack when receiving feedback but you can. Feedback is not the end-point. As Heen and Douglas remind us, feedback should be seen as 'welcome input rather than upsetting verdict'.[10]

Annalise describes preparing herself to receive feedback.

I had prepared myself to feel really down and out or to feel like I had a lot of work to do. I'm my biggest critic. The way I went into it was to try to be specific in what I wanted to know. So don't go into some feedback and say *How did I do?* On a scale of what?

So I'd try to say so *I've just done this task. Can you let me know if I could have done it better? I have done it this way. Would you have done it differently?* So you present them your thought process and then you can receive theirs. And they know where your focus is.

If, after following this advice, you still feel feedback is unhelpful, unrealistic or hypercritical, raise it with those giving the feedback. It is your responsibility to do all you can to make the most of feedback. It is the responsibility of those giving feedback to make it useful, possible and productive.

In summary

Teachers automate effective processes by:

● *Seeing* and *understanding* effective teaching practices.

● *Narrowly defining* specific behaviours to practice.

● *Practising before and during lessons.*

● *Receiving feedback* and *refining* in response to feedback.

Observations, practice and coaching overlap and intertwine; you don't move neatly from one to the next. As we begin to look at different types of teacher knowledge, these ideas will be relevant to specific aspects of pedagogy and subject. My aim in writing this chapter has been to give you a way to be an active participant in your training and development rather than a passive receiver.

Possible next steps

1. **Plan an observation.** Decide what you need to see. Ask others to observe for that focus. Before the observation, arrange a time afterwards where you can talk to the person you've observed. Go into that conversation with questions.

2. **Find at least one way to take ownership of your practice.** Others are responsible for directing and developing you, but that doesn't mean you aren't equally responsible. Take steps to make sure your practice extends beyond those out of lesson times. Make visible notes and reminders for yourself. Record or video your teaching. After a period of practice, return to your coach and ask for clarity if you're not sure what to do next.

3. **Talk through your feedback triggers.** You could do this with your coach if you have that kind of relationship but you don't really *need* to discuss this with a teacher. It would be equally useful with a friend or family member you trust. Articulating your triggers to feedback raises your awareness of them. This is the first step in being able to tackle them.

Notes

1 Kirabo Jackson, C., and Bruegmann, E. (2009). *Teaching Students and Teaching Each Other: The Importance of Peer Learning for Teachers*. NBER Working Paper No. 15202.
2 Papay, J., Taylor, E., Tyler, J., and Laski, M. (2020). Learning job skills from colleagues at work. *American Economic Journal: Economic Policy*, 12(1), 359–388.
3 Ericson, A. (2006). The influence of experience and deliberate practice on the development of superior expert performance. In A. Ericson (ed.), *The Cambridge Handbook of Expertise and Expert Performance* (pp. 683–704). Cambridge University Press.
4 Feldon, D. (2007). Cognitive load and classroom teaching: The double-edged sword of automaticity. *Educational Psychologist*, 42(3), 123–137.
5 Ericson, A. (2006). The influence of experience and deliberate practice on the development of superior expert performance. In A. Ericson (ed.), *The Cambridge Handbook of Expertise and Expert Performance* (pp. 683–704). Cambridge University Press.
6 van Nieuwerburgh, C. (ed.) (2012). *Coaching in Education: Getting Better Results for Students, Educators, and Parents*. Karnac.
7 Knight, J., and Nieuwerburgh, C. (2012). Instructional coaching: A focus on practice. *Coaching: An International Journal of Theory, Research and Practice*, 5(2), 100–112.
8 Santoyo, P.B. (2016). *Get Better Faster*. John Wiley & Sons.
9 Heen, S., and Douglas, S. (2014). *Thanks for the Feedback*. Penguin.
10 Ibid.

Further reading

Heen, S., and Douglas, S. (2014) *Thanks for the Feedback*. Penguin.

PART 3
Knowledge of student behaviour

Early in my one of my first teaching placements, I was left alone – for a moment – with a class for the first time. The class were already working quietly, a benefit of their usual teacher's presence, so I waited anxiously for her return. Whilst she was gone, one student decided to start flicking little balls of paper off his desk and onto the floor. I tried to mask my terror at encountering behaviour I was not prepared for by saying, as firmly as I could muster, 'Stop doing that'. The student looked up, sighed, and asked, quite reasonably, 'Or what?' It was a question for which I was entirely without an answer. Having made his point, he quietly continued and the teacher returned soon afterwards. To begin with, behaviour management felt like something I wanted to avoid. I wanted my classes to be well-behaved. I wanted not to have to deal with paper flickers or their ilk.

Behaviour management, for me, was a minefield of misconceptions. Knowledge of behaviour management often begins in challenging these misconceptions, pre-conceptions and stereotypes. Here are a few of them.

● You need a certain type of personality to manage behaviour.

I have never been an outgoing, shouty extrovert. Those were the people, so I thought, who would find all this effortless. I, on the other hand, was exhausted by just the possibility of poor behaviour in my lessons. Even when I became a senior leader, I felt that I would never have the authority of those who could command a play-ground of children with a whistle and a loud voice.

Behaviour management, however, is not about personality type. It's a set of strategies and these strategies can vary from person to person. Unlike other areas of teaching, these strategies feel more tied to our personality. Are you more likely to defuse a situation with humour or lay down the law? But these are quite superficial questions when compared to the complexity of planning for and managing behaviour across a class because so much of behaviour manage-ment is about how you plan and organise your lessons. You do need to be able to talk with authority, loud enough for a class full of children to hear you. You do, at times, need to act decisively for the sake of the children's safety or the

DOI: 10.4324/9781003281306-9

success of your lesson. None of that is the same as saying behaviour management is the skill of the extrovert. Believing you can manage your behaviour through the force of your personality is a recipe for burnout.

● You need to have a response ready for every possible scenario.

As a trainee, behaviour management felt like a huge set of scenarios that I would have to plan for, rehearsing responses. I never plucked up the courage to do this but I was always eager to sit my mentor down before a lesson and ask endless *What if* questions. Comfortingly though, behaviour *generally* falls into categories that we can prepare for.

Your first line of defence against low level and off-task behaviour is the organisation of your classroom and the planning of your lessons. It's not so much that your lessons have to be 'fun', 'relevant' or any other vomit-inducing sentiment. Rather, we plan for students to behave by creating a classroom built on routine. That routine includes a response to students who don't adhere to expectations, a response that should be guided by your school's behaviour management systems and policy. It isn't cruel or boring to make the foundations of our lessons routine. Whilst unglamorous, this sort of planning makes the most out of our time with the young people in our classes. Routine doesn't mean we can never be spontaneous, never deviate. It is simply the foundation on which we build.

Even when behaviour is more extreme, there are routines and scripts we can embed to help us prepare. A student in one of my lessons once threw a book across the room and then proceeded to kick it into confetti against the wall. I hadn't been trained for this and I confess I just watched in frightened awe. It would have been foolish to spend hours considering how to prepare for future book-kickers. He was the only one.

● You shouldn't smile until Christmas.

Smile as often as you normally would. Smile when a student gets something right. Smile when they do something funny. I'm not sure this advice really exists in any real sense but perhaps some new teachers go into lessons believing they need to be an ogre. Being strict, at least in some quarters, is back in vogue and so it is likely a few will confuse this with draining your face of personality until spring. Even if you don't hear this advice, it points to something unhelpful about behaviour management instruction. Smiling or not smiling will have very little impact on student behaviour. Behaviour change is borne out of more fundamental change in how we plan for and act in the classroom.

Contained within this unhelpful advice not to smile, though, is perhaps a nugget of truth. You aren't there to be a friend. Chummy banter with the students might elicit a positive reaction initially but will make your life difficult in the long run. As we'll see, the strategies we use to manage behaviour are quite different to those we use to win friends.

● For students to behave, you need to show them you care.

Almost inverse to the previous statement, some believe that students can't learn anything until they feel loved. Of course, you should care for your students. Teaching would be a surprising career choice if you didn't. But there does seem to be some confusion about what *care* really means here. It does mean you're interested in them as people. It does mean you want them to do well. It does mean you work hard to ensure they meet their potential. Caring *doesn't* mean putting up with offensive, disruptive or aggressive behaviour. It should never mean working yourself into the ground to make tiny gains with a student who is endlessly rude or deliberately spoils your lessons.

The twin statement of *you need to show them you care* is *teaching is all about relationships*. Teaching is absolutely about relationships but those relationships aren't friendships. A teacher–student relationship works best when students know exactly what to expect from you. Everything, at least in the realm of behaviour, comes back to creating clarity around routines and expectations, as well as certainty of response when students don't meet those expectations.

On our tour of teacher knowledge, I'm focusing on areas where we can develop real understanding of and make tangible changes to our behaviour management. Whilst whole books have been written on the subject of behaviour, it's my hope that these chapters give you a guide to begin building mental models for behaviour management. This section won't answer every question you have about behaviour because it can't. Instead, you will be directed to the two areas in which you can, right now, develop knowledge to improve behaviour.

In this section, we'll answer the following questions:

- How do we prepare for students to behave?

- How do we manage behaviour in-lesson?

None of the answers here guarantees perfect behaviour nor are these answers switches you flick to get immediate good behaviour. Behaviour in a school is also not *wholly* down to you. We must be careful not to abdicate responsibility to manage our classes well, but school systems, policy and routines also play an important role. The following chapters focus on you and what you can do whether you're in a school that manages behaviour well or badly.

Perhaps the biggest misconception about behaviour management is that it is something you master before moving on to your loftier goals. Teaching is always going to be about the management of behaviour because students are young people and, well, they behave in ways you wouldn't expect or predict.

How do we prepare for our students to behave?

When I was a new teacher, I felt the benefit of teaching English in a school that mandated five minutes of silent reading at the start of every lesson. Not many schools do this now, probably because – with entry, settling and getting the students to actually read – 5 minutes often became 15. Starting my lessons was easy: students came in, got their books out (or got a battered one from the box at the front) and started reading. I had some time then to hand out books and resources, to set up my computer and do odd jobs I should have saved for later. Starts of my lessons were anything but good but the reading masked that, and I carried on, clueless about what could have been better.

The *Great Teaching Toolkit* describes how 'Great teachers plan activities and resources so everything works smoothly'.[1] In the myriad of ways we can achieve smooth running of the classroom, a larger proportion than you'd expect happen before students have even entered the classroom. A crucial question to ask is *What should I base my decisions about behaviour on (before the lesson or otherwise)?*

Annalise, a Science teacher, describes her biggest fear going into the classroom.

Ultimately, it's standing in front of a group of students and not being able to be in control of that room. This is the biggest fear, I think, because if you can get that you can build everything else. But you can have all the knowledge in the world. If you can't control the room, then what good is that knowledge?

 DOI: 10.4324/9781003281306-10

What norms are you seeking to create?

Ashley, a secondary Maths teacher in his first year, describes a realisation about behaviour management.

To start with, I thought behaviour management was about controlling everything and waiting to see if they'd be naughty. I was worried about people fighting and throwing things but it's not really that kind of behaviour that's the issue.

It's more about like getting rid of or eliminating the bad habits within the room: somebody calling out rather than putting their hand up, someone turning around talking when they shouldn't be talking. Low level behaviour is what you're going to have to spend most of your time actually dealing with. So I wanted focus on getting rid of those bad habits and getting students into good habits.

I made lists of what I wanted to see to remind me what I wanted and what I didn't.

Behaviour management is both proactive and reactive. Your mental model of managing behaviour is proactive in that you can prepare for behaviour in advance outside of the classroom. It is proactive in that you can teach students positive behaviours rather than just respond to negative behaviours. We shouldn't kid ourselves, though: there are times when we will have to react. We can prepare for these times but that doesn't mean that they will be easy. Whilst the next chapter will deal with the reactive side of behaviour management, this one looks at the proactive steps we can take. These steps stem from a question: *What type of classroom do I want to create?* Such creation doesn't happen because of wishful thinking. It happens through careful planning, thoughtful reaction and intensive work with our students.

Behavioural economist John Elster describes social norms as 'emotional and behavioural propensities'[2] – behaviours and inclinations, driven by motivation to fit in. Often, such behaviours are not rational but instinctual. Every day, teachers see in their students the tensions between instinct and rational forward thinking. Secondary students often know intellectually that school is useful and that education is valuable but they still act in ways that seem to discount this. In fact, adults also tend to discount the potential gains in the future compared with gains in the present but, developmentally, teenagers are more susceptible to this.[3]

So what? That children can act irrationally hardly needs stating. We don't need a body of evidence to remind us to be the voice of reason in the classroom. Fortunately, this is not all we can learn from behavioural economics. In this field, we find methods not just to recognise the norms I've described but also to create them through habits, routines and nudges.

In being proactive about behaviour management, we're not simply trying to *prepare for the worst* – the worst behaviour or our worst expectations. Rather, we want to make changes to our classroom, our planning and our delivery that make it less likely that students will misbehave. Ultimately, we're trying to create habits or norms. Logan Fiorella, Professor of Educational Psychology, describes how 'beneficial habits will continue effortlessly despite fluctuations in motivation or willpower'.[4] We can't overstate the importance of such knowledge for teachers: even when students don't feel like or don't want to learn in your classroom, habits trump apathy and disengagement.

Before you consider what norms you are trying to create, consider the following questions:

- What do you value as a teacher and how do you want to make that a routine?

- What norms already exist in your school? Or, what norms is your school trying to establish?

Let us then turn our attention to the evidence and strategies we can use to harness the power of routine and promote good behaviour in our classrooms.

Remove the friction from doing the right thing

When the British government's Behavioural Insights Team produced a report on how to nudge behaviour in an intended direction, their first piece of advice was to 'make it easy'.[5] As this sounds a bit obvious – *of course I want it to be easy for students to behave* – it's worth considering from another angle: *How can I reduce the 'friction costs', the 'seemingly irrelevant details that make a task more challenging or effortful'?*[6]

As behavioural scientist Katy Milkman explains, 'An engineer can't design a successful structure without first carefully accounting for the forces of opposition (say, wind resistance or gravity). So engineers always attempt to solve problems by first identifying the obstacles to success'.[7] At times, the origin of friction or obstacle can be difficult to identify. In some lessons, it might all feel like friction, making choosing one behaviour or routine difficult. Consciously looking for friction *might* help but a supportive observation (or recording) can highlight what you would otherwise miss.

Below I'll cover three major examples; of course, there are more.

Entry and exit routines

Kate, a secondary Maths trainee, describes how routine has an impact on her classroom.

Routine for the students was so important. Having come from a fairly academic and studious background myself, I was shocked at how much processing power was used by children in mundane tasks. So I made a consistent effort to make routine automated for students. Now, the first 10–15 minutes are entirely predictable from how books are handed out, to expectations for seating and behaviour to how I greet students at the door. Similarly, my final 5 minutes are now automatic based on where I stand in the room – I don't even have to say an instruction for the students. This was all to help reduce the cognitive load placed on students so they can spend as much mental energy on the content as possible.

A large part of the answer to the question of behaviour depends on what your school does about it. Your school may have a particular routine about entry to the classroom – they line up, they go straight in, they stand behind chairs. Such routines make your life and the lives of your colleagues profoundly simpler. If you are lucky enough to find yourself in such a school, embrace the routines even if they feel like they grate against your freedom-loving sensibilities.

Constructing your own routines, where a school does not dictate one, is definitely possible. Your aim is to remove the friction in the process of students entering the room and starting whatever the first task is. When students have to go and get their books or resources at the start of every lesson, when they have to look for them because they seem to move around, we're making it harder for students to get started. We're making it more likely that students will act out.

The Behavioural Insights Team encourage us to 'harness the power of defaults'.[8] You might not like the idea of *every* lesson starting in the same way but there is power in a routine that happens (at least almost) every lesson. Routines may feel constricting but their effects are often liberating: time has been saved, behaviour has been managed almost effortlessly, students spend lesson time on the right things. A lesson entry is a good time to create a default: students come in, sit straight down, push books along a row and then get started on a task on the screen.

For a while I was teaching in five different rooms. I know teachers who have had to teach in *so many* more (the highest I've heard being around 13). Five still felt like a lot to me. I didn't know what to do at first; I'd arrive panting, sweating and stressed from one room to the next. Behaviour in the initial moments of those lessons was always precariously close to chaos as I set up resources, frantically searched for books hidden by another teacher and started the first task.

If you're moving from room to room, it's likely you won't have a say about the layout of the space. I would have liked to change the layout of some of those rooms I was teaching in but I couldn't. Instead, I focused on what I had control over: resources and first activities. I got into school early and logged on to each computer in turn and set up my lessons for the day. That way I just needed to log in for students to see the first task on the screen. I made different piles of books for each row in the classroom and told students on the end of those rows it would be their responsibility to pass the books along. Because these strategies worked so well across five rooms, I continued using them even when I went back to teaching in one. My argument isn't that you should get in early and pile up books in a specific way, but a plan of some kind can help massively. I've known teachers print out a task on a slip of paper so that students can complete something whilst the room is prepared. I've known teachers breeze into a room and write a question on the whiteboard to similar effect. Try out different approaches but aim for a routine that works over time.

Setting tasks and managing transitions

Alex, a secondary English trainee, describes how he's learned to make his instructions easier to follow.

If you set a task and you say, 'Five minutes off you go', that might give no clear indication as to how the students should proceed with that task. If you say, 'You have five minutes to do this task in silence, and I expect at least three questions to be done by the end of it, I will be coming round in one minute's time to survey the class. Anybody that does not have at least the first one down in that time will be choosing a consequence'. All the expectations are clear. It's up to the students now whether they meet those expectations. Students know what to expect from you.

Training schemes usually, if only for a time, mandate a lesson planning proforma. These often have a box for what you're working on, some information about the class (which you can copy and paste from the previous plan), and the sequence of activities for the lesson. These plans can have you playing Nostradamus when they ask you to set out the length of time each task will take, which is a brutally unfair thing to ask a new teacher to decide.

What is missing from these forms tends to be what will happen in the gaps or transitions between the activities. Any time you set a task or transition from one activity to the next, there is both the possibility of calm and chaos. Planning transitions and structuring the distribution of resources can feel like additional work, additional planning, but these things will save you immeasurable time and hassle in the future. You can prepare for transitions by:

- Checking all resources are ready before the lesson.

- Putting out resources for the *next* task during the *current* task.

- Giving time reminders and warnings. For example, *In five minute's time, we're going to be packing away. By then, I'd expect you to...*

Dead time between tasks is a breeding ground for off-task behaviour and even if students do behave as you set up the next task, the time you've spent doing this could have been folded into a prior moment in the lesson. Time can be saved and learning maximised. Equally, if instructions are given but are unclear, students may start a task but fail to engage properly or quickly – at best asking lots of questions, and at worst disrupting the lesson.

What, then, avoids this potential disruption or loss of time? In short, clarity and specificity. Knowing you need clarity and specificity or trying to remind yourself of those things in the moment is unlikely to be helpful. We prepare for behaviour when we plan our expectations around a task. Going into a lesson, for the tasks you will set, you should know:

● **How long the task will last?** I'd make this a rough estimate and respond to what you see in the students' work but if you struggle with timing, you may want to use a stopwatch.

● **Where and how the students will complete the task?** On the sheet? In their books? In full sentences? In notes? What does 'notes' mean? One way to answer these questions – particularly for more complex tasks – is to model how you expect students to approach a task. This can be particularly effective under a visualiser when you demonstrate work in the same format as the students: if they are using a sheet, show them how to work on the sheet; if they are working in an exercise book, use your own exercise book under the visualiser.

● **What are the expectations of and constraints on student behaviour during the task?** Start with noise. Are students allowed to talk? Who are they allowed to talk to? Are they allowed to move around the room? If students get stuck, what should they do?

The questions above can help you to create scripts like the examples below. Remember, your aim is friction reduction.

> Example 1: You have 10 minutes to complete all of the questions on page 120 of the textbook. Your answers should be written – with working out – into your exercise book. You must not talk any louder than a whisper to the person sitting next you, and only to that person if you get stuck. Go.
> Example 2: Complete the passing drill I just showed you with your group as many times as you can in two minutes. You should only be talking to people in your group. Off you go.
> Example 3: Write your own paragraph, like the one I've modelled. If you get stuck, you're going to use the sentence starters and notes in your book from this lesson to help you. You won't put your hand up. This task will be completed in silence because I want to see what you can do on your own. You have ten minutes. Begin writing now.

In addition to the above, we remove and reduce friction when the starts and ends of tasks are clear. Notice each of the examples has a clear start to it. Deciding a word or phrase to start a task is as much for you as it is for the children. If you say 'Off you go', emphasis on the *go*, every time a task starts, it helps you to stop continuing to talk until your instructions fade out as you find yourself wandering around the class. After the 'Go', pausing at the front of the room can help you to assess if your instructions have been successful. If everyone looks puzzled or if the instructions of *where* to complete the task – Not on the sheet! – aren't followed or if everyone starts talking even though silence was the expectation, then you have grounds to halt the task and reiterate instructions.

Sarah, a new Year 4 teacher, describes making her instructions clear.

It's important to be clear on what you expect from the children. Telling them Step 1, Step 2, Step 3 and then keeping it simple. So, when they know what they're doing, there are fewer behaviour problems. For example, I might say, *After you've finished your work, I want you to read your book quietly or do your times tables.* So they're not looking round or having a chat.

Ending tasks

Just as we shouldn't continue talking after our planned instructions have ended, we shouldn't end a task by starting to talk, gradually winning the attention of small numbers of students at a time. Instead, make the ending clear. If you use a countdown timer, that could be the buzzer noise as it ends. The upside of the buzzer is that it is definitive and clear to students; the downside is that once you've started a countdown, you cede control of the end of the task to the buzzer.

Teachers often use a verbal countdown at the end of a task, perhaps because they've heard others use one. Countdowns can be a source of friction rather than a solution if you get to zero and the class aren't doing what you've asked of them. Classes can be taught to respond appropriately to the countdown but we should expect to put in the hours of communication, practice and repetition.

Narrating the countdown is often effective at getting students to follow an instruction in a short space of time. A narrated countdown communicates and reiterates the expectations between the numbers: *Silence in 3... pens down in 2... everyone looking this way, silence in 1... zero.* Early in my career, this became my signature move to the extent that, at one school, a student used to yell, 'Silence in THREE' at me across the playground. Although students yelling at you across the playground is usually not a good sign, I was cautiously optimistic that this particular student had become aware of the routine.

Planning a set of instructions or narrated countdown can be scripted and then practised as discussed in Chapter 5. The more you do this in the short term, the less you'll have to do it in the long term. Friction against the behaviour we want is likely to deter students from it.

Decide on common cues to prompt the right behaviours

Habits are sometimes described as the behavioural responses to cues in our environment. Although it's probably more complex than this – habitual behaviour interacts with our goals and personality[9] – cues can be useful in the classroom. Certain contexts demand certain actions; habit researchers Wendy Wood and David Neal give the example of buckling your seatbelt, an action demanded by the act of getting into a car but not one you think a great deal about.[10] In your classroom, you don't have the luxury of relying on an already universal action like the buckling of a seatbelt. Work is required to get anywhere close to that kind of automaticity. Cues are your way of highlighting the easy behaviour and removing the friction.

As students enter the room – whatever the time of day, whatever they've just done – set it up so the cues are visible. Exercise books are out on tables. Resources are easily accessible. A resource is handed to students as they enter. A countdown tells students to start quickly. Settled, immediate work is the aim. One-off usage won't turn any of these into a cue or achieve the result you're after. Repetition is the breeding ground for habit cues.

Some poor behaviour is the cued response to the friction you're working to eliminate. Students have nothing to do or instructions are unclear; students engage in some kind of off-task behaviour: they talk, they move around, they shout across the room.

Keep at it

If your aim is to establish a behaviour as the norm, you need to be in it for the long haul. We can always move away from behaviours we don't think are getting the desired result, but we shouldn't be quick to move on to the *next thing* until students are in the habit we want them to be. One study found it took around six weeks, the length of an average half-term, to establish a regular gym habit.[11] We should probably expect something similar in our classrooms.

If, for example, you want students to pack up in a particular way, you need to introduce the new system to the students, make a big deal of it for a long time, get students to do it again when it isn't right and praise it when it is. If we've made any change or introduced a new strategy with a class and it doesn't feel like it's working, ask yourself how long you've been at it, how much you've practised it, and how often you're returning to it. Even weeks after you've introduced a routine, demonstrate to students that it's *still* important and that you *still* care about it. Set a reminder or schedule an email to yourself; find one way to force yourself back to a routine a few weeks after you start it. Reminders like these could pleasantly surprise you when they come at a time when you have established something in your class you can be proud of. They could also remind you before you lose something that it is worth pursuing.

Distinguishing between a norm you should keep going with and one that can be shelved is difficult. You have sunk time and energy into creating it. Base your decision to leave a norm behind on:

- The realisation you don't want to or can't create this norm.

- The discovery of a better way (through observation, conversation or training) that you can achieve this norm.

> **Georgia, a trainee PE teacher, describes the thing she found helped the most when it came to setting up routines to manage behaviour.**
>
> I'm always at lessons on time with everything ready. Everything is planned. I know what I'm doing but I make sure the class do too. I let them know what they're going to do. They know what to expect. I always have a task to help them settle down because I'm already there.

Use the power of timing

I love meeting a new class at the start of the year. These are moments of such potential. Every time is an opportunity to reinvent yourself as a teacher or, if that is too strong, to take at least one step forward. And, whilst I've rarely lived up to my own expectations of what I could achieve in an academic year, I've also found it easier to make at least some kind of change for the better. I've got a little bit stricter, perhaps. Or worked hard to teach a new topic well.

Katy Milkman describes the 'fresh start' effect, a phenomenon where people find it easier to change at natural transitions or landmarks in the calendar. Milkman describes how these fresh starts are 'helpful for kick-starting change' but warns that they can disrupt 'well-functioning routines',[12] particularly where those routines are newly established. The 'fresh start' effect has two important applications for teachers.

A new term is a good time to introduce a new habit or break an old one

I once worked for a headteacher who would make no major changes to school policy until September. If the behaviour policy was proven to be woefully inadequate in February, you just had to buckle up and hold on until September. Perhaps this headteacher, like I had with my classes, realised a new term is a good time to make a change. Unfortunately, not all changes can wait until after a holiday.

A new term, therefore, is a good time to make the big changes you want to make to your practice. You've realised you've been too lenient and now you want to raise expectations. You've been tentative about live-modelling under the visualiser but now you're going to start. You've wanted to discuss and share more student work during lesson time but have felt a barrier to doing so – a new term is a fresh go at breaking down that barrier.

Before the end of a term, consider what changes you want to make in your classroom. Consider the norms you want to create or recreate. Consider the cues you need to set up for yourself and for your students. Note these things down for future-you to be reminded of when you return after the break.

A new term is an important moment to review and consolidate habits you want to keep

The end of a term is also a good time to reflect, consolidate and take pride in the success you have achieved. Unfortunately, habits and norms only recently formed are at their most fragile when we take a break from them. If a questioning technique, an exit routine, a behaviour management script had a modicum of success during the term, make a note of that success before you leave. Leave yourself a note to explain to future-you what you've been doing and why you think it's worked. Don't leave to chance your ability to sustain success into a new term.

Prepare for the class(es)

Part 6 will go into more depth on knowing your students. For now, it's worth noting that to make actions easy, to use the power of identity, to use praise sincerely, you need to know your students:

Know their names. Knowing a student's name when they don't feel you should never ceases to have impact. Place a seating plan in front of you whilst teaching and use the names as often as you can. Photos help you to learn names over a brief period of quizzing.

Know their needs. Support plans and pupil passports (named differently from school to school) offer strategies to work with some students. At times, advice given is vague: *break content down.* Concrete direction can be followed easily: *Sit at the front* or *Don't get this student to read aloud.* Following such plans reduces friction.

Know the data. Bias and assumption cloud knowledge of students. Past performance tells us something but not everything. Data might need to be explained to you. A conversation about specific content and how to pitch it is likely more useful than a spreadsheet at this stage.

Be wary of 'getting to know you activities', or at least spending time excessively on them. Teachers aren't short of time with students; relationships don't form because we've played a couple of games with a class. Teachers are responsible for *knowing their classes* but those relationships are best developed within the boundaries of the rules, expectations and norms of the classroom. We've spent time considering routines and habits so that you have the space to teach and develop those relationships.

In summary

Behaviour management is more than the sum of the routines you build but you're unlikely to manage behaviour well without routine. If you look around your classroom and despair at the lack of routine, don't panic. Effective teachers aren't usually managing behaviour through the force of personality. They've created successful routines that happen automatically. Within the framework of those routines, we'll still have to respond to student misbehaviour as it arises whilst promoting positive behaviour. That is what we'll turn to next.

Possible next steps

1. **Be clear with yourself on norms and routines.** If you haven't done it before, write down as much as you can about how you'd like students to behave in your classroom. Consider which of these are coming from you and which from your school's procedures (prioritise whole school behaviours first).

2. **Identify a point of friction.** Where and when do students behave in a way you don't intend? Is it when they're handing out resources? During class discussion? In extended independent tasks? Of course, identifying friction is only half the battle. Once identified, talk to others about how they deal with similar friction. Invite your coach or mentor to look at this area specifically.

3. **Script and practise a clear instruction.** You can't do this for every instruction – imagine how long that would take! But, with new or complex activities, a script can help clarify – for you and them – what is expected. An unrehearsed script is unlikely to help. Practise by yourself or with a coach to reveal possible issues.

Notes

1 Coe, R., Rauch, C.J., Kime, S., and Singleton, D. (2020). *Great Teaching Toolkit Evidence Review.* Cambridge Assessment International Education.
2 Elster, K. (1989). Social norms and economic theory. *Journal of Economic Perspectives,* 3(4), 99–117.
3 Lavecchia, A.M., Liu, H., and Oreopoulos, P. (2016). Behavioral economics of education: Progress and possibilities. In E.A. Hanushek, S. Machin and L. Woessmann (eds), *Handbook of the Economics of Education* (Vol. 5, pp. 1–74). Elsevier.
4 Fiorella, L. (2020). The science of habit and its implications for student learning and wellbeing. *Educational Psychology Review,* 32, 603–625.

5 Behavioural Insights Team. (2014). EAST Four simple ways to apply behaviour insights. www.bi.team/wp-content/uploads/2015/07/BIT-Publication-EAST_FA_WEB.pdf (accessed 22/11/2022)

6 Ibid.

7 Milkman, K. (2021). *How to Change*. Penguin.

8 Behavioural Insights Team. (2014). EAST Four simple ways to apply behaviour insights. www.bi.team/wp-content/uploads/2015/07/BIT-Publication-EAST_FA_WEB.pdf (accessed on 22/11/2022)

9 Wood, W., and Neil, D.T. (2007). A new look at habits and the habit–goal interface. *Journal of the American Psychological Association*, 11(4), 843–863.

10 Ibid.

11 Reed, J.A., and Phillips, D.A. (2005). Relationships between physical activity and the proximity of exercise facilities and home exercise equipment used by undergraduate university students. *Journal of American College Health*, 53(6), 285–290.

12 Milkman, K. (2021). *How to Change*. Penguin.

7 How do we manage the class's behaviour during a lesson?

> **Alex, a secondary English trainee, describes reacting to poor behaviour in the classroom.**
>
> There are some weeks where you come away from a lesson and you really question your career choice because you think *Why am I doing this?* Sometimes your classrooms can really feel like a battleground. Even when you feel like you're doing things in the kids' best interests, they really see you as an authority figure in opposition to them. And you have to work hard to overcome that. And there are some weeks it can be a demoralising job if you don't have that kind of self-security to go, *You know what? It's not personal.*

There are so many stories I could start this chapter with, examples of my inability to predict or manage student behaviour. The time I knew a student was about to start a fight, stood in the way and saw it start anyway. The countless occasions students have said something witty and withering and I've just stood there, stuttering and red faced. I once tried to convince a boy that he was sure to injure himself if he continued climbing the fence. By the time I'd explained how dangerous it was, he was over the fence and walking home.

Perhaps you'll already have your own stories of situations that could have gone better. Struggles with behaviour are universal yet somehow our own difficulties can become a personal source of shame. Managing behaviour gets easier but that doesn't mean it's easy. You can slip into a rhythm with classes that feels effortless, only to be jerked from it when a student arrives riled from the events of break and ready for confrontation.

In this chapter, we'll look at how you can manage behaviour in your classroom, during lessons. We'll work through everything from the minor to the more extreme. In our search for knowledge that can help us face the challenges and problems in the classroom, we'll focus mainly on your school's behaviour policy. To do that, we need to step back and consider your responsibilities and the responsibilities of leaders in your school.

 DOI: 10.4324/9781003281306-11

Whole school versus individual teacher

You've done some of the work to mitigate poor behaviour. Your classroom is ready. What more can individual teachers do to tackle poor behaviour? And what is the responsibility of leaders? Behaviour is sometimes passed back and forth between teachers and school or pastoral leaders. A student misbehaves in the classroom; the teacher, rightly, sanctions them. A leader looks at a spreadsheet of this week's sanctions and wonders why so many sanctions are being given in particular classes to particular students. Leaders mostly don't look at behaviour in this way to get at teachers; they have a wider responsibility to create a positive culture across the school. Behaviour tsar Tom Bennett describes the 'key task for the school leader' as creating a culture. When Bennett describes the features of the most successful schools, he focuses more on leader responsibilities than staff behaviours. Leaders are a visible presence. They set clear expectations. They support staff.[1]

Further research supports the idea that leaders play a vital role in managing behaviour. For example, leaders use knowledge of students' lives and difficulties to pre-empt poor behaviour. Teachers don't always have this knowledge. Behaviour interventions, activities run *outside of lessons*, are also tools in the leaders' arsenal to tackle poor behaviour.[2]

Leaders' responsibilities could be summarised as follows:

- Creating a culture of positive behaviour.
- Providing clarity on what is and isn't acceptable.
- Being a presence around the school, challenging poor behaviour and promoting positive behaviour.
- Supporting staff to manage behaviour, including the delivery of training.

Teachers' responsibilities include:

- Keeping children in their classrooms (and around school) safe.
- Following the school's behaviour policy.
- Creating a classroom environment where learning can happen.
- Challenging poor behaviour in and out of the classroom.
- Knowing the students you teach, forming relationships built on consistency and clarity of expectation.

Simply put, it is your responsibility to manage behaviour as best as you are able, including following the school's behaviour policy. It is a school leader's responsibility to support you as you do this.

Use the policy

> **Rachel, a Year 6 teacher in her first year, describes her school's behaviour policy.**
>
> At my school, the behaviour policy and also how you teach behaviour are really specific. We all follow the same system. And we all use the same strategies, and I think that works really well. So, because of that, it's much easier here to just teach, whereas when I went to my placement school, even though it was a really good school, that type of policy wasn't in place.
>
> We have the silent corridors here. We do *Fantastic Walking* and things like that and that really helps because there's no chatting or messing about in corridors. We do have to teach them those habits in the curriculum, the behaviour curriculum.
>
> We also do *Fantastic Listening* at our school. Instead of saying, 'Stop your work now and listen' I'll say 'Fantastic Listening' and straight away they need to put hands together, sit up straight and face forward. You'll get the odd one who has a pen in their hand. When that happens, you say, 'I am waiting for one'.

I thought I was terrible at managing behaviour until I worked in a school with a clear policy. In the school where I worked for the first two years of my career, a large comprehensive in Bristol, teachers managed behaviour through the strength of personality. For the first time in my life, I realised mine wasn't that strong.

In a school of almost two thousand students, I regularly found a child doing something inappropriate, only to have them run off when I started speaking. I'd see them again months later when it felt rude to bring up their past misdemeanours. My tutor group had its base in the science labs and, to the enduring irritation of the technicians, would turn on the gas taps when they got bored of PSHE. Our aim was to keep students in lessons for as long as possible, or until they did something so terrible that our defence for sending them out could be cast iron.

My second school was quite different. There was a clear system, a graduated approach, we were to use with all students in all classes. The headteacher was clear: he didn't want anyone doing anything else. I used the system and, to my surprise, found I could manage behaviour quite well.

Sometimes there are two behaviour policies: the intended policy and the enacted policy. The intended policy sounds good but the way it is enacted leaves much room for improvement. Or, even when the enacted policy works quite well, it feels distant from what is written down. The knowledgeable teacher seeks to understand the policy, intended and enacted. To do that, we read it. We talk to leaders (ideally, this would be part of your induction). Most importantly, we use it.

Learning about the policy is important but it isn't possible to understand it until you've seen it in action. If you can, observe teachers using the policy. Don't observe the easiest classes. Root out those classes and students that could pose a challenge and examine what experienced teachers do about it. If a consequence is given or a warning appears to be withheld and you're not sure why, ask. Understand the enacted behaviour policy by engaging with those who do the enacting each day.

I once worked with a new teacher who said the first thing she wanted to do was to co-construct a set of rules for her classes. A nice idea but one that failed to acknowledge the school already had a set of expectations and a process for dealing with poor behaviour, alongside a process for recognising effort, achievement and positive behaviour. There may be rare occasions when creating your own set of classroom rules is necessary but the first port of call is always the behaviour policy.

Why are we talking about a policy when the aim is to understand how you should act in lessons? The behaviour policy, when properly understood (and when properly implemented by school leaders), should clearly direct your behaviour in lessons. It won't tell you what to do in every situation, but it should be your map to traverse the range of behaviours you are likely to encounter.

Practise using the behaviour policy

Kate, a secondary Maths trainee, describes her experiences of getting to know a behaviour policy.

My experience of a behaviour policy from the schools I had taught in was very different to the one here. I did however have the opportunity to visit [my school] for two weeks prior to teaching so was able to see it in action before I had to apply it. This is something I would recommend to anyone if they have the chance.

Even so, I felt a little daunted so I printed and laminated a little A5 copy of the sanctions for certain behaviours. In the first few weeks, I would show students this and blame the policy rather than my interpretation. Once I became familiar with [the policy] I found I became less reliant on this and students respected the sanctions being given.

Georgia, a PE trainee, describes a similar experience.

I printed out a summary of the behaviour policy in grid form, laminated it and stuck it in my planner so that it was transferable, then by the end of the first term I no longer needed to refer to it. Over time, it becomes second nature and you are able to develop the refining of specific behaviours with scripted speech involved.

Annalise, a Science trainee, also used a prompt to refer to the behaviour policy.

I knew at the start the children knew more than I did about what constituted what sanction. They have been familiar with it longer than I had. To combat this, I kept the sanction table in the behaviour policy on my laptop open for reference to ensure I was confident [of the] sanctions as well as being clued up if I was challenged by a pupil.

Practice prepares us. Not for every eventuality, but for the processes we'll repeat. It's true, you can't prepare for everything, but warnings, consequences, the act of resettling a class or calming a student are all scriptable moments.

Your practise should answer the following questions:

- How do I promote positive behaviour through clear instructions?

- How do I settle a class when needed?

- How do I give warnings?

- How do I call for support when needed?

- How do I give a consequence or send a student out of the classroom?

- How do I respond to (rare cases of) extreme behaviour (e.g. a fight)?

Unfortunately, you can't practise in VR. When my wife was training to be a GP, they'd hire actors to play patients. These actors would cry on demand or get cross when a diagnosis wasn't to their liking. Whilst a helpful colleague may play the part of the recalcitrant youth, it is often the case that you can't rehearse what is unpredictable. Teacher trainers (and schools) don't seem to have the budget for actors. Perhaps it's the difference between one actor (who can play many patients) and the 30-odd you'd need for a realistic classroom. The predictable part of behaviour management is not the students' behaviour. It is yours.

If your training, policy or growing experience can provide effective answers to the questions above then these can be rehearsed to the point of automaticity.

Natalia, a secondary History teacher in her first year, describes applying the behaviour policy.

So for me it's about realising that, yes, there's a school behaviour policy and there's a way to follow that as a teacher, but at the same time I don't have to implement it in the exact same way as everyone else.

There's the way my mentor would, or that another teacher would, implement it. I don't have to think, *This other teacher wouldn't accept this kind of thing.* I felt that I was very in my head comparing myself to what I considered to be the stronger teachers in terms of behaviour management. Sometimes I can take a situation a little bit lightly, have a laugh about that with my student for a second. And so you know, if they're being cheeky, I can have a little giggle and they will appreciate that and then they'll stop.

What if my school's behaviour policy doesn't work?

A policy may fail to answer the questions above so, before we turn to *what* we will be practising and *how*, it's worth considering what to do in those circumstances.

Equally, it's worth considering why some behaviour policies go unused or ignored. Teachers, not just new teachers, fail to use school behaviour systems for all sorts of reasons. They don't like the system. It's too strict or not strict enough. They want to do their own thing. At times, there might be genuine concerns that the behaviour policy doesn't manage behaviour well. If it doesn't work, *why should I use it?*

I once worked in a school where the behaviour policy had buckled under the weight of detentions set. Students walked into detentions months after wrong-doing totally unaware of what they had done wrong. At another school, we weren't even able to set detentions. That was done as a last resort by staff above my pay grade.

In these ways, behaviour policies can fail because staff are deterred from using them. When a leader, or anyone else for that matter, asks why you're giving so many sanctions or detentions, it can feel like sanctions or detentions are actively discouraged. Even when, in reality, these things are mandated by the behaviour policy, a codified expectation of what staff are meant to do.

A policy not working will also look different in different schools. One sign is, obviously, student behaviour, but a more telling one is *how* students respond to the language, sanctions and consequences of the policy itself. If one student shrugs when given a detention, it doesn't mean much. If no student cares about the consequences set, the policy isn't having the desired effect. The knowledge you develop of the policy is not just what is written on the page.

If it feels as though your policy behaviour policy isn't working, there are several actions you should take.

Talk to and observe other teachers

If others don't feel as you do, seek to understand before critiquing or rubbishing. A behaviour policy at your current school might be different to one at a placement school. Different doesn't mean terrible, ineffectual or wrong. Our aim is knowledge, an understanding of how better behaviour has been achieved in the same corridors and classrooms we inhabit.

List the questions you have. *What happens when I send a student out? What kind of behaviour gets a student a suspension? Is it acceptable for a student to...* Ask colleagues who know the policy well. Ask to watch them. I once watched a teacher who was so much better at behaviour management than me; it was a revelation. Her classroom was calm. Her students were happy, engaged and committed but also compliant. Observing her, I noticed how little she said. Even when giving a warning, her language was precise and to the point. She didn't have to say more because she was clear, was known to follow through and, therefore, was respected by the students. The point of this story is not to say less and, as we'll see, asking for clarity is not enough; we need to know *what* we're being clear about. But, watching her, I started to understand where my enactment of the policy was haphazard or ungainly. I didn't just take the principles of *clarity* or *precision* from the observation. I took phrases I could use later that day, in lessons of my own.

Give feedback to leaders

The best leaders want to know as much as possible about what it is like to learn and teach at their schools. They want to know this because, for them as well as you, knowledge is the key to expertise. Like all humans, your school's leaders might bristle at the thought of hearing that the behaviour policy isn't working. Receiving such feedback from a new member of the profession might not be easy either. Leaders might not believe your feedback. A leader's identity might be tied up in the success of what they've implemented.

Your feedback could take the form of questions, requests for advice or support, or observations you've made about the enacted behaviour policy. Firing off a feedback email to a senior leader can feel like a quick and easy way to 'help'. Email, though, bats a problem to someone else and misses our opportunity to engage and understand the intentions of a behaviour policy. Go to see someone; arrange a meeting if you need to. Be in the same room with them.

Be clear on your own expectations in the meantime

Even where a policy is non-existent, or feels that way, where sanctions feel ineffectual, where feedback leads nowhere, you are still the teacher of your class. You have a responsibility to manage it as well as you can, a responsibility to the quiet majority who turn up, behave and want to learn. Read back through the questions listed above. Your answers are your expectations. Clarity for students begins with clarity for you.

If this section has frightened you with the thought of the behaviour policy crumbling beneath you on day one, please don't panic. Of course, most school behaviour systems are neither perfect nor are they awful. A symptom of seeking to manage complex behaviour in a complex organisation is a set of practices that will often work most of the time, for most students. If you've worked through the steps above and feel unsupported, unsafe or burned out, if possible, it might be time to look for another school or talk it through with your training provider.

The rest of the chapter will help to consider how to implement those expectations whatever your situation.

Settling a class

> **Annalise describes one of the biggest lessons she's learned when it comes to behaviour management.**
>
> If I speak louder, the disruption gets louder again. So I find myself now lowering my voice as a method rather than increasing the volume. I'll start the lesson with talking quite loudly. Once unpacking sounds and the book shuffling has stopped, I try to make a choice in turning my volume down when I'm asking for the students to turn the volume down as well.

When I was a trainee, I was fascinated by a homemade 'Wheel of Noise' a teacher had stuck on their classroom wall. A, now quite floppy, cardboard arrow could point around the wheel at various 'levels' of sound from *silence* through to *whisper* and then to *group conversation*. The wheel didn't give a section for 'Chaotic Hubbub' but, in that school, it was hard to achieve anything else.

Certain types of behaviour are often called low-level disruption. 'Low-level' reflects the minor, often quiet, nature of the behaviour: chatting rather than working or quietly distracting others, for example. 'Low-level' is an unhelpful label, though, as this behaviour wastes hours of lesson time if it goes unchecked. Teachers try to manage this behaviour by shushing, by shouting and by creating ineffectual craft projects that hang neglected on the wall.

Part of the problem, as it so often is, stems from the need for clarity for the students and ourselves. If we say 'Quiet' when we mean 'Silence', we confuse students when we get cross about an expectation that goes unfulfilled. A classroom rule I'm fond of is that students should not get out of their chairs without permission. At times, I've got cross with students getting out of their seats only to remember I haven't actually taught or told them not to. Like a lot of behaviour management, then, managing low-level disruption works better proactively rather than reactively. A teacher once told me about all the strange ways he'd try to get a class's attention when they went off-task – standing on tables, clucking like a chicken, that sort of thing – but he was reacting to behaviour rather than planning for it. I would not recommend these strategies.

As we saw in the previous chapter, managing low level disruption becomes part of our planning. Scripts for instructions include direct comments on behaviour expectations. Such scripts don't always lead to the desired behaviour but they make it easier to respond to undesired behaviour.

For example, if you've asked for silence, quite clearly, and not got it:

1. Narrate a countdown to focus back on you. *Silence in 3… Looking this way with pens down in 2… 1 and zero.*

2. Watch and wait to ensure expectations are met.

3. Reiterate explanations and warn class of consequences where they aren't met. *Year 9, the expectation was silence. We've not managed that. We're going to start the task again. Anyone talking will immediately receive a warning. Off you go.*

4. Follow through. If students start talking when you've asked for silence, they should receive whatever warning or consequence mandated by your behaviour policy. *Alice, you're talking. That's a warning.*

The same principles apply to classes who are only meant to be talking to their groups, only meant to be on one part of a court or field, only meant to get out of their seats to get resources.

Clarity of expectation, warning and consequence

In the previous chapter, we looked at how planning clear instructions prepare the ground for students to behave. Clarity makes positive behaviour easier for students and managing behaviour easier for you. A student speaks when silence was the expectation. A student shouts out when your expectation is hands-up. A student is rude or unkind about another member of the class and the school expectations are clear. Clarity from you or school policies helps to define which behaviours will be encouraged and which will be challenged. Clarity of expectation with no follow through when those expectations aren't met is likely to erode student trust in your ability to manage their behaviour. If you've said students should ask to get out of their seats and they're constantly getting out of their seats with no consequences, some of them will start to believe that what you say doesn't matter.

Knowledge of how to use this clarity is really knowledge of students and situations. Who needs a quiet warning, given so only they can hear? Who needs time to make the right decision? When does the class need to hear you and see you give the warning? Behaviour is a sequence of problems set by questions like these. The sections below offer strategies that do work but you need to learn how they work for you, when they work and with which students. This comes with practice.

Clarity of warnings

Students need to be clear on where a warning will lead, even when the school policy dictates what you do. Ways to make warnings clear include:

- Use the language of the behaviour policy (for example, if you're meant to say C1, warning, demerit etc., say those words).

- Use the language of choice – give students ownership and responsibility for their decisions.

- Be clear about the consequences.

  Example 1: If you continue to talk over others, you'll be choosing a lunchtime detention.
  Example 2: You've chosen your first warning because you haven't completed the task.

It's worth noting down the warnings that you give to avoid getting lost in what you've given and what you haven't. At times, it's enough just to say *That's a warning*. Brief and to the point works well when you know a student won't react and you can return to them later.

Clarity of consequences

> **Alex describes giving consequences and punishments without being drawn into long, drawn out arguments about them.**
>
> I think I've gained more wisdom about where to fight battles. Sometimes you get students where you give them a [consequence] and they 100% deserve it. They want to challenge you on it because they have to stand up to authority. And sometimes you just have to learn to go, 'I actually don't want the conflict'. You stick to your stance and you let them take the punishment and you don't give the satisfaction of trying to stand up against you and make you question why you've given it to them in the first place.

Our aim with consequences is to diffuse rather than escalate. If we're too quick to jump on every behaviour that follows the warning or consequence, students can go from ten minutes at lunch to a five-day suspension. That said, certain behaviours can't be ignored: direct rudeness and defiance need consequences.

When giving a consequence:

- Use the language of the policy.

- Continue to use the language of choice.

- Remain calm and in control. Delay giving the consequence if this isn't possible. If a student has wound you up to the point that you're cross, it's better to move away from that student for a moment (if their behaviour allows), returning to them when you can calmly and clearly give the consequence.

Unlike a warning, it may not be possible or desirable for all these things to be shared with students in the moment. For example, you may give the consequence as set out by a policy (a C, a detention, whatever) but give the student a chance to calm down before talking through their behaviour.

In the first instance, you may just make clear the consequence.

Example 1: You're talking over me for the second time. You've chosen a C1.
Example 2: I've now had to stop the lesson twice because you were talking over myself and others, you've chosen to lose five minutes of your break time.

If you have the chance, then or afterwards, to talk through the student's behaviour, discuss how it affected the lesson and ask lots of questions to prompt their understanding, all the better. Such conversations are usually not possible, or not done well, during the lesson because you will still have to be teaching.

Sending a student out

> **Alice, a Year 5 teacher in her third year, describes using her behaviour system to call for support.**
>
> One afternoon, one boy was turning round, scowling at another student. The next minute he was up and going across the room to another student. Then they were at each other. At the time, I didn't have a TA in the classroom. If anything ever happens like that, we have a system with red and yellow cards where we can get support. Yellow card is *Can you come to my classroom in five minutes time?* Red card is *I need you now.* The rest of the children were shocked so thankfully they didn't react. I got between the boys and got another child to take the red card next door. A leader came and got the boys.

The ultimate consequence in the classroom is the removal of a student. In some schools, sending a student out is a rare occurrence; in others, it is a daily battle. Whilst our aim should never be to *get students out*, a teacher who is tentative about removing persistently disruptive, rude or dangerous students is likely to have a chaotic or unsafe classroom.

Without meaning to sound like a broken record, your school's behaviour policy should dictate how and when a student is removed. Often the behaviour policy will answer questions about when the student is removed, where they are removed to and who is notified. If it doesn't answer these questions, seek your own answers from leaders.

Preferably, sending a student out should be a well-signposted act. The students in the class and the student in question should be unsurprised by the removal. Here, warnings serve a vital function. Warnings set a destination the student is heading towards unless their behaviour changes. That way, a sending out can be framed as an unfortunate result of the student's continued choices.

> Example 1: Unfortunately, as warned, you've continued to distract others. You need to stand outside.

At times, you'll want to make the reason clear for the student and the class. At others, it's more effective to leave it brief.

> Example 2: John, stand outside please.

Brevity has the benefit of removing any anger or frustration you feel from the language used. If a student is leaving, it helps no one to hurry them up or remind them they've ruined your lesson or your day (even if they have). If the student refuses to go, you'll need to call for additional support.

As always, we need to use, and practise using, the behaviour system and the language it encourages.

Example 3: John, that's a red card. You need to go and sit outside Mr Smith's office.

At its best, the system removes the need to come up with your own snappy phrases. You know you'll have to say 'red card' or 'C3' or 'removal room' or 'Mr Smith's office'. Your job is to put those into a clear, concise phrase. Although you might feel a little silly, practising the phrasing in your classroom by yourself is really helpful.

When the student returns the next lesson, the slate must be clean and students must have the opportunity to re-enter the classroom and improve without past behaviour hanging over them. When possible, a quick chat with the student before they return – even if it's on the door as they come back in – to repair and rebuild can be really valuable.

How do we promote positive behaviour?

Discussing behaviour management can feel overly negative, constantly preparing for the worst. We do need to plan for good behaviour but we can also plan for, and practise, the promotion of good behaviour.

Use praise

When you're first teaching and a student does something you ask or answers the most basic of questions, you can begin to gush with praise. 'Perfect', 'Thank you so much', 'What a wonderful idea!' I began to talk in a way so far removed from my usual style of communicating I was worried they would realise I was being insincere. Perhaps they did.

A knee-jerk view of reward sees it is the physical – often packs of sweets or chocolate bars you spend your own money on. Logan Fiorella cautions us that 'a feeling of accomplishment [is] generally superior to relying on expected external rewards'.[3] He goes on to say that simple praise 'can play an important role in habit change if the rewards are *uncertain* or *unexpected*'.[4] Further research suggests that young people will respond better to the immediate, rather than distant or future, rewards.[5]

Praise is the main way you can motivate through reward. Although praise is given in the moment, and although it often isn't planned, used well it is a way of proactively creating the environment you want in your classroom. To avoid insincerity, this praise should:

● Be (or appear) spontaneous.

● Be specific, related to aspects of what the student has been learning.

- Focus on creating a sense of accomplishment.

- Point students towards the intended identity of the classroom.

Examples of 'spontaneous' praise are hard to show you because, in their nature, they will emerge from the moments in your lesson, the responses from your students and work that is produced. Praise can both focus on the content students are learning and the positive behaviours they exhibit.

Subject-focused praise

> Example 1: Lucy, your use of the word 'timbre' there was spot on. You used it correctly and without me reminding you to! I want to hear more of our subject terms in class discussion. Thank you, Lucy.
> Example 2: Sammy, you've converted these fractions to percentages with no mistakes! That's incredible. I bet you're ready for something even more challenging now.

Subject-focused praise can feel distant from management of behaviour. But praise is motivating.

Positive behaviour praise

We need to be careful we don't praise students for things that should just be basic expectations. That said, where possible, thanking students for getting it right should be heard more often in our classrooms than reprimand and correction.

At the start of a lesson we can use praise to set the right tone for the class:

> Example 1: Thank you, back row. You've all settled down and have written the title and date really nicely... Thank you, Travis – it looks like you've already started which is excellent... Thank you to the vast majority of the class – already silent and working.

It might feel silly to thank students for what you've just asked them to do but giving instructions and then noticing the students who follow them well is incredibly powerful. Try it.

During independent writing, we can use praise to encourage classroom habits we are teaching.

> Example 2: Year 4, you are using your purple polishing pens beautifully. I really like what I'm seeing in Meera's work. She's corrected the spellings like we talked about but she's also replaced one of her adjectives with an even better word.

Sometimes this kind of praise works well if you can project a student's work under a visualiser or show the class in some other way.

> **Sarah, a new Year 4 teacher, describes how she tries to focus on the positive in her class.**
>
> I narrate the positives. Instead of focusing on the children doing something wrong. You focus on a child doing something right, explaining what they're doing. When I do that in my classroom, everyone wants to do what that child is doing. Obviously, there are some children who have problems with that. It doesn't work with every child.

Use the power of identity

Intrinsic motivation is the motivation to act that comes within ourselves as opposed to a response to external reward. Habit expert, James Clear, explains that the 'ultimate form of intrinsic motivation is when a habit becomes part of your identity'.[6] Identity is a powerful motivator to act or not and schools face an uphill battle to create an identity focused on learning rather than social approval.

The language we use is a powerful tool in creating an identity norm. High performing schools seem to have their own language as well as a set of ingrained routines. I recently visited Yate Academy in South Gloucestershire, a school which has achieved results amongst the best in the country. Leaders at Yate have created a set of 'mantras' outlining the commonly held beliefs and aspirations of the school: 'At Yate, we...' The mantras cover the punctual, hard-working, community-focused nature of the school.

At a whole school level, properly embedded, you can see how a set of mantras like this could use the power of identity to promote positive behaviour. Schools, leaders and teachers can pay lip service to such strategies without putting in the work to embed them in the long term. The Behavioural Insights Team recognise that we are motivated by 'mutual support' and committing to others.[7] Harnessing the power of language, then, supports the creation of a shared identity.

An individual teacher doesn't have the power of the whole school approach and, in your first year, it may feel like you don't have the headspace to create a set of mantras for your classroom. This is fine. As elements of teaching become easier, though, your use of language is one route to consider as you progressively problem solve behaviour and motivation issues in your class.

I was recently talking with a trainee about the behaviour issues in her class. We talked about routines and sanctions, aspects of her teaching she was aware needed more and continued practice. Our conversation ended and dwelt upon the source of the negative behaviour as she saw it: students struggled with Science and gave up quickly. She was aware that, with hard and focused work, she was on the road to achieving compliance from the class but she wanted more than compliance. In your first years of teaching, with some classes, compliance is a massive victory, but there's a horizon beyond compliance: commitment. It's unlikely that consequences or detentions *on their own* will reach the commitment we want from students (that's not a reason to stop issuing them).

Out of our conversation, and from her not me, came the idea that scientists make mistakes and learn from them. This trainee wanted that nugget of truth to be understood, to be the lived reality of the class. We acknowledged that the Science classroom is quite different from the lab beyond school. We weren't trying to turn the former into the latter. She started playing around with the language of the classroom: 'In this class, we think like scientists', and 'Scientists make mistakes; so will we'. I'm not arguing that using phrases like this will solve your behaviour problems. But shaping a students' identity whilst they're in your classroom will take conscious effort.

None of this means we should apply a label to a student until they believe it. Labels should be approached with caution in education, but the language of identity can be incredibly powerful. Katy Milkman describes how 'When we're labelled "voters" (instead of people who vote), "carrot eaters" (instead of people who eat carrots whenever they can), and "Shakespeare readers" (instead of people who read Shakespeare a lot), it influences how we act, not just how we describe ourselves'.[8]

In summary

Knowledge new teachers develop spans from the lofty academic heights of the curriculum to the internal and existential questions of what we actually want. You might be ambitious for your students to develop strong intrinsic motivation to do well in your subject. Until we've laid the groundwork – and that is our main aim starting out – we can't achieve those ambitions. The behaviour policy – intended and enacted – is what we need to know to solve the initial problems of behaviour in our classroom. I won't lie and tell you that knowing the behaviour policy well will prevent all poor behaviour.

Behaviour management is both proactive and reactive. Proactively, we plan for clear routines and social norms which promote positive behaviours. We get to know our behaviour policy well so we can manage behaviour consistently. Our knowledge of policy should drive our instructions, warnings and consequences towards clarity and consistency of response to student behaviour.

Possible next steps

1. **Check your understanding of the behaviour policy.** It's easy to think we know something because we've been around it for a while. Do you know how, when and why consequences are given in other classrooms? If it's new to you, laminate a summary of the policy and stick it where you'll see it.

2. **Script and practise warnings and consequences.** Whilst you can't rehearse every type of behaviour that might come up, you can make automatic the

language of the policy. Make it easy for your mouth (and brain) to get through language you're likely not used to (demerit, red card etc.).

3. **Tally up the ratio of praise to reprimand.** All this talk of consequences and warnings is essential but can present an unbalanced view of the classroom. How are you also working to create a positive atmosphere in the classroom? Use praise and the language of identity. If the positive side of behaviour management is proving difficult to embed, script and practise it as you have for the instructions, warnings and consequences.

Notes

1 Bennett, T. (2017). *Creating a Culture.* https://assets.publishing.service.gov.uk/government/uploads/system/uploads/attachment_data/file/602487/Tom_Bennett_Independent_Review_of_Behaviour_in_Schools.pdf (accessed on 04/06/2022).
2 Moore, D., Benham-Clarke, S., Kenchington, R., Boyle, C., Ford, T., Hayes, R., and Rogers, M. (2019). *Improving Behaviour in Schools: Evidence Review.* Education Endowment Foundation.
3 Fiorella, L. (2020). The science of habit and its implications for student learning and wellbeing. *Educational Psychology Review*, 32, 603–625.
4 Ibid.
5 Lavecchia, A.M., Liu, H., and Oreopoulos, P. (2016). Behavioral economics of education: Progress and possibilities. In E.A. Hanushek, S. Machin and L. Woessmann (eds), *Handbook of the Economics of Education* (Vol. 5, pp. 1–74). Elsevier.
6 Clear, J. (2018). *Atomic Habits.* Penguin.
7 Behavioural Insights Team. (2014). EAST Four simple ways to apply behaviour insights. www.bi.team/wp-content/uploads/2015/07/BIT-Publication-EAST_FA_WEB.pdf (accessed on 22/11/2022).
8 Milkman, K. (2021). *How to Change.* Penguin.

Further reading

Bennett, T. (2020). *Running the Room.* John Catt.

PART 4
Pedagogical knowledge

When I was training to teach, I had close to no idea what *pedagogy* was. People – our trainers and other trainees – would ask, 'What's the pedagogy behind that?' and I'd just fluster and change the subject. Or they'd say 'Pedagogically speaking…' and I'd zone out for a minute because what they were saying seemed unhelpful for planning tomorrow's Year 9 lesson. Discussions about pedagogy, to me, seemed like a distant piece of theory I had to endure rather than something relevant to the moment. Of course, I was wrong. Whilst pedagogy can become theoretical and distant, we can't escape it. Every time we plan, every decision we make about how to teach in the classroom is underpinned by pedagogical thinking. We can either do this implicitly, drifting along without intellectually engaging, or we can make this thinking explicit. Pedagogy is the thought underpinning your behaviour in the classroom.

There isn't a curriculum of pedagogical knowledge for teachers. Perhaps such a curriculum is not possible. Too often this means that new teachers' pedagogical thinking is strung together from the strategies left over after a long period of trial and error. Some teachers and researchers have sought to break down teacher behaviour – pedagogy – into its component parts.[1] These attempts at codification can be helpful but they generally give a set of broad behaviours to follow rather than a framework with which to make pedagogical decisions.

Pedagogy is not synonymous with evidence-based practice; they haven't always gone and won't always go hand in hand. But, in seeking to offer you a framework of knowledge for your pedagogical decisions, we can look to no more helpful a place than what evidence says about learning. That hasn't always been the most obvious direction to look.

Education has, even in the recent past, seemed resistant to evidence. More recently, the tide – in England at least – has begun to turn. Pointing to a time, a place or a person as originator of this sea-change is difficult. Recognising the effects of the change is much easier. Founded by the Sutton Trust in 2011 with a grant from the Department for Education, the Education Endowment Foundation (EEF) aims to tackle disadvantage through the application of evidence. To achieve this, the EEF trials strategies and reports on the results, produces guidance reports,

DOI: 10.4324/9781003281306-12

and offers a toolkit of evidence-based approaches for schools. Brought on the same tide, founded in 2013, researchEd runs conferences that aim to 'bridge the gap between research and practice in education'.[2] At these conferences, you're just as likely to hear from a teacher as you are from a researcher or policy maker. Whilst both the EEF and researchEd delve into evidence beyond the classroom – they cover everything from attendance to teacher training – both have forced pedagogical decisions to become about the evidence available to us.

Pedagogical thinking will always have a limit. It's clear why. Lee Shulman describes how pedagogical skill is 'useless' if it is 'content-free'.[3] You can't think pedagogically without considering the content to be taught. Some might even argue persuasively that thinking pedagogically is next to useless[4] and that thinking about subject and curriculum are more worthy of our time. Christine Counsell, one of the UK's leading curriculum thinkers, warns against 'an intransitive pedagogy, a pedagogy without an object'.[5] An established teacher may well think more in terms of the merging of content and pedagogy. A new teacher should build up a mental model of the behaviours which promote learning.

To do that, this section will seek to answer three questions:

- What does 'the evidence' say about learning?

- How should Cognitive Load Theory affect our pedagogical decisions?

- What changes long-term memory for our students?

What you won't find in this section is an explanation of *every* teaching behaviour, what you need to know about it and how to do it. These chapters will, instead, provide a framework to think about pedagogy. They will help you to create a mental model of learning and the learner which can direct future decisions.

Notes

1 For example:
  Rosenshine, B. (2012). Principles of Instruction. *American Educator*, Spring.
  Lemov, D. (2010). *Teach Like a Champion*. Jossey-Bass.
2 ResearchEd. (n.d.). About us. https://researched.org.uk/about/about-researched/ (accessed 10/01/2022).
3 Shulman, L. (1986). Those who understand: Knowledge growth in teaching. *Educational Research*, 15(2), 4–14.
4 Stuart Lock has written a blog called Pedagogy is Overrated (https://mrlock.wordpress.com/2017/06/23/pedagogy-is-overrated/) and Adam Boxer has written one called Teaching and Learning is Dead (https://achemicalorthodoxy.wordpress.com/2019/02/19/teaching-and-learning-is-dead/). Both make the case for curriculum over pedagogical thinking.
5 Counsell, C. (2018). In search of senior curriculum leadership: Introduction – A dangerous absence. https://thedignityofthethingblog.wordpress.com/2018/03/27/in-search-of-senior-curriculum-leadership-introduction-a-dangerous-absence/ (accessed 05/01/2022).

What does 'the evidence' say about learning?

My friend turned to me one Inset Day and said, 'The word "Research" has become a bit meaningless in education, hasn't it?' I can't remember what we were being asked to do in the name of The Evidence. It was almost certainly workload inducing, untenable and destined to be quietly dumped onto the scrapheap of bad ideas. But it was, we were told, backed by Research. Infuriatingly, *The evidence says...* is not the helpful phrase it could be. In some utopian dream of education, research provides teachers with The Answers. Even more infuriatingly, a side-effect of the evidence-revolution in education has been the rise of those who will use vague references to research as the flimsy support for their flimsier ideas.

Part of the problem is the breadth of what might be considered 'evidence'. Is a study based on interviews of teachers in small, rural primary school evidence? Is a large quantitative study of a classroom strategy in several secondary schools useful for primary teachers? A national survey of students might be considered evidence but should such a survey inform decisions I make in my classroom? And where does all this evidence come from? The problem of breadth is really a problem of different kinds of evidence. Randomised controlled trials might be conducted using classroom or whole-school approaches. With these trials, we can say *X is likely to work (or not)*. Teaching also draws on evidence of what works from cognitive and behavioural science, which provide principles which underpin effective learning. How far, then, can teaching and teachers learn from the evidence from fields beyond education?

These questions prompt several important acknowledgements:

1. **Evidence rarely provides an absolute answer.** As the new teacher – you – develops knowledge of evidence-based pedagogy, arrogance about *the right* classroom strategies should be avoided at all costs. Instead, this knowledge gives us a lens through which to view our planning and our practice. This knowledge might hint at why what we're doing is working, or why it isn't. This knowledge might guide but it rarely gives a single answer to a question about classroom strategies.

DOI: 10.4324/9781003281306-13

2. **It's easy to expect too much of evidence.** Sometimes teachers ask questions of evidence we know can't really be answered. *What does 'the evidence' say about the types of questions I should ask Year 9 on Friday afternoon? What does the evidence say about how to teach boys [insert particular problem topic]?* You might get lucky and find a specific study on *just* the question you were thinking of but, invariably, niche questions in teaching and learning don't sit upon mountains of evidence.

3. **Evidence doesn't offer one way to teach.** On the one hand some research might confirm that certain styles of teaching aren't effective in promoting learning. For example, inquiry learning – where students must discover information or processes for themselves, with minimal input from a teacher – has widely been discredited.[1] Regularly asking students to learn about topics or acquire new skills with minimal guidance is a bad idea. To some, the evidence about the failures of minimally guided instruction makes the case for a type of teaching where, whilst the teacher doesn't simply lecture the students, lessons are firmly led from the front, by the teacher. Even if we, as I do, see merit in this argument, what this teacher-led approach looks like can vary massively.

4. **But we ignore the evidence at our students' peril.** Arrogance is a real danger when we increase our understanding of how learning happens. At the other extreme, if we remain indecisive or ideology clouds our view of what the evidence is telling us we take the risk of making decisions that put the brakes on learning in our classrooms.

What *can* we get from 'the evidence'?

The four points above offer a negative view, focused on what the evidence *can't* or *doesn't* help us with. If evidence is only viewed this way, we can end up overly cautious of seeking evidence out or applying what we find. Tim Cain, Professor of Education, has a particular interest in how research meets the practice of the classroom. He offers several ways that teachers can forge a positive relationship with research.

Firstly, teachers should look beyond 'the personal experience of individual practitioners or the cumulative assumptions and practices of a profession, both of which tend to be untested'.[2] Secondly, by providing 'conceptual frameworks', research can support teachers to understand and reflect on student learning. These 'conceptual frameworks', like the mental models we have been discussing, generate insights and rules of thumb as evidence is understood further. It is not that evidence trumps experience every time; instead, you plan and teach lessons in light of both evidence and experience. This section on pedagogy will help to build your conceptual framework of learning by focusing on foundational principles – things we must know – to plan for effective learning. Finally, Cain argues that research 'can raise the quality of debate within a school and thereby improve the school as a learning organisation'. In such a debate, we must hold lightly to our position and be prepared to have preconceptions challenged.

Project Follow Through

American history tells a cautionary tale. In the late sixties, one of the largest experiments ever to be conducted on education in America began. Across more than 180 schools and with upwards of 70,000 students, researchers examined which teaching methods had the greatest impact on student learning. This was Project Follow Through. Ostensibly, the experiment pitted child-centred, child-directed learning against Direct Instruction from a teacher. Child-centred teaching was about freedom for children to learn at their own pace, to dictate their own learning journey. Direct Instruction was the opposite: a teacher followed a carefully structured and often scripted curriculum engaging all students in the same activities.

In the child-centred approach, in a reading class for first graders, children largely direct their own learning:

> [Children] might be found scattered around the room; some children are walking around, some are talking, some painting, others watching a video, some looking through a book, and one or two reading with the teacher.[3]

In turn the teacher has a facilitative role:

> The teacher uses a book that is not specifically designed to be read using phonics skills, and, when a child misses a word, the teacher will let the mistake go by so long as the meaning is preserved to some degree.[4]

In contrast, in the Direct Instruction classroom:

> Some children are at their desks writing or reading phonics-based books. The rest… are sitting with the teacher. The teacher asks them to sound out challenging words before reading the story. When the children read the story, the teacher has them sound out the words if they make mistakes.[5]

In which class do students more effectively learn to read? Is it close? No. It isn't. Students who direct their own learning don't learn as much as those taught directly. The two groups were compared with a control group. In some cases, the child-centred approach didn't fare as well as the control group. In everything from problem solving in Maths to reading comprehension, the Direct Instruction group achieved the best results. There were even hints from the research that the Direct Instruction approach has a positive effect on students' self-esteem.[6]

Why hasn't Project Follow Through had the seismic impact it deserves? It's complicated. The Direct Instruction approach is complicated; it isn't just a teacher telling students things (as it is sometimes caricatured). Intensive development and training time are required to make Direct Instruction approaches viable. Whilst the experiment was large, it covered measurable subject-areas – English and Maths in particular. Applying the lessons of Project Follow Through would not be as simple as deciding to apply those lessons, particularly for the individual teacher.

But some would offer less diplomatic reasons for its failure to make inroads. In the angrily titled 'Why education experts resist effective practices', Douglas Carnine bemoans the entrenchment of unevidenced positions based on ideological rejection of ideas because they come from the wrong voices or draw the wrong conclusions. Recalling the failure of Project Follow Through to win the argument for Direct Instruction, Carnine describes education as an 'immature profession' because expertise is based on 'the subjective judgments of the individual profes- sional'.[7] You can see his point. Why should opinion trump evidence?

Direct Instruction has come to mean many things, from the scripted lessons from Project Follow Through (with capitalised letters – Direct Instruction) to any teach- er-led approach (often called, confusingly, direct or explicit instruction). Evidence supports the behaviours of direct teachers, things like reviewing content regularly, checking student understanding, modelling processes and obtaining a high suc- cess rate.[8] Often, when we list these behaviours direct teaching can seem simple or obvious. Don't all teachers do this? The short answer is no. A longer answer might explain that, as in Project Follow Through, certain types of pedagogy are treated with scorn for reasons other than their efficacy.

The labels *child-centred* and *Direct Instruction* imply something that isn't so clear cut. What is child-centred about teaching in a less effective way? Teachers imbued with a sense of their moral purpose must seek out the most effective teaching methods. The knowledgeable teacher recognises what evidence does and doesn't say, what it can and can't do. The question is learning. The tentative answer is evidence-based pedagogy. What that answer looks like might vary depending on how we define learning.

What is learning?

It's an obvious question with a slightly elusive answer. Teaching is quite clearly about making learning happen. When you go into the classroom, you are trying to achieve learning. But what is learning? What will it look like if anything? What tangible changes will there be in students because of your teaching? Let's look at some definitions.

An internal model of an external world

Neuroscientist Stanislas Dehaene sees learning as forming 'an internal model of the external world'.[9] Helpfully, Dehaene's definition recalls the mental models you're already familiar with. These models help us to navigate the world, reduce errors, discover possibilities, recall information quickly and hypothesise. Dehaene explains that this learning is often unconscious. A common complaint about our school days is that we remember nothing from them. Dehaene's expansive definition of learning includes the perceptions and ways of thinking that make up our mental models.

Dehaene's understanding of learning is a bird's-eye view; there's some distance between it and the day-to-day practice of our classrooms. The next definition brings learning a little bit closer to the classroom.

A change in long-term memory

A straightforward, but regularly controversial, definition of learning is that it is a change in long-term memory.[10] In a paper drawing on evidence from cognitive science, Paul Kirschner, John Sweller and Richard Clark use this definition to challenge minimal guidance approaches to teaching. Provocatively, they go on to say, 'if nothing has changed in long-term memory, nothing has been learned'. Think about that for a moment. At the risk of sounding ridiculous, *How does that definition make you feel?* I ask because it's not uncommon to bridle when confronted with what feels like a cold view of learning. It's not uncommon to feel uncomfortable. I initially felt uncomfortable with this definition because, looking back on my early lessons as a teacher, I'm sure lots of my students wouldn't have remembered much at all. It's not uncommon, in our discomfort, to reach for examples that will challenge or undermine the definition.

Whatever our feelings about it, this definition can radically affect what we do in the classroom. Before we get to that point, we need to understand what the definition *doesn't* mean. Talk of memory somehow usually leads to talk of facts. Focus on facts leads to accusations of rote learning. And soon this is no definition of learning but a description of regurgitation. In this way, the definition can be dismissed without ever being refuted. But this is not simply about factual learning.

As we've seen already, knowledge extends beyond the parameters of what we can list on the page. A student practising their free-throws in basketball is committing the process to memory. A student who has been taught orthographic drawing in D&T, who has practised it to automaticity, has committed it to memory.

A change in long-term memory is a powerful definition because it points to some tangible ways in which we can change what we do. It forces us to move from 'I taught it; they learned it' to 'I taught it; how do I make sure it sticks?' It's ok to want a more expansive definition of learning as long as we let this one challenge us. Cognitive science offers an answer to why humans often forget and sometimes remember what they're told or what they do. Before we turn to those strategies, let's spend a moment considering what can't be defined as learning.

What isn't learning?

I was in an interview for Assistant Headteacher of Teaching and *Learning*. The Chair of Governors had just asked me what learning looked like and I could tell my answer wasn't going well. None of it was going well. I continued talking about *what learning looks like* even though I couldn't quite make sense of the question. Looking back, I think I spoke a bit too much – for her liking – about what I do as a teacher to make learning happen. She stopped me mid-sentence. Always a good sign in an interview…

'Yes', she said, pointedly. 'But what does learning *look like?*'

As it turned out, she meant: if learning is happening, what can you see? It dawned on me suddenly that viewing learning as an invisible process taking place in the mind would make it difficult to answer this question well. Mercifully, they sent me home at lunch.

The governor's question reveals a problem we all encounter when we talk about learning. To what extent are we talking about learning? To what extent are we talking about fluff that sounds exciting but ultimately isn't learning? Professor Rob Coe has helpfully created a list of the things we can often mistake for learning. He calls these 'proxies for learning', things that look like learning but don't guarantee it. These proxies aren't bad things; it's not that we must avoid them. They're just easy to mistake for learning. They are:

- Students are busy: lots of work is done (especially written work).

- Students are engaged, interested, motivated.

- Classroom is ordered, calm, under control.

- Curriculum has been 'covered'.

- (At least some) students have supplied correct answers.[11]

We *want* our classes to be engaged and ordered. We *want* students to get the right answers. We *want* to get through the curriculum. But none of these things mean that students have learned anything.

Coe offers a 'better proxy for learning': 'Learning happens when people have to think hard'. Of course, this is still a challenge. My three-year-old daughter has already mastered the tilt of her head, her hand to her chin and an exaggerated 'Hmmm' to signal she is thinking. It would be easy just to turn thinking into another proxy where we look out across a class and ask ourselves 'Do these children look like they're thinking?' Perhaps we could count up the number of hands reaching for chins. In this way, I don't see how 'thinking hard' can be a proxy for learning because, unlike other proxies, it's difficult to see.

So thinking hard becomes something we don't necessarily look for *during the lesson*; it's something we plan for *before the lesson*. Understanding some evidence about teaching or learning can't answer every single pedagogical question your classroom poses. This understanding gives us a lens through which to view our actions and those of our students.

Planning for proxies

To take Coe's proxies as an example, if you're planning activities for a lesson you could ask yourself two sets of questions. In the first set, you ask:

- How can I make sure the students are engaged?

- How should I keep the students busy for the whole hour/day/morning?

- What sorts of activities will keep them calm?

- What do I need to cover?

Asking these questions isn't wrong; it's just that there isn't a direct line between the answers and student learning. Coe's 'better proxy' would lead us to ask different questions:

- What do I want students to learn?

- How can I get them to think hard about that?

- What might get in the way of thinking hard and what could I do about it?

- How will I know that they are thinking hard?

After we've asked these questions, we could turn back to some of the others if they seem useful. Grounding your thinking in what learning is and what it isn't is vital to getting your planning right. Armed with these definitions and proxies, we have a target to aim at and a measure of our success.

   An important caveat lingers behind our answers to these questions. In a school where behaviour is poor or difficult to manage, we celebrate those times when students busily engage in lessons and get through content. The second set of questions are easier to answer and the answers are easier to put into practice when behaviour is well managed. Whilst as a new teacher it's important to develop a solid mental model of learning, this will only help you in a classroom where students are ready to learn. If necessary, return to Part 3 and look at the steps you can take to embed positive behaviour.

In summary

We could go on about evidence in education for much longer. In many ways, this chapter skirts the sides of a mountainous terrain of viewpoints and controversies. No teacher can expect evidence to answer every question about the classroom. No teacher should blindly follow every new trend packaged as evidence. We must question and interrogate. We should, however, do this from a place of knowledge, knowledge of what learning is and isn't, what evidence does and doesn't suggest.

Thinking hard about evidence-based learning leads us to plan lessons where students must think hard. Perhaps even more helpfully, evidence-based thinking helps us to avoid getting confused about proxies for learning, potentially good things that can masquerade as learning.

To really use our understanding of what learning is and isn't – and how we get more of it in our classrooms – we should delve further into what makes learning happen. If learning is a change in long-term memory, we need to understand what prompts and causes those changes.

Possible next steps

1. **Reflect on proxies.** Look back at a lesson you taught today or this week with the list of proxies:

   ○ Students are busy: lots of work is done (especially written work).

   ○ Students are engaged, interested, motivated.

   ○ Classroom is ordered, calm, under control.

   ○ Curriculum has been 'covered'.

   ○ (At least some) students have supplied correct answers.

   To what extent have these things driven your view of learning in those lessons? Look ahead to lessons coming up tomorrow or later in the week. How will you ensure these proxies don't colour your view of success in the classroom? Stick them up somewhere as a reminder to yourself.

2. **Plan for thinking.** Rob Coe's better proxy was 'thinking hard'. Whilst this is exactly a proxy because it's difficult to observe 'hard thinking', it's worth planning for thinking. As Daniel Willingham tells us, 'memory is the residue of thought'. Look at upcoming lesson plans or resources. Student thought will be directed by activities you plan, the resources they use and your explanation and instruction. Unthinkingly planning an activity that keeps students busy but doesn't direct their thinking is easy to do in a rush. Slow planning down to focus solely on the thinking students will be doing. To grapple with content – to think deeply about it – students need content-rich lessons. Reading, clear and planned explanations, rich demonstrations and well-structured talk can all give students time to dwell on what they are learning.

Notes

1 Kirschner, P.A., Sweller, J., and Clark, R.E. (2006). Why minimal guidance during instruction does not work: An analysis of the failure of constructivist, discovery, problem-based, experiential, and inquiry-based teaching. *Educational Psychologist*, 41(2), 75–86.

2 Cain, T. (2019). How research can inform teachers and teaching in schools. Bera blog. www.bera.ac.uk/blog/how-research-can-inform-teachers-and-teaching-in-schools (accessed 27/06/2022).

3 Carnine, D. (2000). *Why Education Experts Resist Effective Practices (And What It Would Take To Make Education More Like Medicine)*. Thomas B. Fordham Foundation.

4 Ibid.

5 Ibid.

6 Ibid.

7 Ibid.

8 Rosenshine, B. (2012). Principles of Instruction. *American Educator*, Spring.

9 Dehaene, S. (2020). *How We Learn*. Penguin.

10 Kirschner, P.A., Sweller, J., and Clark, R.E. (2006). Why minimal guidance during instruction does not work: An analysis of the failure of constructivist, discovery, problem-based, experiential, and inquiry-based teaching. *Educational Psychologist*, 41(2), 75–86.

11 Coe, R. (2015). What will it take to develop great teaching? www.ibo.org/globalassets/events/aem/conferences/2015/robert-coe.pdf (accessed 21/01/2022).

How should Cognitive Load Theory affect our pedagogical decisions?

You often hear students tell you *I learn best when...* but how the sentence is finished usually speaks to preference rather than efficacy. *I learn best when I'm listening to music. I learn best when I'm sitting with my friends. I learn best when I'm eating.* Students will often come into your room and make you feel like the only teacher who doesn't let them do X. *Miss Clark always lets us sit where we want, eat what we want, do what we want, and listen to music. Why don't you?* Although students won't always accept it, your answer is that you know more about the best conditions for learning than your students.

Constructing a mental model of learning based on the evidence available to us is vital. Our intuitions about learning can be limited or unsupported. Cognitive Load Theory has quickly become an all-encompassing way of understanding the learning process. What follows is a brief introduction with some practical steps for implementation in the classroom.

What is Cognitive Load Theory?

The originator of Cognitive Load Theory, John Sweller, describes how Cognitive Load Theory is founded on the premise that 'human cognitive processing is heavily constrained by our limited working memory which can only process a limited number of information elements at a time'.[1] Because of this, our cognitive capacity becomes overloaded when we attempt to process too much new information at once. As a guide for teachers explains, Cognitive Load Theory is grounded in two principles:

> The first is that there is a limit to how much *new information* the human brain can process at one time. The second is that there are no known limits to how much *stored information* can be processed at one time [my emphasis].[2]

 DOI: 10.4324/9781003281306-14

Cognitive Load Theory doesn't simply diagnose a problem. It points us towards the solution: long-term memory. The conclusions we draw from Cognitive Load Theory are both simple and complex:

- We must teach in a way that doesn't overload cognitive capacities. It isn't helpful to speak of minimising cognitive load. To learn, as we'll see, we need to think hard. Zero cognitive load probably means you aren't thinking much at all.

- We must teach in a way that takes account of what we know of long-term memory. This will be the focus of the next chapter.

These conclusions are simple because they are straightforward and logical. They are complex because you could spend your career trying to optimise your teaching to achieve these two ideas and still have work to do.

At a glance, Cognitive Load Theory is an appeal to simplify but there is hidden complexity to our applications of it. Cognitive load affects the mind and the learning process in different ways; there is *intrinsic load*, the focus needed to learn, the required load during a task, and there is *extraneous load*, anything superfluous or unnecessary for learning. But cognitive load research goes beyond simply pointing out how students are likely to become overloaded. As we'll see it offers teachers specific strategies and principles for how to teach.

Before we get there, let's just look at some examples. A Year 5 student has been tasked with comparing the National Parks they have studied. In separate lessons, the student has learned about the Lake District and Pembrokeshire. Ideally, because of those lessons, knowledge about the parks is now 'stored information'. The intrinsic load in the comparison task is the generating or finding of the similarities and differences between the parks. Extraneous load could come in several forms: superfluous information in resources or unnecessary, distracting images.

In a Year 6 music lesson, students might be learning about rhythm by tapping out a repetitive beat. Students have learned what the word *rhythm* means and have watched their teacher tap a rhythm with two fingers on the edge of a desk. Now it's their turn. Paradoxically, the intrinsic load – what students must focus on and learn – is the beat they are tapping but this may also be a source of extraneous load as other students' unrhythmic tapping becomes a distraction. Involve ukuleles and the extraneous load is likely to become unbearable.

Cognitive Load Theory underpins the work we're doing in this book to develop expertise. Your working memory is limited too. Whilst you have more embedded in your long-term memory than your students, making teaching manageable is about embedding knowledge and process into your long-term memory.

How should the principles of Cognitive Load Theory inform my teaching?

The problems posed by the classroom, the persistent challenges of teaching, start with how we will get students to learn content they don't know and aren't interested in, all while those students are distracted by the environment, their peers or even the teacher. You may have students who, lesson to lesson, don't seem to recall what you tell them.

Mary Kennedy's persistent challenges remind us we need to 'portray the curriculum' and 'enlist student participation'. Whilst knowledge of behaviour (from Part 3) and knowledge of curriculum (from Part 5) both will help us to face these challenges, addressing the challenges offered by cognitive load help to cut to the heart of how learning happens, and whether it's happening in your classroom. As you read this introduction to cognitive load, there's a real ironic danger it backfires and leads to cognitive overload for you. In particular, what makes sense on the page might be overwhelming to apply.

My advice to stop that happening would be:

● Read the chapter through once, taking in what you can.

● Once you've done this, turn again to the chapter as you plan a single lesson. Refer to the principles as you decide on content and activities for your lesson.

● Refer once more to the chapter as you plan another lesson. Look again at the strategies for managing cognitive load. Plan a lesson considering at least one of the following: a Worked Example, a Completion Problem or the Split Attention Effect.

Plan for intrinsic load

Daniel Willingham's maxim 'memory is the residue of thought' takes on richer meaning in the light of Cognitive Load Theory. Coupled with Rob Coe's encouragement that learning happens when students have to 'think hard' we have a good idea of what it means to maximise intrinsic load. Two things determine intrinsic load: how complex the information is and how much the learner already knows.[3] In this way, intrinsic load is not a given for a topic or task. Not every student experiences intrinsic load in the same way. Knowing this gives us two ways to think about intrinsic load. In the long term, we can increase a student's capacity to manage more complex information by 'changing the expertise of the learner'[4] (in other words, by teaching them). In the short term, we can change 'what needs to be learned'. Through planning, we can focus on the specific components we need students to learn; we can break content and tasks down to make the learning process more manageable.

It is the aim of all lesson planning: to focus students' minds on what it is we want them to learn. Look at your planning or resources for upcoming lessons. Consider the question *What will students need to think about here?* at every stage of the lesson. Whilst *planning for intrinsic load* is our guiding principle, the following strategies shed more light on how we do this.

Manage element interactivity

Cognitive Load Theory contains within it the truth that human beings find it difficult to hold more than four[5] new pieces of information in their minds at one time. Without meaning to, we can give students too much to juggle in tasks and activities we plan. Something which seemed straightforward to us strains the limits of their working memory. As John Sweller and colleagues point out, 'Working memory is simply incapable of highly complex interactions using novel... elements'.[6] Sweller concludes that teaching which requires the combination of lots of unfamiliar elements is likely to fail. Element interactivity, therefore, is the term used to describe how different knowledge, instructions and information interact.

What does element interactivity look like? Firstly, it can be described as high or low, depending on the design of a task or the content to be learned. Sweller gives the example of learning a language. Learning individual bits of vocabulary from a new language can be difficult but the element interactivity is low. One word in the target language interacts with an equivalent (or two) in the native language. A languages teacher would be quick to tell you that they don't spend lessons just working through the dictionary one word at a time. Understanding the grammar of a new language forces language learners to manage a dangerously high number of elements. Not only is vocabulary important; now word endings, tense, voice: the relationship between words becomes the thing the learner is holding in their minds. Students will be more than capable of tackling complex grammar when their knowledge of vocabulary and tense – built separately and over time – have been embedded in long-term memory.

When we plan a task, the process is usefully seen through the lens of element interactivity. All we're doing here is assessing the complexity of the task; to begin with, we're not simplifying it nor are we making it more complex. Ask:

- How many *new* elements do students have to think about at once?

- How much will students have to combine or use the *new* elements together?

- What knowledge or skill do students have embedded in long-term memory that they can use in this task? How can I prompt them to do this?

If students will have to use various things which are new to them in combination, it's likely they'll be overloaded. This doesn't necessarily mean they *all* won't be able to do the task. Some might but it probably isn't worth the risk. We can always accelerate the learning where students are finding it manageable. A room full of students with their hand up because they feel they can't do it is counterproductive.

Alex, an English trainee, describes trying to meet the needs of his class by reducing the elements they'll have to manage in one go.

You have to get enough knowledge of the class to know what works for them and what doesn't. It's trying to be able to recognise, 'That didn't work. That was too hard for them. They found that too easy or didn't apply themselves to it properly'. It's about gauging that. I always start with the mentality of how it is for the weakest person in the class, how they are going to approach this challenge then work backwards from there. Well, OK, if I've got a student in my class who is very slow to draw a table which I want them to draw, I need to print off the table so that it's there for them. That's one step. Then what's the next weakest person going to do? Well, they are very poor at finding quotes, so maybe I'll give one example of a quote just as a good example.

Assessing element interactivity is not even half the battle. We have to do something about it. Whilst it is unproductive to make things easier for students, where our tendency is towards complexity, we should consider how to *break content down*.

Break content down

Alice, a Year 5 teacher in her third year, talks about learning to break content down.

When I first started, I would have a PowerPoint with content and all the questions and activities would be at the end. Now, I have a slide and then questions. I split it up. I don't have all the questions at the end of the PowerPoint.

How has this affected student learning?

Now student attention is there. They're more with it. It's fresh in their brains. I would say by splitting it up into small chunks, it's going in for them. And they're not getting bored with it. They listen to me and then they go on a task. Then they listen to me and then they go on a task.

It's easy to tell you to break content down but harder to specify by how much or into what kinds of pieces. Here again, Cognitive Load Theory challenges our intuitions and the preferences of our students. Students might prefer to play a match than practise passing drills. They might prefer to write the full story rather than practise individual sentences. They might prefer to ferociously debate the interpretations of a historical event than encounter each of them in detail and gradually. We too might prefer to give them the freedom of the former rather than spend time in the latter. In doing so, though, we guarantee slow progress towards proficiency in netball, story writing and debating. It's true that we may demotivate students if the drill and the practise never lead to a finished product. But success too is a motivator and success is unlikely without breaking down and practising the component parts.

There are two broad approaches to consider when *breaking content down* into manageable stages:

- The 'part-whole approach' – 'where the individual elements of the material are introduced to the learner first, before the integrated task is introduced'.[7]

- The 'whole-part approach' – the whole or bigger task is introduced to students initially but the teacher breaks it down into sub-tasks or elements.

Even when you've settled on an approach, *How far should I break this content down?* is a fair question and one we will return to below. If we remember that learning happens when students are thinking hard, we must direct their thinking. Deciding on how far to break content down will take a bit of trial and error.

It's also important to remember we can both break down content – what we are teaching – and tasks – the way we are teaching. We need to see this distinction because it's possible to have lots of mini-tasks focused on big unwieldy bits of content. Breaking down both will help students to manage cognitive load. Let's look at two examples, one for breaking down content and one for breaking down tasks, both focused on teaching a play.

When teaching *Macbeth* as a GCSE text, I want students to know something about King James I. I could give a short explanation about all those things and then expect students to know them. Perhaps I'll find some reading that reflects what I want them to know. But there's a problem. In my mind, King James I might be *one thing* about Macbeth. In the students' minds, King James I is a subtopic of *Macbeth* with several strands. To break this content down, it first needs to be defined (by me or by the curriculum):

- King James I had become king three years before *Macbeth* was written.

- King James I was Scottish.

- King James I was Protestant.

- King James I believed in the *divine right of kings*.

- The year before *Macbeth* was written, an attempt was made on the life of King James I by a group of Catholics – the Gunpowder plot.

If I make a list like this or if the curriculum provides one for me, I can start to see what is manageable together and what should be separated. Students can handle learning when King James I became king and that he was Scottish in quick succession. I may group other content that works naturally together. For example, I could save the concept of the *divine right of kings* until we reach Act 2 Scene 2 where the concept relates to what we will be reading. The Protestant and Catholic conflict that acts as the backdrop to his reign will, however, take more careful thought and planning. Students will need to understand the terms Protestant and Catholic but also the historical background. The introduction to the Protestant/Catholic content will, therefore, be broken down into its own lesson, a topic worthy of attention in its own right. Even this lesson needs to be broken down. Definitions of words and reading of historical context offer further divisions.

Let's turn our attention to the breaking down of tasks and processes. If I want students to write analytical paragraphs about the play we're reading as a class, I could just get them to write the paragraphs (with lots of sentence starters for support) but if I really want them to retain and re-use what they've learned, I'll focus on the different teachable elements. We might spend a lesson on introductory sentences where we try to accurately express a supported, personal interpretation about Macbeth, ambition or evil. Following this, a lesson on how to use and embed quotations will be necessary to embed and manipulate the content students are discussing. Of course, the aim is fluent analysis and I should not teach the parts without aiming to reach the whole.

The following sequence of questions might help you to consider how best to break content down:

● What end goal am I working towards?

● What component skills and knowledge is that goal made out of?

● Which components are priorities for teaching individually? These could be the things students *need* to get right to reach the goal. They could also be things most relevant to future topics and tasks.

● Having chosen a priority to focus on, how can I get students to think about or practise *just* that part? Which activities will best create intrinsic load focused on the relevant component?

Kate, a secondary Maths trainee, describes a topic she broke down for her classes.

Often students struggle with [percentages]. However, I believe it's a really attainable topic for all learners. There are definitely multiple avenues you can take to teach the topic but I found working with manipulatives really helpful. For example, to find 65% of a rule we need to using 'building blocks'. If a red block is worth 50%, a green block 10% and a yellow block 5% (three of the most useful building blocks) how can I make a tower worth 65%? Students can then add these together to find the desired percentages.

Minimise the extraneous

In my misspent early years as a teacher, I kept a few activities held in reserve for difficult classes I wanted to keep busy (and behave). One such activity was the board game sequence of lessons. My students made board games about anything I could vaguely relate to the topic at hand, including some truly awful ones about Shakespeare and English grammar. I vividly remember the first time a particularly difficult class were cutting and sticking in near silence. If only for a moment, I thought I'd cracked teaching but, of course, the class were learning nothing.

If this sounds like fun to you – I can assure you it wasn't – I'm not against some project-based or open-ended activities for students. But setting students off on open-ended projects over the course of several lessons is an inefficient use of time and of the teacher's expertise. From a cognitive load perspective, the core problem with these approaches is their failure to minimise the extraneous. Students get bogged down in design and complex systems of rules; they barely think about Shakespeare or grammar at all.

Extraneous load can be found in the design of our tasks, the detail of our explanation, the presentation of our resources. The teacher who shares a self-deprecating joke over a silent and focused class is adding unnecessarily to their cognitive load. Perhaps this is where the cognitive load informed classroom starts to feel to you like a humourless vacuum but it doesn't have to be. Maybe the class can handle the joke *and* what they're doing. It isn't necessary to remove your personality from every moment of your lessons. It isn't necessary to stop telling jokes. I've told a lot, particularly bad ones. But our knowledge of Cognitive Load Theory forces us to reflect on our decisions and actions.

When planning tasks or designing a resource, even when thinking about your classroom, consider how to minimise extraneous load. Anything that is likely to distract students from thinking about what you want them to is worth cutting back. In planning, this is about considering each moment of the lesson and looking for any point where students may have their attention drawn to something which won't aid learning. Resources should not contain the superfluous or distracting, both in terms of visuals and writing.

To some, the idea of 'designing your classroom' will feel alien and unwelcome. It certainly did to me. In my third year of teaching, I had clearly done so bad a job of making my room look nice that two colleagues came and did all my displays for me, unintentionally teaching me to leave the 'design' of my room to others for the rest of my career. If someone tells you that your displays or room could have a bit more colour or excitement, look them straight in the eye and say, 'I'm doing my best to minimise extraneous load'.

Teachers concerned about extraneous load should be careful not to eject every interesting story or tangent from their lessons. Minimising extraneous load is not about removing the colour, the detail or the life from the topics we teach. Shakespeare offers fascinating tangents, stories and language to explore. As does, in my opinion, English grammar. When our tasks or resources take us too far from these things, we're likely to be minimising the intrinsic and maximising the extraneous.

Aim for independence

Cognitive Load Theory has become the main bit of research underpinning the argument that teaching should be an explicit or direct affair. I agree that what is called explicit or direct teaching – highly interactive teaching led by the expertise of the teacher, full of lots of questions and practice – is the best bet and a suitable classroom norm. That doesn't mean you can never set projects or work in groups. Whatever, and however, we're teaching, our aim should be to build those chunks of content back into something recognisable as knowledge or skill.

At one school I worked at, some students engaged in an extended project that culminated in an exhibition in the sports hall. I wandered that exhibition in awe, listening to students explain their projects, confidently rich in detail. One boy in particular sticks in my mind because of his passion for black holes, something about which I know almost nothing. I asked question after question only to have them all answered energetically. Schools can and should make space for this kind of independence and see it as the natural destination of education.

What classroom strategies does Cognitive Load Theory encourage?

Thus far, our focus has been principles but it would be a reductive reading of the Cognitive Load Theory research to *just* look at these. Much of this research investigates specific strategies that manage cognitive load well whilst embedding new knowledge and process into long-term memory. Practical applications of Cognitive Load Theory are not simply the good intentions to manage load a bit better. It should prompt real change in your classroom. Some of the strategies below are things you can fold into your planning from tomorrow.

Again, consider how they might solve the problems you're facing *right now.* If they don't seem to, return to them in the future. Students struggling with complex processes might benefit from the Worked Example Effect. Students who 'don't know how to start' can engage in Completion Problems, initially being guided through the steps of a task. Students who are overloaded by your explanations might benefit from your knowledge of the Split Attention Effect. Knowledge of these things expands your repertoire of strategies for guiding students towards competence and skill. None of these are *tips or tricks* to try in the classroom in that superficial way. They are solutions to the complex problems of thinking and learning. Consider whether they solve the problems you are facing before throwing them at your planning.

The Worked Example Effect

Worked Examples are completed examples of problems or questions. Worked Examples are not simply resources available to students if they are struggling. They are objects of study. Steps are revealed; strategies highlighted. You could see how Worked Examples could be powerful in Maths where tasks frequently aim at a specific solution but require mastering several steps. Complex division or multiplication are processes where students can benefit from the specificity afforded by a clear Worked Example. However, Worked Examples can be used across subjects. Where tasks or questions must be approached in a particular fashion, the Worked Example can provide the blueprint for independent practice.

Worked Examples work best when:

- They make clear *every step* a student will take.

- They are a focus for discussion.

- Discussion brings clarity about a process.

Some discussion questions might focus on the approach in general, like 'Why might this strategy work?' Or, for two comparative examples, 'What are the differences between the approaches? Which approach do you prefer and why?' Worked Examples should also have questions that focus student thinking on the subject content being taught. In an example of an analytical paragraph on *Oliver Twist*, questions could explore how the paragraph communicates Dickens's intentions or how the paragraph unpicks the quotation.

It's unlikely your first attempts will produce perfect Worked Examples but they should highlight what students might struggle with and where your examples or explanations have been unclear. As you start to find Worked Examples that work, you can collect them for future use. Research also suggests that two or more Worked Examples might be better than one so don't expect a breakthrough with students after one short example.[8]

A Worked Example can't complete a task *for* a student. We need to hand over responsibility – at times, gradually – to our students. That is where Completion Problems come in.

Completion Problems

In a Completion Problem, part of a solution or process is revealed, leaving the rest to be completed by the student. An almost finished diagram, a table with some data, a question with the beginnings of an answer, the first two sentences of a paragraph. One frequent classroom refrain is, 'I don't know how to start'. The Completion Problem gives the student the help they need to get going. Our aim is to gradually hand over responsibility to students so that they can do such tasks with no Worked Example or Completion Problem necessary.

A geography teacher might want their students to confidently analyse climate graphs. In the last lesson, climate graphs have been introduced. In this one, students will have to work independently to draw inferences from the graphs. One way to do this would be to reiterate what a climate graph is – a graph showing average temperature and rainfall – and get students to answer a couple of questions about them. Some students might struggle; others might have missed or misunderstood the explanation. Cognitive load from the multiple sources of information – the task, the graph, the new concepts – is probably too much. Instead the teacher projects the climate graph and the question which follows it under the visualiser. The teacher starts to answer the question, modelling their approach (more on this in Chapter 14). A sentence is started – everyone copies it – and then students are expected to finish it.

A Completion Problem is a good middle step between a Worked Example and independence. Have a look at an upcoming lesson plan. Where is independence expected? If students are ready for it, fine – let them carry on. At times, though, what they need is the bridge between an example and competence. They need either one or more Completion Problems.

The Split Attention Effect

Students often must split their attention between two sources of information: the board and their book, the teacher and their friend, the clock and their work. The Split Attention Effect refers to a more specific tension: between the modes of communication used to explain and teach. A diagram often has labels helping to explain it. When the labels are separate from the diagram, John Sweller explains that, 'Learners must mentally integrate the two sources of information in order to understand the solution, a process that yields a high cognitive load and hampers learning'.[9] Integrating labels with a diagram reduces this split attention.

Implications of split attention extend beyond an integration of labels with diagrams. Two researchers of the Split Attention Effect differentiate between visual working memory and auditory working memory.[10] Visual working memory scoops up what we've seen, including what we've read. Auditory working memory does the same with what we hear. Integrating labels with a diagram may reduce split attention but both labels and diagram enter visual working memory. Students may need to combine and manipulate information from a diagram. Working memory may buckle before students think in a way that will support learning. Students manage cognitive load better when information is channelled to both visual and auditory working memory. Not only that, students are able to connect and think about content when we use both channels.[11]

If this all feels a bit theoretical, consider what students are expected to attend to in a single lesson. Attentional issues abound where resources, particularly PowerPoint, brim with competing information. Initially, evaluating a resource's attentional demands before a lesson or reflecting on explanation after a lesson can weigh heavily on *your* cognitive load. Focus on:

- Integrating text and diagram in resources.

- Avoiding text heavy resources that you plan to explain verbally.

- Considering the balance between auditory and visual working memory in explanations.

- Scripting and then practise explaining a diagram or picture with no text.

- Removing PowerPoint slides or other aspects of a resource that are *for you*. Print and use them as an aide-memoir if you need. Don't submit students to text heavy resources just there to remind you what to talk about.

Knowing about Cognitive Load Theory will only matter if it affects what you do in lessons. Recalling vaguely that splitting students' attention is unhelpful as you explain a diagram with a complex key and set of notes improves nothing. Our understanding of Cognitive Load Theory should help us to pre-empt the pitfalls of cognitive overload in the planning stage of lesson delivery.

How should this affect my teaching?

Improve your reflection

We've been examining the knowledge needed to face the challenges of the class-room. Ideally, this knowledge would prevent most of the problems we face but often it works differently: we look back at a lesson, initially unsure of what went wrong. Students got stuck or didn't get through as much as we expected them to. Students failed to answer what we considered basic questions in a mini-assessment. Students struggled with content they know well but perhaps in an overly compli-cated task. Cognitive Load Theory is a core element of your mental model of how students learn. Apply it to your classroom and shine a light on student learning *and* these problems.

In lessons, and after them, we can reflect on learning by considering how well we (and our students) are managing cognitive load in any given moment. You may realise a crucial task had students handling too many elements at once and decide to return to that topic in a subsequent lesson.

When you grow in confidence, you can start to do this in the lesson. As an explanation lands you may realise you're expecting too much of students in one go. Pause it and start at least part of a task. If students were going to answer five questions or complete a task with several steps but this seems too ambitious, break it down in the moment.

Pre-empt cognitive overload

Better than reflection, plan with cognitive load in mind. Look at upcoming lessons. Is content broken down into manageable chunks? How will element interactivity affect student thinking here? Am I demonstrating processes using Worked Examples? Am I handing over responsibility using Completion Problems? Are there any points in a lesson where student attention will be split?

In summary

Knowledge of cognitive load adds a layer of thinking to your planning, making it richer and, in all likelihood, more effective. You continue, of course, to think about content. Activities and classroom routines are still important. Not every activity can include a Worked Example or Completion Problem. It isn't always possible to completely focus student attention. Cognitive Load Theory, in this way, doesn't solve all your problems but it gives insight into the learning experience that you quickly find you can't do without.

Cognitive Load Theory can feel both obvious and profound. Obviously, we should spend time breaking content down for students. Obviously, we should gradually hand over independence to students. But these things haven't always been obvious. Rather than planning a series of gradual steps, teachers have been rushed towards extended and open tasks: writing full stories in English, conducting experiments in Science, making an argument in History, problem solving in Maths. Cognitive Load Theory provides both a set of principles and strategies to shape your planning. Applicable immediately, these principles and strategies will take a career to master.

Possible next steps

1. **Optimise, don't minimise, cognitive load.** Students need to think hard in lessons. The application of Cognitive Load Theory is not to make things easier. If students really know the content we're looking at in a lesson, we should expect more from them. If we're introducing a concept for the first time, we should break it down and carefully manage element interactivity.

2. **Plan some Completion Problems.** In lessons coming up, where would students benefit from a bridge between your explanation and their independent practice? Don't simply *plan to do a Completion Problem*. Include in your plan the task you'll focus on, what you'll write or say and where you'll leave students to continue. Where you leave students will depend largely on how new this is to them and how much they've covered before. After modelling a process for the very first time, you might use a Completion Problem where students are taken through the whole process again with only the very final step left for them to

complete. If students have completed similar problems before or spent time in the content, you might just give them the very first step.

3. **Plan against split attention.** Upcoming resources are a good place to look for possible split attention. Pre-empt it where you can. Do this by considering where students are being asked to pay attention – the screen and their books, a printed knowledge organiser and their textbook, the labels of a diagram and the diagram itself. Reduce the moments where students must move from one source of, potentially unfamiliar, information to another.

Notes

1 Sweller, J., Merrienboer, J., and Paas, F. (2019). Cognitive architecture and instructional design: 20 years later. *Educational Psychology Review*, 31, 261–292.
2 Centre for Education, Statistics and Evaluation. (2017). *Cognitive Load Theory: Research that Teachers Really Need to Understand.* New South Wales Government.
3 Sweller, J., Merrienboer, J., and Paas, F. (2019). Cognitive architecture and instructional design: 20 years later. *Educational Psychology Review*, 31, 261–292.
4 Ibid.
5 This number is disputed: research places it between four and seven.
6 Sweller, J., Paas, F., and Merrienboer, J. (1998). Cognitive architecture and instructional design. *Educational Psychology Review*, 10(3), 251–296.
7 Centre for Education, Statistics and Evaluation. (2017). *Cognitive Load Theory: Research that Teachers Really Need to Understand.* New South Wales Government.
8 Kalyuga, S., Chandler, P., Tuovinen, J., and Sweller, J. (2001). When problem solving is superior to studying Worked Examples. *Journal of Educational Psychology*, 93(3), 579–588.
9 Sweller, J., Paas, F., and Merrienboer, J. (1998). Cognitive architecture and instructional design. *Educational Psychology Review*, 10(3), 251–296.
10 Mayer, R., and Moreno, R. (1998). A split attention effect in multimedia learning: Evidence for dual processing systems in working memory. *Journal of Educational Psychology*, 90(2), 312–320.
11 Ibid.

What changes long-term memory for students?

A common classroom conversation goes something like this:

> I say, 'You'll recognise this from last week –'
> 'What?' says at least one student.
> 'Last week. We introduced this. We're just recapping'.
> 'I've literally never seen this before in my life', says the student, gesturing at the PowerPoint or resources. 'I've never even heard of…'

Even when I get them to turn to the page, to the date, in their exercise book when they *were* in and they *did* the task, they still look blankly, happy to continue arguing that they've never heard of what I'm talking about. Memory is a funny thing. And students don't have it easy – their experience of school is different to ours. We focus on one subject or one class. We spend more time anticipating lessons and more time reflecting on them. Students move from lesson to lesson, to break time drama, to home, to all the other activities of their lives. I can't guarantee you won't have conversations like the one above but knowledge of memory provides a foundation to explore the problems and solutions of learning in the classroom.

If learning is a change in long-term memory, we must seek to understand what changes long-term memory. I recognise for some that is still quite a big *if*. Remember:

- Long-term memory contains more than *facts*. This isn't simply about learning dates, concepts or terminology.

- If learned meaningfully, facts don't sit in mute isolation; they connect and form webs of knowledge called schema.

- Other definitions are available. Dehaene's forming 'an internal model of the external world' is a useful contrast whilst driving at a common truth.

- Even if you still don't fully accept the *change in long-term memory* definition, it usefully informs some pedagogical decisions.

 DOI: 10.4324/9781003281306-15

● Cognitive Load Theory is based on evidence that working memory is limited and long-term memory is limitless. Students can fail to learn when we overload their working memory capacity. We must, according to Cognitive Load Theory, attend to how students retain information in their long-term memories.

When we looked at *Developing Teacher Knowledge*, the following strategies were introduced.

1. Retrieval practice, our attempts to retrieve memories without (or with minimal) prompts or aids.

2. Spaced practice, our attempts to practice a specific, narrow skill with feedback that helps us to improve.

However, we'll examine them now considering the classroom rather than our personal study. Our aim here is that we understand the basic principles, can apply them to our classrooms and have a plan for how we will do this.

Retrieval practice

What is it?

Testing, particularly high-stakes testing, is commonly seen as a Bad Thing because of the pressure it places on students to demonstrate what they've learned. Testing can be a quiz at the start of the lesson. It might be an end of unit assessment of what students have learned during a half-term. Testing is also a method of gaining knowledge in order to adapt to what students show us they can and can't do, and do and don't know, known as formative assessment (more on this later). When surveyed on their views of the uses of testing, teachers still tend not to link testing to memory and retention.[1]

The 'Testing Effect' describes the observable phenomena where people remember more of what they are tested on compared to non-testing. In turn, 'retrieval practice' refers to how, as teachers, we exploit the Testing Effect to benefit long-term learning. Every time a memory is searched for and found without significant direction or support, our ability to retrieve that memory strengthens. When we try to remember something, we conduct a kind of imprecise search for it. This search extends from a source or prompt, like a piece of terminology, towards a target, the definition. Retrieving the definition strengthens its connection to the terminology we started with. Benefits of retrieval extend beyond individual memories. When we retrieve, the connections between the network memories in the same topic strengthen. And memory here doesn't solely mean individual, isolated facts. It includes concepts, complex ideas and understanding of processes. All can be retrieved and strengthened.

What mistakes can we make with retrieval practice?

Despite a well-established body of evidence and growing use in the classroom, quality of retrieval practice varies wildly. Knowledgeable teachers will see past the superficial and potential pitfalls outlined below.

See it as one part of the lesson

Too often, helpful concepts backed by evidence get diluted in their transition to the classroom. Retrieval is one such concept. The idea of *testing* leads understandably to the idea of a *test* but then, for many, testing and retrieval become a quiz, and then a five-question quiz at the start of the lesson.

Retrieval includes quizzing but it also includes any activity where students are forced to recall something they have previously learned without, or with minimal, support.

Some examples include:

- Explaining an unlabelled diagram to a partner.
- Writing out everything you can remember about a topic.
- Describing the connections between two previously explored names, terms, dates or ideas.
- Summarising a concept in a specific number of points.

Retrieval happens well at transition points in the lesson. The start of the lesson may work for routines but the middle or the end may work for the content you're teaching.

Move to retrieval before learning

Retrieval won't work where students don't know something. It's a method of review not delivery. If retrieval reveals a lack of knowledge or ability, the task should be stopped and we should focus on re-teaching activities. Where we are concerned that students aren't ready for retrieval, we can pre-empt potential retrieval failures by increasing the cues and prompts. For example, in a language task where students had to translate English words into another language, providing the first letter or letters of the target word led to effective retrieval and long-term retention.[2]

Spend too much time on it

Starting a lesson with a retrieval activity is not necessarily a bad use of time nor is it inherently a good use of time. Some schools mandate quizzing at the start of lessons. This is fine if the quizzing is high quality. However, such a quiz can eat into time for new content to be introduced. A five-question quiz can quickly take up 15 minutes of a lesson once students have come in, done the questions and corrected answers. One temptation is to rush them through it. Another is to avoid feedback, perhaps thinking the process of retrieval is enough without sharing answers or corrections. Both temptations should be avoided. Even when students have retrieved something accurately, it helps retention to give feedback and share answers or ideas.[3] Wherever retrieval takes place in our lessons, it must be efficient. Specific parameters are given; time limits are rigid; feedback is quick and clear. Before moving on, let's look at how to use time efficiently in two different retrieval activities.

Quizzes

If you're using a quiz for retrieval, don't be restricted by an arbitrary number of questions. Ask questions focused on what you want students to remember. I can't tell you how long a certain number of questions will take to answer and give feedback on: it depends on the questions (and the answers). We'll re-examine what we want students to remember when we look at the curriculum in the next section. It's worth planning more than one quiz at a time so that you can map questions into the future rather than dwell on what will be asked in a single lesson. Quizzes tend to target an individual's ability to retrieve on their own. For this reason, silence should be the norm. Explain the quiz. Explain what it is for (and keep on explaining, until the students are bored of hearing it, that retrieval strengthens memory). Explain the time limit and that silence is expected.

This might sound something like:

> We're starting today's lesson with four questions to see what you can remember from the last two weeks. The more you try to remember these things, the easier you'll find it to remember them in the future. You have two minutes to answer the four questions on the screen. You will do this in absolute silence. Off you go.

Pause at the front of the room. Don't be tempted to move around. Don't interrupt the silence. Show the class you're watching them and do watch them. If there are more questions, or students need more time, once the class are settled and silent you can move around to check their answers. When time is up, go through the answers quickly but clearly. Hands-down questions will give you a good idea of how the class have got on. If an answer seems to have stumped everyone, you have a couple of choices. You can pause the lesson and re-teach or revisit a concept in some depth again, possibly adding another question to check understanding further. Alternatively, you can give the correct answer and move on, knowing there will be time to return to the mistake in the future. If you're unsure, it's worth just giving the answer and moving on, making a note of what they struggled with.

Pair discussion

One way for students to retrieve is to explain what they've been taught to someone else without the use of notes or too many other reminders. Unfortunately, pair discussions can waste a lot of time. They waste this time when pairs don't talk about what they're meant to, when they have too long to talk, and when the responsibility between the two speakers is unbalanced.

Because it's likely you'll explain the pair discussion in the moment (unlike the quiz questions you've thought about beforehand), it's vital you're clear on what you want students to retrieve. This could be the underlying principles behind a scientific concept, the tone or tempo of a musical genre, the correct usage of a new piece of vocabulary or something else. Be clear with students about what you're wanting them to retrieve – *I want to see if you can remember the factors influencing the declining number of Sweat Shops*. Be clear about time limits and give less time than you think they need – *You have 30 seconds to explain to your partner...* Sometimes it's useful to label individuals (1 and 2 or A and B) and give direct instructions to each person in the pair. For example, A might talk during the 30 second time limit but B might be expected to feedback to the class. It's important that both retrieve the target content otherwise the task won't have the desired effect.

A final mistake made with retrieval practice is rushing to it before embedding what has been taught. At times, retrieval is not the answer; further teaching, practice, checks of understanding and feedback are required. Students are better served by depth of study in the present, not the assumption they'll get it or top up their understanding when it comes to retrieval.

How do we use retrieval practice well?

Tie it to the curriculum

Retrieval is only meaningful as an ongoing strategy rather than a one-off. It may help students remember something in the following lesson or following week, but our eyes should be fixed on the long-term impact. The curriculum should define what needs to be retrieved and which memories require strengthening. Where the curriculum is well-planned, it (or the leader in charge of it) may direct what retrieval should focus on. It may not.

If schemes of work or resources don't arrive to you with this kind of definition, you may need to make decisions about retrieval yourself. Too often, in reaching for something to retrieve (usually for a quiz) we simplify content or place too much importance on the basics. Even worse, we can make retrieval trivial through a focus on the surface or tangential features of recent lessons. A story might have helped students to understand a concept but, if we don't expect them to recall that story in the long term, questions about it should feature in our retrieval.

Curriculum should drive retrieval. If we hold a narrow view of knowledge – that it's just facts and vocabulary – we might find our retrieval contorting into a misshapen and deficient version of our curriculum.

Increase the complexity

It's no bad thing to get students to recall definitions for important vocabulary but if this is where our retrieval rests, we'll find students unprepared for the complexity of thought and understanding our curriculum demands. It might be quicker and easier to design a quiz full of definition recall but we should also expect students to use those words accurately, to use them in combination, to understand correct and incorrect uses.

Students forced to recall basic individual items regularly are likely to remember them. Unfortunately, stringing a few bits of rudimentary vocabulary or content together in a student's mind won't ignite creative or critical thinking. Asking students to repeat a definition they've heard every few lessons will automate the definition but not necessarily the understanding. Retrieval practice can progress from recalling a term, through to using it, and beyond to using it in conjunction with other important bits of content. Retrieval tasks increase in complexity when they incrementally expect more of students: a multiple-choice question might be a good start to check and strengthen a student's understanding of a word or process.

Alice, a Year 5 teacher in her third year, talks about different ways she uses retrieval practice in her classroom.

I have this thing called hot-seat. The children love it. They think it's a game and don't actually realise it's retrieval. Basically, I sit a child on a chair and the rest of them question that child. We use a points system to track how many questions are answered. They thrive off it because it's not just the ones in the seat who are retrieving; the others have to think of the questions.

We also use speeches. At the end of the lesson I'll say, 'You've got five minutes to plan a speech on…' and I'll give them a topic. It may be to do with the lesson or the lesson before. They love that because they get to give a speech in front of the class. They all do fantastic listening for their friends. I'm at the back, listening. They absolutely love that.

We also do a brain dump where they put everything they can remember about a topic on their whiteboards.

A possible unintended consequence of delving into the research on retrieval is the fear that a 'right' way to do retrieval is always just out of reach. Another study or paper or speaker may come along (or already exist *out there*) ready to give definitive insight. Nerves about applying research with fidelity are understandable but, in this area, probably unwarranted. A recent large review of the retrieval research, examining different types of retrieval practice, found that all classrooms and schools 'yielded a benefit from retrieval practice'. The researchers concluded that 'educators should implement retrieval practice, with less concern for the precise format or timing' of retrieval tasks set.[4]

Spaced practice

What is it?

Spaced (or distributed) practice is the repetition of any activity where the gap between repetitions is greater than nothing.[5] Repetition leads to better retention than massed practice, an extended period of uninterrupted practice. The optimal gap between practice sessions is debated and disputed, with some arguing the longer the better while others warn that left too long nothing will be remembered. Whilst the definition of spacing includes any length of gap, there is evidence that spacing *within* lessons – practising something at the start of the lesson and returning to it at the end – does very little to aid retention.[6] Reaping the benefits of spaced practice appears more likely when we take the long view, embedding it over time rather than during a single lesson.

How do we do it?

Teachers should have some control over what is practised in their lessons, but not all the control. A curriculum defines the direction students are travelling in, and their ultimate destination. Practice tasks should be obvious as you examine the resources of the curriculum. It *should* be obvious but it isn't always. Even when a rigorous curriculum sets out what your students should practise and when, if *your* students struggle with a process, responsibility to fix it lies with you, their teacher.

Break practice down

Writing an essay isn't, initially, useful practice. Getting students to play badminton for an hour isn't practice. Designing a product from scratch, with no direction, isn't practice. This is all sink or swim. Practice demands, as Cognitive Load Theory does, that we break content down into the components that make up the whole.

A badminton match is made up of stance, serve, forehand, backhand but also position on the court, perception of opponent, knowledge of rules and potential strategy. Even in this list, further dissection is possible. A teacher's job is to break tasks down into practicable chunks.

Ask how many different elements – knowledge, steps in a process, instructions – students will have to juggle to do what you are asking. Focus on practising these separately. Our aim is to string them together, to reach alchemy of knowledge and skill. Students who have been taught your subject for some time don't need every single element broken down. They are likely to find this frustrating and tell you so. We don't practice to make everything easier for students; we do it so that students master what we teach them.

Return to practice regularly

Time is tight. Each lesson is overfilled and colleagues warn you there isn't enough time to 'get through' the content. Is it worth spending lesson time returning to what you've already studied?

For a long time, teaching analytical writing, I would teach a paragraph structure. Students would then write paragraphs to varying degrees of abject failure. To me, a paragraph was a reasonable chunk to practise. For the students, I may as well have been asking for an essay. A paragraph is so many individual things: the knowledge underpinning it, rules of structure (and how you're allowed to break them), grammatical and sentence level skills (like embedding quotations). Practising the whole before students have mastered the parts is overwhelming for you as well as for them.

Reading through my students' early paragraphs, I was struck by how they struggled with so much. Opening sentences were a problem. Students used phrases that made me shudder – *This makes the reader want to read on* – and phrases I would never have taught them – *The writer says the quote...* Confusion about quotations revealed fundamental misunderstanding. Efforts to get students to write these fully formed paragraphs too soon had wasted time. Students didn't *know* more. They couldn't *do* more and yet time had moved on.

We don't have time to return to everything so we decide based on two questions: *What do we want students to do automatically?* and *What are students struggling with?* The former can be asked proactively, informed by the curriculum. The latter we return to regularly and adapt based on our findings.

Build practice up

We don't teach the components forever. Practice of the individual aims at mastery of the whole. As students attain proficiency, combine elements. My failure with early paragraphs wasn't permanent – students should *never* write paragraphs – nor was it universal – students shouldn't write *any* paragraphs.

Our aim is not that students do the same task *ad nauseam* until they've got it. Practice works cumulatively into more complex tasks. Practice also varies when we vary the type of task whilst focusing on the same component. My realisation that students couldn't learn everything they needed for effective paragraphs by writing lots of paragraphs doesn't mean we leave every complex task until we're sure students can do it. Approaching these tasks with our knowledge of practice, we teach and focus on an element and recognise that *our* focus will rest there.

Why don't they remember this?

At a certain point, all teachers will ask themselves why a class or a student can't remember something they've been taught. If this is you, don't worry. One of our persistent challenges in the classroom is 'exposing student thinking'. It's not uncommon to be disheartened by a lack of thought or understanding or retention. After a whole term of teaching her, one of my students couldn't remember the name of the play Macbeth starred in so you're probably not doing too badly. It's easy to feel that problems of retention shouldn't trouble the research-informed teacher. Unfortunately, they do.

If we've experimented with the strategies in this section and some groups or some students are struggling, we shouldn't be surprised. We should turn back to the principles of progressive problem solving. Progressive problem solving harnesses our knowledge to solve our problems. At first, we use retrieval or spaced practice because we know these things are *good bets*. Because the classroom is complex and so are they, at least some students are likely to struggle to remember some of what they've been taught. Defining the problem is essential. Is it that students don't remember what we want them to? Is it that their memory is superficial or surface level?

Which additional avenues can you explore when you feel that practice and retrieval aren't leading to memory? The problem we're trying to solve is likely to fit into one of these categories:

1. **We haven't been practising the right things in the right way**, a possibility even when we think otherwise. Michael Pershan, a Maths teacher, describes the conflict between students doing 'a bunch of problems on a page' and genuine retrieval or practice of Maths facts.[7] Students should be able to remember basic addition and multiplication facts, helpful knowledge to think and problem solve in Maths. Pershan explains how, depending on their method, students might be retrieving and practising or they might be counting or laboriously noting down their working. Both routes will get the answer but neither will strengthen the memory.

2. **We haven't taught the knowledge or skill sufficiently in the first place.** Retrieval and spaced practice only work, only can develop in complexity, when students have learned something in the first place. Where they haven't, retrieval and practice become a sort of second teaching where students grasp some knowledge just a little bit tighter.

Refocus your practice

Picture a sports hall filled with badminton nets. Students start the lesson by grabbing a racket and a couple of shuttlecocks and serving *to* their partner. Serving has been a problem for the teacher. Students just weren't getting it so this extra practice has been planned for them. Except there's a problem. Students aren't practising serving or at least not practising it well. No expert badminton player steps up to serve thinking, *How can I direct this serve at my opponent's racket?*

To refocus this practice, the teacher explains where students can serve that will pose an immediate challenge for their opponent. She demonstrates these one at a time before students practise them. Monitoring and individual coaching corrects potential errors and misconceptions before the class move onto the next serve. Teaching in light of the research on practice doesn't mean that students won't play mini-matches at the end of the lesson. They will simply do so with a variety of serves beginning to enter their repertoire. The same research reminds us that students will need to return to these serves later for them to be useful. With the same group the following week, the teacher starts with serve practise again but calls out the names she has given the serves to move quickly through them.

So often, we think students are practising when they aren't. Or, more accurately, students practise and learn a skill counter to our intentions. We want students to work something out in their head but they write something down. We want students to write unaided but sentence starters remain on the board. We want students to shade for definition competently in art without asking us before every stroke of the pencil. Audit the tasks you've planned, checking they practise the right knowledge and watching for loopholes and shortcuts that undermine your aims.

Prioritise reading

Cognitive scientist Daniel Willingham argues that 'Books expose children to more facts and a broader vocabulary than virtually any other activity'.[8] Willingham's case is not simply that reading supports general knowledge; he makes it clear that the knowledge gained from reading provides the foundation for the skilled activities we want students to master. Simply put, 'Factual knowledge must precede skill'.

Students need a rich experience of subject matter before we expect them to retrieve or practise in that domain. Moving too quickly to quizzes and narrow practise activities may be the cause of shallow knowledge, weakly connected in our students' minds. If students are struggling with a particular topic, go back to the resources that introduced the topic. Were students exposed to complex and interesting texts? Were these texts accompanied by lively, interesting discussion or debate? There are other legitimate ways to enrich and introduce content but it's hard to argue any of them are as important as reading.

Use homework for spaced practice and retrieval

Homework varies from school to school and many have not yet decided what exactly it is for. Although homework can serve more than one master, the one it should be most devoted to is retention of taught content, an aim achieved best through spaced practice and retrieval. In some schools, homework is set for you. If this is the case, make sure you're clear on what is set and what it is for. Where freedom allows, set in line with the principles in this chapter. Define what you want students to know and do well, based on what you teach in the curriculum. Decide what students can do on their own. Set simple tasks which retrieve and practise. Several online platforms offer ways for this to largely be done for you but the idea remains the same: students should spend additional time retrieving and practising as well as learning new content. As homework is unsuited to the introduction of new content, it is ideal for the review of what has already been covered.

Memory is vital to learning. Don't, as I foolishly did as a new teacher, make the argument from ignorance that *I don't want students to remember. I want them to understand.* How will they understand if they don't remember? This chapter has focused on two main strategies because they are straightforward and easily adopted. Dwelling on these strategies is not the same as saying your lessons should *only* or *mainly* be filled with quizzes and narrow slices of practice. They shouldn't. Teaching is more than these things but it's unlikely to get very far without them.

In summary

Pedagogy is the thinking underlying our decisions and strategies employed in the classroom. Where possible, our pedagogy should be informed by the best available evidence. Whilst this section has not been a comprehensive summary of 'the evidence', it has highlighted some important pillars to any mental model of learning:

- Evidence can't answer all our questions but it can open some avenues to pursue whilst closing others down.

- Learning changes our long-term memory. More expansive definitions of learning are available but this one has the benefit of focusing our minds on what might bring about tangible change in the classroom.

- Things that teachers often fixate on in the classroom – activity, busyness, completion of tasks – are proxies for learning, not bad in and of themselves but no indicators of learning.

- Cognitive Load Theory is one of the best explanations of why students learn and remember, and why they don't. In both the principles it sets out and the strategies it promotes, Cognitive Load Theory should underpin our planning.

- Retrieval and practice both offer applicable ways to make learning stick. We must not pay lip service to these strategies but embed them with thought and care.

Possible next steps

1. **Increase retrieval complexity.** If you do a quiz or some kind of retrieval regularly, look back at your plans and resources. As students make progress in the curriculum, match that progress with increasingly complex retrieval. Students

had to list non-renewable energy sources a week ago. Now, based on lessons since, they have to compare them with what they've learned about renewable energy.

2. **Define and practice.** So often, I've just got students to do some activities and not carefully defined what I wanted them to practice. Maybe this is a symptom of teaching English where content and skill aren't clearly defined. Nebulous approaches where we expect students to gather up skills almost incidentally from our lessons are bound to lead to failure in retention and frustration for students. Pick out one skill you want to practice. Make it definable. Create a clear success criteria. Get students to practise that thing and nothing else. Set up a task so you can give feedback to all or almost all, even if that feedback is simply, 'You've got it, well done'.

Notes

1 For example the authors of the study here describe how only a fifth of teachers surveyed linked testing to retention, with most seeing it, rightly but not exclusively, as a way of finding out what students know. Yang, C., Luo, L., Vadillo, M., and Shanks, D. (2020). Testing (quizzing) boosts classroom learning: A systemic and meta-analytic review. *Psychological Bulletin*, 147(4), 399–435.
2 Fiechter, J., and Benjamin, A. (2017). Diminishing-cues retrieval practice: A memory enhancing technique that works when regular testing doesn't. *Psychonomic Bulletin and Review*, 25, 1868–1876.
3 Rowland, C.A. (2014). The effect of testing versus restudy on retention: A meta-analytic review of the Testing Effect. *Psychological Bulletin*, 140(6), 1432–1463.
4 Agarwal, P.K., Nunes, L.D., and Blunt, J.R. (2021). Retrieval practice consistently benefits student learning: A systematic review of applied research in schools and classrooms. *Educational Psychology Review*, 33, 1409–1453.
5 Carpenter, S.K., Cepeda, N.J., Rohrer, D., Kang, S.H.K., and Pashler, H. (2012). Using spacing to enhance diverse forms of learning: Review of recent research and implications for instruction. *Educational Pyshcology Review*, 24, 369–378.
6 EEF. (2021). *Cognitive Science Approaches in the Classroom: An Evidence Review.* https://educationendowmentfoundation.org.uk/education-evidence/evidence-reviews/cognitive-science-approaches-in-the-classroom (accessed 26/02/2022).
7 Pershan, M. (2021). *What People Get Wrong About Memorizing Math Facts.* http://notepad.michaelpershan.com/what-people-get-wrong-about-memorizing-math-facts/ (accessed 20/03/2022).
8 Willingham, D. (2009). *Why Don't Students Like School?* Jossey-Bass.

Further reading

Lovell, O. (2020). *Cognitive Load Theory in Action.* John Catt.
Willingham, D. (2021). *Why Don't Students Like School?* Jossey-Bass.

PART 5
Subject knowledge

Views about teaching have changed dramatically over time. One such change provides insight into the role of subject knowledge in teacher training. In the late nineteenth century, elementary teachers in California were expected to pass a rigorous written exam to qualify. Prospective teachers had to be well-versed in arithmetic, grammar, geography – so far so good – as well as penmanship, industrial drawing and vocal music.[1] Whilst your average primary teacher might still just look down this list, nod and get on with it, such tests are almost entirely absent from teacher training today. What is interesting about this test is its unwavering focus on subject knowledge. Nothing in it examines generic teaching skills or pedagogy.

What would you put on a test for teachers? It's hard to know, isn't it? As a new member of the profession, which areas of your knowledge received the most scrutiny in your training? Perhaps it has been your subject knowledge. Or your knowledge of educational theory. You may feel that the greatest scrutiny has been directed to your actions in the classroom.

Around a hundred years after that Californian test of subject knowledge, American assessments of trainee teachers had changed dramatically. A test usually still existed for trainees but it now assessed knowledge of planning, organisation and policy. Subject knowledge had gone. I'm sure the trainees and the trainers considered the subject but it had lost its core status. The trend in America is mirrored around the world. Subject knowledge has been important, less important and now, it seems, is regaining prominence in the teaching profession. Two separate but parallel narratives have brought subject knowledge back into focus after that period in the cold.

Narrative 1: Cognitive science and knowledge

One Christmas, I received a book that genuinely changed how I saw teaching. It didn't change anything immediately. This was no Damascene conversion. Gradually, as I went back to it, I realised I'd got teaching completely wrong. The book was *Why Don't Students Like School?* by Daniel Willingham. Willingham, a

DOI: 10.4324/9781003281306-16

cognitive scientist, promises to 'answer questions about how the mind works and what it means for the classroom'.[2]

I was never – as far as I can remember – taught how to teach. We didn't work through the 'learning to teach' curriculum from start to finish because such a curriculum did not exist. When I started teaching in 2009, truths about teaching were cobbled together from moments in lectures and initial lesson feedback. One observer told me she loved how little I spoke to my classes. I didn't explain that I was terrified of speaking to them so I kept students as busy as possible. A lecturer gave us a complicated equation we could use to figure out how long we were allowed to speak to students in a lesson dependent on their age. It became clear that learning was something you tricked students into.

There were so many texts I had looked forward to teaching but I realised quickly that English teaching wasn't concerned with specific texts, periods or movements of literature. Content was less important than the skills students developed along the way. It didn't matter if you were teaching *Romeo and Juliet* or rap lyrics because we weren't teaching the content. What mattered was students' ability to analyse or express an opinion or create something new.

So when Willingham told us, based on research from cognitive science, that 'Factual knowledge must precede skill',[3] he was challenging an ingrained and long-standing status quo. He was describing a well-founded principle of cognitive science: we need knowledge to apply skill. When I was training to teach, the absolute pinnacle of good teaching was 'higher order' thinking. Creating, synthesising, analysing, problem solving and others were all more important than simply knowing. It's hard to disagree. I haven't met a teacher who doesn't want their students to reach the dizzy heights of the 'higher order'. A difficulty arises when we try to skip the steps of 'lower order' thinking. You can't synthesise knowledge you don't have. You can't problem solve in an area you don't understand. Strange as it is to say it now, that's exactly what teachers were asked to do when I was training. Skip the knowledge and go straight to the complicated stuff. It doesn't make any sense now, and it didn't then.

Knowledge, and in particular the knowledge held by the teacher but not their students, became incredibly important. But this didn't happen, for me, right away. For a long time, I struggled to see how facts could be important to the English curriculum. The word itself – facts – is possibly part of the problem. In English, I thought, students needed understanding rather than facts. We tend to see facts as an isolated, potentially interesting but ultimately minor part of cognition. Your mind doesn't see things this way. Knowing when *Romeo and Juliet* was written, its genre or themes, its historical background – none of this is isolated in the mind of a student of literature. Instead, a web of knowledge, a schema, builds the more you get to know.

I realised students need to know things. To some, this might feel like an underwhelming realisation. To me, it was ground-breaking. Whilst the profession has moved on, it would be wrong to miss the turn cognitive science has caused.

Cognitive science made knowledge, and therefore curriculum, central but that didn't end the conversation. Cognitive science prompted the questions *Which knowledge?* and *Whose knowledge?* but couldn't answer them.

Narrative 2: The curriculum renaissance

Cognitive science has encouraged curriculum into the limelight, but it can't take sole credit. There are plenty of voices who argue for the supremacy of the subject and the curriculum whilst paying little attention to the cognitive arguments. Despite wanting the same thing, or at least a similar thing – subject and curriculum to be central – these arguments are often made from drastically different positions.

Many have looked to Matthew Arnold, nineteenth-century school inspector and poet, as they've sought to reignite the curriculum fires. Michael Gove borrowed Matthew Arnold's phrase and argued that students should learn 'the best that has been thought and said'.[4] We should return, thought Gove, to teaching students a traditional curriculum unashamedly. Being a fairly blunt instrument, Gove didn't seem to wrestle with the less palatable views of Arnold's expression. The idea of 'best' is often exclusionary and elitist. Arnold's overriding desire is to civilise the barbarian. Teaching the 'best' in this way becomes, for many, an imposition of values and ways of thinking.

Gove's curriculum legacy has been baked into the most recent Ofsted inspection framework in England. Amanda Spielman, Ofsted's Chief Inspector, also a fan of the 'best',[5] put curriculum at the heart of school inspection. Ofsted must ascertain whether schools 'construct a curriculum that is ambitious and designed to give all learners... the knowledge and cultural capital they need to succeed in life'.[6] Teachers, in turn, must 'have good knowledge of the subject(s) and courses they teach'.

To be fair to the curriculum, these arguments had already been made outside of the corridors of power. Over a decade before Spielman's inspection framework, in his aptly named *Bringing Knowledge Back In*, Sociologist of Education Michael Young argues from the left that knowledge is the right of the many, not the few. Where knowledge has been the preserve of the elite and of private education, Young argues knowledge offers an avenue to equality. Knowledge doesn't belong to the powerful; knowledge offers power to those without it. In this view, subject and curriculum aren't an imposition of values but a way of understanding and accessing the world and all its opportunities.

To some, these narratives have run their course. Curriculum, they say, is a fad. Or, if not the curriculum, then the work that has gone into it. Carefully crafted (and wholly ignored) statements of curriculum philosophy written by harried middle leaders are read by no one. Low-rent art projects present the curriculum as a tube map or an incomprehensible web (where a bullet point list would do). Narratives rise, fall and are replaced. If subject knowledge or curriculum were fads, we could expect to see them fall again as rapidly as they had ascended. Of course, the curriculum – like assessment or behaviour management – can never be a fad. The current focus on curriculum may be dropped as faddish but that would be our fault for allowing one of the central aspects of what we will always do to become superficial and cheap, or overwrought and unsustainable.

Difficult though it is to imagine, curriculum will give way to another inspection focus, another politician's priority, another solution to an ill-defined problem. If you've made it this far, I hope it is clear that knowledge is vital for the expert teacher. Which knowledge could be more vital than the knowledge of the content being taught? If some new fad grips the profession soon, trying to wrestle your attention from the curriculum, remember that subject is central. This is the peak, the focal point, of our examination of teacher knowledge. Pedagogy without content is empty. Knowledge of how students learn is useless unless we direct this knowledge to the content learned.

All that said, there is confusion about what kind of subject knowledge makes a great teacher. With that in mind, this part will seek to answer these questions:

- What types of subject knowledge do we need and how do we develop them?

- What do we need to know about the curriculum?

- How does knowledge of the curriculum affect our planning?

- How do you use all that subject knowledge in the classroom?

Notes

1 Shulman, L. (1986). Those who understand: knowledge growth in teaching. *Educational Research*, 15(2), 4–14.
2 Willingham, D. (2010). *Why Don't Students Like School?* Josey Bass.
3 Ibid.
4 For example, this phrase is found in the DfE's National Curriculum at www.gov.uk/government/publications/national-curriculum-in-england-framework-for-key-stages-1-to-4/the-national-curriculum-in-england-framework-for-key-stages-1-to-4
5 For example, in this speech to a curriculum conference: Spielman, A. (2019). Speech at the 'Wonder Years' curriculum conference. DfE. www.gov.uk/government/speeches/amanda-spielman-at-the-wonder-years-curriculum-conference (accessed 24/10/2021).
6 Ofsted. (2021). *Education Inspection Framework*. www.gov.uk/government/publications/education-inspection-framework/education-inspection-framework (accessed 19/11/2021).

What types of subject knowledge do we need and how do we develop them?

I decided to train as a teacher when I realised that after university, I wouldn't be able to talk to people about poetry all day. Unfortunately, I found early in my career that English teachers don't *just* spend their days talking to people about poetry. The knowledge I'd gained at university didn't seem relevant. I stood in the store cupboard trying to choose a text to teach Year 7 from a selection of books I'd never read. I was given a half-term's topic titled *Animal Poetry* but had to muddle through after being told I could choose the poets, poems... or animals. It wasn't all like this. My favourite moments became the times I had to think deeply about the texts I was teaching and make plans for students to think deeply too. I didn't know if working on that knowledge made me a better teacher but I knew I wanted more of those times and more of that thinking.

Being Head of English allowed me to devote large chunks of time to reading, thinking and planning around the topics I loved. As I made being a Head of English more about the content of *what* was taught, my team followed – some willingly and some begrudgingly – and we found knowledge to be addictive. The more we sought to know deeply what we were teaching, the more we wanted to know. There were department meetings where we read an essay about *Macbeth* and discussed how it should shape our teaching of Year 10. There were discussions and debates about what students should study and when.

My point is that teaching becomes a rewarding job when knowledge is central, and nowhere is this truer than subject knowledge. This isn't a one-time thing, nor is it something only for the uber-keen. Not only is it rewarding; it's essential for your continued development, particularly – but not limited to – the start of your career.

In this chapter, we'll look at three types of subject knowledge:

- Degree knowledge – The knowledge we gain in higher education.

- Subject knowledge – This is your knowledge of the whole domain of the subject you teach. Often the domain is different to, or at least much larger than, the curriculum you teach.

DOI: 10.4324/9781003281306-17

- Pedagogical content knowledge – This is your knowledge of pedagogy – your classroom behaviour – merged with your knowledge of your subject. If your subject is writing heavy – like English or history – your pedagogical content knowledge might be full of writing frames and models, how they can be used as well as their limits. Every subject will have content to explain and some useful ways to think about explanation. Questions will vary in use from subject to subject.

Degree knowledge

No teacher takes the same route into teaching. Training and prior qualifications are diverse. In secondary school, teachers often teach outside of specialism and must develop subject knowledge on the job. Even if you have a relevant degree, if you've entered teaching from another profession, it may have been years since you've had to think about the object of your study. In primary, being a subject specialist, at degree level, across the curriculum is impossible. Concern about how prepared you are to deliver the content of the curriculum well is understandable.

It's worth pausing to consider how this study prepares you and how perhaps it doesn't: to what extent does what we arrive in teaching with shape our success and the success of our students? Reflect, for a moment, on the mental model you have of your subject or subjects, or had when you started teacher training. The extent to which this mental model maps well onto the school curriculum will depend on the subject and on your route into teaching. It's natural to feel, as a subject expert, you should be ready to encounter relative novices in the classroom. Remember, the most useful knowledge is that which solves the problems or addresses the challenges of the classroom. Degree knowledge, whilst useful and enriching, might do that but not all the time.

Academic degrees are often framed as a kind of foundation, particularly for secondary teachers. You might even believe subject knowledge is less of a priority because it is something you have studied recently. Pedagogy, on the other hand, is probably entirely new to you. Whilst there is some evidence that a better degree will lead to better teaching, there is little consensus. For example, one large-scale study in America saw no link between university test scores and eventual teacher quality.[1] The same study found little evidence that having done postgraduate qualifications predicted more effective teachers or teaching. More recent research does challenge this, arguing that having specialised or done postgraduate study in the subject you teach is correlated with better student outcomes.[2]

Why then is this type of knowledge useful or necessary? Lee Shulman describes what he calls 'syntactic knowledge'; this is the 'structure of a discipline [and] the set of ways in which truth or falsehood, validity or invalidity, are established'.[3] Like grammar, syntactic knowledge provides the rules of a discipline. A good teacher doesn't just know what the students are going to learn really well. A good teacher understands the reasons why the things they're teaching are important or true. At times, depending on your subject, you might feel like a degree is next to useless, irrelevant and detached from what students are learning in your class-room. What you've gained from it may feel like it is lying dormant but this knowl-edge shouldn't be underestimated. Where you've studied the subject you will be teaching, making a list of this background, syntactic knowledge as you encoun-ter it can usefully bring to the fore those things you already understand that are helping.

What then of teachers who don't arrive in teaching with a relevant degree? Or of primary teachers who could never have studied all the things they are going to teach? Many very successful teachers start their teacher careers as 'non-specialists'. You or a mentor or a training provider can assess what the absence of a particular qualification might mean for your development. Syntactic knowledge can still be developed but be careful of seeing further study as the silver bullet.

Annalise, a Science teacher with an Anatomy degree, describes her route into teaching.

I graduated three years before starting [training]. So I was already self-conscious because I'm speaking to other trainees who are fresh out of university, the terminology is still at the tip of their tongue. All of their ideas are still ready to go. Whereas I've taken three years away. I did very little work in Science between leaving university and coming into this role here because I was focused on hospitality.

It was also different for me because I had an anatomy degree. A large amount of an anatomy degree is communicating using Latin words, which I'm quite keen on and it's something I bring into the classroom now. I'm trying to incorporate it to give me a com-fort zone I think, and hopefully support the students who are interested in that.

Conflicting research in this area reminds us of something we can easily ignore: degree knowledge is not the same as teacher content knowledge. It would be fool-ish to suggest that we don't need or want highly qualified teachers. It would be foolish not to go into teaching pleased that you have built the prerequisite knowl-edge through study (or slightly concerned that you haven't). But this research about qualifications and degree knowledge:

- Reminds us that a good degree or further study is no guarantee you will be a good teacher.

- Encourages us that whatever our background we can be successful (even if we don't have the 'right' degree).

- Warns us that we can't rely on previous study. We're breaking new ground. We can use what's come before but we'll need to do something with it.

Subject knowledge

A qualification points to something: subject knowledge. The degree or degree result is always only a proxy for knowledge. What about the knowledge itself? Even then, the types of knowledge we need, the types of knowledge we want for our students vary further.

As you'd imagine, no one is arguing against this content knowledge. Research papers and investigations don't stack up against content knowledge. And researchers have been fascinated by teachers' content knowledge for a long time. Subject knowledge has been assessed, compared, tested, improved, all with the aim of understanding teacher expertise. The message from this research is that 'more content knowledge is always better'.[4] This knowledge is a 'core component of teacher competence'.[5] This knowledge is not just necessary; it is a 'significant predictor' of student achievement.[6] The essential thread running through teaching, and through this research, is content knowledge – knowledge of the subject or subjects taught.

But that isn't the *only* message or a complete message. The *Great Teaching Toolkit* has, whilst reviewing this research, described the relationship between teacher content knowledge and student learning as 'modest to weak'.[7] Writers of the *Toolkit* are not arguing that subject knowledge is unimportant. Improving subject knowledge is not no-impact but it can be low-impact. Extensive research into Maths teachers, for example, did link improving teacher subject knowledge with improved student learning but, understandably, the biggest effect was felt by those with the worst knowledge to begin with.[8] You can see the issue. When a teacher starts out, a boost in subject knowledge leads to a boost in quality of teaching. If you're a non-specialist, a primary teacher or just beginning to teach with understandably large gaps in knowledge of a much larger domain, subject knowledge will help you.

Where further development is concerned, however, there is a problem. The content has no borders. If we just stroll around this borderless domain, we'll pick up some knowledge along the way but the progress may be slow – for us and our students. It will help you because, however much you've studied, there will be elements of the domain which are incomplete in your mind but it will help slowly. Subject knowledge development, therefore, is a good bet for new or non-specialist teachers but it will not remain a good bet *on its own* if our aim is expertise.

Subject knowledge is:

- Important for effective teaching *but…*

- Not the be all and end all – continued development will see limited immediate returns.

- A massive field – whatever the discipline – and something we're never going to master.

How do we develop subject knowledge?

To start, a warning: growing your subject knowledge can be what you enjoy the most. It can also be something that offers limited returns the more you develop it. Time spent developing your subject knowledge doesn't necessarily equate to a proportional development in your teaching ability. You could read a whole book on your subject and find that little changes in your practice. Not reason to stop reading altogether but certainly a reminder to be realistic, to pace ourselves. Perhaps, when it comes to subject knowledge, we should look to the long term. Subject knowledge development, in this way, probably doesn't help us solve the immediate problems of the classroom unless we truly don't understand what we're teaching this week. Rather, it prepares us to solve future problems by expanding the options, ideas, concepts, analogies, stories – the knowledge – we can call upon in future.

You can build subject knowledge by:

Auditing what you know

When I was completing my PGCE, I had to fill out a subject knowledge audit. It massively depressed me. There were vast swathes of English Literature that I hadn't covered or had barely covered in my degree or previously. I went into a meeting with my university tutor with trepidation, concerned about the amount that I'd have to get done to 'catch up'. The tutor looked at it, said it was fine and we spoke about something else. For some time after, I felt a bit bitter about that. I thought he should have challenged me more. But should he? I had limited time and maybe it was shameful I hadn't read any Sylvia Plath but I wasn't immediately teaching her poetry. In this way, a broad audit can be unhelpful.

As a new teacher, the curriculum at your first school is the best mirror you can hold up to your subject knowledge. The curriculum helps narrow the domain so you're not auditing *everything*. Colleagues can help narrow that further by directing you to the priorities.

As you examine what you'll be teaching, you are prompted to reflect on what you know (and what you don't). To manage your time, and your cognitive load, you'll have to narrow down your focus to what is most immediately important. Examine each unit, topic or subject you'll have to teach. It might be clear which bits of content need immediate work. There's also a danger that it feels like every aspect of the curriculum is in urgent need of attention. Focus on the areas you haven't ever studied, read or learned anything about. Make a list in order of importance – what is coming up and where is your knowledge worst? Remember, this isn't *just* about confidence levels. Instead, you're assessing whether you have the necessary knowledge to teach a topic. Don't ask *Do I understand the resources?* Ask *Could I explain this topic? Could I model a process from this topic confidently?* Don't confuse *developing subject knowledge* with *developing knowledge of lesson tasks and processes*.

Once you've got your list, you can start to focus on what you don't know. Return to Chapter 4 and look at the strategies for developing knowledge there. Decide on one or two that can help with your study and get started. The ideas below may also help.

Reading widely

Teachers should be readers. We should read about strategies for the classroom. We should read about subject. We should seek to understand how young people learn. Being a critical teacher-reader means interrogating what we're reading. It means asking *Does this chime with my experience? Will this help in my classroom? Is this my understanding of the subject matter or the best way to communicate it?*

Teachers should be readers because we should be intellectually engaged in what we do but we must acknowledge a couple of things. First, not everything you read will be transformative. Second, reading is a long-term strategy. Re-reading is unlikely to support retention or improved understanding in the short term.[9] Teachers should be career-long readers but that doesn't mean several weighty tomes are the only answer to the gaps in knowledge for next term's scheme of work.

If you've audited your knowledge, you might decide you need to read around two upcoming topics. As a time-poor teacher, your choice of reading material is crucial. Your choices of when to read and when to stop are equally important. If reading about your subject feels like a leisure activity, it might fit effortlessly into your evenings and weekends. If the thought of picking up a book on a weeknight feels like attending a lecture or research for an essay, subject knowledge reading might best be left for the brief time available in the school day. In this case, articles and summaries serve you better than, even highly recommended, books.

A chasm stretches between subject knowledge and the classroom, and *what we know* doesn't always feel like *what we need* for teaching. What kind of knowledge could bridge that gap?

Pedagogical content knowledge

Knowledge of subject is a bit of a Russian doll. We study a subject through various tiers of education, and perhaps informally. The residue of this study is subject knowledge but even then, we must admit that subject knowledge gained from study isn't quite like subject knowledge used in the classroom. The question then becomes not *Is subject knowledge important?* but *What kind of subject knowledge is important for the classroom?*

Lee Shulman describes pedagogical content knowledge as 'subject matter knowledge *for teaching*' [his emphasis] and the 'ways of representing' the subject that help students to understand it.[10] Pedagogical content knowledge includes any knowledge that enables analogies, explanations, illustrations and demonstrations.

Teachers with this knowledge recognise which aspects of a topic will be particularly challenging and what strategies will best meet this challenge.

Pedagogical content knowledge takes the generic elements of pedagogy – like questioning – and turns them into classroom behaviours. It acts as the bridge between the background – what we've studied, learned and understood – and the foreground – the classroom where that knowledge will be used. But it isn't just about what you *do*; your knowledge changes your perception and understanding of what students say and do in lessons. A teacher with pedagogical content knowledge will be more able to recognise a student's mistake[11] or interpret a student's answer.[12] Vitally important to effective teaching is understanding how what you know of a subject is becoming what students know of it.

New teachers must develop pedagogical content knowledge whilst planning and delivering early lessons. There's a sense in which it will *just happen* if you wait for it. As someone looking to accelerate their journey towards expertise, this won't do. It's not uncommon to hear about a new teacher with a PhD or other further study who is struggling to break through to the simplicity required to teach successfully. Like many anecdotes, the lesson here doesn't reflect the reality or possibility for all new teachers. There's no reason why serious qualifications and study should hold you back from being a great teacher; they may well help. The problems with large quantities of subject knowledge arise when coupled with deficient knowledge of how novices progress in your domain.

The curse of knowledge is a cognitive bias born of the assumption that others possess the same knowledge as you. Expertise in your subject – whether signified by a qualification or not – in this way can lead to a blind spot. Experts can struggle to verbalise a thought process because working, problem solving and thinking in the domain of their expertise has become implicit.[13] Not that such a blind spot should convince us to shun content knowledge but it should cause us to reflect on how ready our knowledge is for the classroom.

Developing pedagogical content knowledge should change something in the classroom – an explanation, feedback to students. Perhaps because of this, at least some evidence indicates that developing pedagogical content knowledge is a good bet for improvement for new teachers (and a better bet than simply developing your subject knowledge).[14] Pedagogical content knowledge is most likely to be lacking from your current mental models of the classroom. Compare what you know – the topics you're going to be teaching – with how you'd teach it.

Pedagogical knowledge:

- Is amalgamation of subject knowledge and classroom actions and behaviours.

- Includes explanation, modelling, feedback, questions and adaptations to student responses.

- Won't necessarily follow from large quantities of subject knowledge (but large quantities of subject knowledge can help us to develop it).

How do we develop pedagogical content knowledge?

> **Kate, a secondary Maths trainee, describes how she focused on improving subject knowledge.**
>
> There are definitely topics I've had to go home and study. I don't have bulletproof Maths subject knowledge just because I have a degree. You can become very used to *your* way of teaching Maths. But I think there is a never-ending set of possibilities of how to explain something to the student. So you have to keep going back to it.

Although pedagogical content knowledge has a lot to say about what *we* do in the classroom, it also speaks to how students encounter the subject. Teachers need, Shulman explains, 'an understanding of what makes the learning of specific topics easy or difficult: the conceptions and preconceptions that students of different ages and backgrounds bring with them to the learning of those most frequently taught topics and lessons'.[15] Pedagogical content knowledge is forged through understanding how students will experience, misunderstand and make progress in your subject, allowing this knowledge to shape our decisions in the classroom.

One of the main challenges we face in the classroom is making content meaningful for children. It's a problem that will never leave us. Developing pedagogical content knowledge is *a* method of trying to solve that problem, taking something abstract and turning it into a tangible classroom resource, activity or explanation.

Co-planning

Colleagues' subject knowledge and knowledge of planning is invaluable. Whilst it's not possible to observe the planning process in the way we might observe a lesson, there is much to learn from interrogating how experienced teachers plan. Most schools will have at least partially resourced curricula. Resources offer a framework or suggestion for what might happen in your lesson. Seeing the route the resource will take into your classroom is not always easy. At times, it can feel like these resources are a drain on your time rather than a help. Early in my career, I would look at the resources available – usually a PowerPoint presentation for each lesson – and start to delete the slides I didn't like or activities I didn't think would work. Slowly, I'd reach the point where all that was left was the title slide and maybe a bit of reading. Some of these resources weren't fit for purpose, like the hour of Citizenship I was meant to fill with a single slide that said 'Democracy?' on it. But, with others, I lacked understanding of what to do to make them work.

Your expert and experienced colleagues may well have forgotten their early steps into the difficult process of navigating from a point in the curriculum through the resources available to a real and successful lesson. At times, this makes recently qualified teachers the font of wisdom for the new teacher. Teachers who have recently qualified are able to call upon the recent experience of learning how to adapt the resources or curriculum documents into teachable lessons. The onus is on you to ask them and investigate how they do this. Much of what they offer will explain how subject knowledge is brought into the classroom. How much content can fit into a lesson? How challenging should I make this? How many questions should I set for them to practise?

In some schools, PPA is shared or planning has its own semi-regular meeting. Often, this is called collaborative planning. Embrace these times if you're lucky enough to experience them. If these aren't available to you, manufacture them. Collaborative planning is not someone else planning for you. If you can plan with a more experienced colleague, make the most of this process by being proactive: plan something and talk through it with them.

Ask your mentor which teachers are best to talk to about certain topics or areas of teaching and learning. Talk to the teachers who use nothing but the whiteboard and a pen. Talk to those who use PowerPoint or booklets. Talk to the teachers who weren't subject specialists when they arrived but are now thriving.

Engaging in the subject community

Beyond the walls of our schools, communities of teachers offer help in everything from planning to applying research. Subject communities bridge the gap between the academic subject and its curricula counterpart. Ruth Ashbee defines a subject community as 'the people involved in the discourse around a subject both formally and informally, through organised groups and ad hoc arrangements'.[16] The dual emphasis within the definition is useful: there are formal groups and institutions we can turn to as well as an informal web of knowledgeable educators, generously willing to offer us their support.

Many subjects have their own subject association you can join. Benefits of these organisations – and levels of quality – vary wildly so check with your colleagues if they've used, or found useful, resources from them. If the formality of these subject associations is not for you, plenty of informal networks have sprung up in recent years, reflecting the increased connectedness of teachers. CogSciSci describes itself as 'a grassroots group of teachers and other education professionals looking to promote the use of cognitive science in school science teaching'.[17] The group freely offer training, resources and guides for teachers across a range of Science-based topics. LitDrive, an informal English community, 'provides an extensive bank of classroom materials for teachers to upload, share and adapt for use in their classrooms', as well as articles, CPD and mentoring.[18] Core subjects have it easier. The Science and English groups here aren't replicated at the same scale in D&T or Music. Equally, a large group is no guarantee of quality. Whilst you might find a Facebook group full of specialists in your subject, realising it's just a forum for moaning about the exam spec can be a bit disheartening.

Formal or informal, these groups should:

1. **Support your ability to plan effective lessons.** This is not simply, or even mainly, about taking someone's resources to save you time although the impact of that cannot be underestimated. More than reducing the workload burden, resources from other teachers demonstrate how to approach a particular topic, examples of sequence, explanation or models. Such resources might give a flavour of the amount of practice another teacher gives to a topic or the way new content is connected to old. It's not unusual for these groups to include blogs or articles from teachers on how they've dealt with planning certain topics. Subject communities expand the number of colleagues' minds you have access to which can only help you as you plan new units and encounter subject areas for the first time.

2. **Make links between the domain and the classroom.** Curriculum giant Michael Young gives us further cause to consider engaging with the subject community. To Young, this is not simply about gaining lesson ideas from others who teach our subjects. Young expects all teachers to have a 'relationship with knowledge'[19] and for those teachers to want the same for their students. For Young, this relationship is not simply built on transmission of knowledge to our students. Such a relationship is a relationship with the ways that knowledge is created, articulated and perpetuated.

In summary

Subject knowledge isn't easy to pin down. It's what remains from your school and university days. It's what develops as you teach and plan and learn from colleagues. Subject knowledge *on its own* won't make you an expert teacher because great teachers aren't those with deep but detached knowledge of subject. Subject knowledge you arrive in teaching with must be funnelled through the curriculum.

We could continue examining subject knowledge from further angles or create further divisions. In fact, two more chapters will be devoted to one more type of subject knowledge: curriculum knowledge. Depending on the subject you're teaching and your prior study or qualifications, you might find that your knowledge doesn't map well onto what is taught in your school. Knowing your curriculum is more than just knowing what will be taught. Chapter 12 will answer the question *What should I know about the curriculum?*

Questions for reflection

● Have your qualifications (A-Level/degree) prepared you to teach your subject(s)? Where might they be deficient and why?

- How closely related are the content you have studied and the school curriculum? If you're not sure, talk to someone in your department or phase team or whoever's running your training.

- Have you conducted an audit of your subject knowledge? For the subject or phase you're teaching, what would an audit like this look like? Often, this is part of a training programme. If it hasn't been, talk to your mentor about how this could work.

- If you have conducted an audit, what has it revealed? In broad domains, like History or Literature, you might feel like there's too much that you don't yet know. Be careful of feeling like you need to rush to develop every area.

- How confident do you feel about taking what you already know and explaining it or adapting it to be manageable and understandable for students? Don't worry if you aren't sure about this; the next chapter will look at some strategies.

- If you've begun to teach, how have you already tried to develop this pedagogical knowledge? Where have there been barriers to students understanding what you've been explaining or modelling?

Possible next steps

1. **Audit your knowledge to identify one priority.** Compare your knowledge with the content of your school's curriculum. Select *one* thing – no more – that will be your subject knowledge priority. Spend time with the resources you have to teach. Ask colleagues for articles or blogs or books (or summaries of these things), whatever you can handle in the moment.

2. **Book in some co-planning.** In some schools, more commonly in primary schools, this will already exist in a designated time. If this isn't the case in your school, overcome the awkwardness and ask someone. Book this if a difficult topic is on the horizon, if you're teaching something new after half-term, or just because you want to gain experience from someone who's been doing the job a little bit longer than you.

3. **Investigate subject communities.** A subject community can help to combat the feeling you don't know *how* to approach certain topics or moments in your curriculum. At times, subject communities offer resources, particularly useful for those without resourced curricula, but this is not their primary aim. More than a compendium of resources, a subject community should offer a conversation about the subject and how it interacts with students in the school curriculum.

Notes

1 Harris, D., and Sass, T. (2007). *Teacher Training, Teacher Quality and Student Achievement*. National Center for Analysis of Longitudinal Data in Education Research.

2 Lee, S., and Lee, S. (2020). Teacher qualification matters: The association between cumulative teacher qualification and students' educational attainment. *International Journal of Educational Development*, 77, 102218.

3 Shulman, L. (1986). Those who understand: Knowledge growth in teaching. *Educational Research*, 15(2), 4–14.

4 Mitchell, N., Alibali, M., and Koedinger, K. (2001). *Expert Blind Spot: When Content Knowledge and Pedagogical Content Knowledge Collide.* Institute of Cognitive Science Technical Report.

5 Baumert, J., Kunter, M., Blum, W., Brunner, M., Voss, T., Jordan, A., Klusmann, U., Krauss, S., Neubrand, M., and Tsai, Y. (2010). Teachers' mathematical knowledge, cognitive activation in the classroom and student progress. *American Educational Research Journal*, 47(1), 133–180.

6 Hill, H., Rowan, B., and Ball, D. (2005). Effects of teachers' mathematical knowledge for teaching on student achievement. *American Educational Research Journal*, 42(2), 371–406.

7 Coe, R., Rauch, C.J., Kime, S., and Singleton, D. (2020). *Great Teaching Toolkit Evidence Review.* Cambridge Assessment International Education.

8 Hill, H., Rowan, B., and Ball, D. (2005). Effects of teachers' mathematical knowledge for teaching on student achievement. *American Educational Research Journal*, 42(2), 371–406.

9 Dunlosky, J., Rawson, K., Marsh, E., Nathan, M., and Willingham, D. (2013). Improving students' learning with effective learning techniques: Promising directions from cognitive and educational psychology. *Psychological Science in the Public Interest*, 14(1), 4–58.

10 Shulman, L. (1986). Those who understand: Knowledge growth in teaching. *Educational Research*, 15(2), 4–14.

11 Ball, D., Hoover Thames, M., and Phelps, G. (2008). Content knowledge for teaching: What makes it special? *Journal of Teacher Education*, 59(5), 389–407.

12 Hill, H., Rowan, B., and Ball, D. (2005). Effects of teachers' mathematical knowledge for teaching on student achievement. *American Educational Research Journal*, 42(2), 371–406.

13 Mitchell, N., Alibali, M., and Koedinger, K. (2001). *Expert Blind Spot: When Content Knowledge and Pedagogical Content Knowledge Collide.* Institute of Cognitive Science Technical Report.

14 Baumert, J., Kunter, M., Blum, W., Brunner, M., Voss, T., Jordan, A., Klusmann, U., Krauss, S., Neubrand, M., and Tsai, Y. (2010). Teachers' mathematical knowledge, cognitive activation in the classroom and student progress. *American Educational Research Journal*, 47(1), 133–180.

15 Ibid.

16 Ashbee, R. (2021). *Curriculum: Theory, Culture and the Subject Specialisms.* Routledge.

17 CogSciSci (n.d.). About. https://cogscisci.wordpress.com/about/ (accessed on 23/05/2022).

18 LitDrive (n.d.). Our story. https://litdrive.org.uk/our-story (accessed on 23/05/2022).

19 Young, M. (2020). From powerful knowledge to the powers of knowledge. In C. Sealy (ed.), *The ResearchEd Guide to Curriculum.* John Catt.

What do we need to know about the curriculum?

When I was Head of English and planning a curriculum with a team of English teachers, I made a lot of mistakes. I tried to do too much at once. We tried to reinvent a curriculum in the space of one academic year. We soon realised that this was a bad idea. We could create resources easily enough but the curriculum is not simply the sum of your resources. Curricula exist as a shared understanding, often written out in a document, of what will be taught and when it will be taught and why it will be taught in this order. Shared understanding does not emerge from a rush of resource creation. It emerges over time, through careful planning driven by ongoing dialogue.

At the outset of this chapter, it's important to make something clear: I don't think a new teacher should be in the business of curriculum creation. The idea that you can learn to teach – an incredibly complex task – whilst learning to create a curriculum from scratch – an equally complex task – is nonsense. And you don't have to master the latter to achieve the former. Teacher training rarely gives time to the theory and practice of curriculum creation, nor should it.

That said, intellectual engagement with the curriculum, as you find it in your school, is vital. It would be very unusual to find a school where little to no curriculum thinking had happened, but levels of work will vary from an overview or broad plan right through to resources for every lesson you teach. Your job is not to plan a curriculum from scratch; it is to teach the curriculum well. With that in mind, it is worth asking *What do I need to know and understand about the curriculum?* and *How do I use that knowledge and understanding in my planning?* We'll answer the former in this chapter and the latter in the next.

Curriculum metaphors

The complexity of curriculum thinking and planning prompts us to often see the curriculum through a metaphor lens but metaphors for the curriculum are bewilderingly varied.

DOI: 10.4324/9781003281306-18

Archipelago

Andy Tharby, English teacher and writer, uses one metaphor which diagnoses the problem with a lot of curriculum thinking. An archipelago curriculum, Tharby explains, 'is taught in atomised topics that are vaguely linked by a shared discourse or a generic set of "skills"'.[1] More problematically, 'there is little expectation that children retain what they have learnt beyond an end-of-term assessment, the subject becomes more like a pleasurable holiday cruise around the islands than a learning experience'.

When I was a new teacher, a shared spreadsheet dictated when each of us taught different topics through the year. So one person taught the novel *Private Peaceful* in September; another would teach it in July. Sometimes the bland unit on comprehension could be whistled through in the short May half-term; sometimes you'd have to stretch it over one of those long, dark Autumn terms. We cruised round these islands – many of which were worth a visit – but these journeys were incoherent meanderings.

The archipelago is a good metaphor for many curricula, but it doesn't capture every subject well. A Music or Art teacher may recognise the archipelago in the curricula they've taught. A Maths or Science teacher probably won't. A Maths teacher's curriculum is not unconnected and, while some elements are diverse and disparate, most hang together in a logical sequence.

Spiral

To capture a journey that repeats and revisits, Jerome Bruner used the image of a spiral. In a spiral curriculum, you visit a topic in one year and return to that topic with added complexity the following year. Bruner was keen for students to understand 'the fundamental structure of whatever subjects we choose to teach'.[2] This poses an interesting question – *What is the structure of my subject or subjects?*

To some, subjects fall into two broad categories: hierarchical and cumulative. In hierarchical subjects, knowledge is connected through a sequence of progression that demands students master one element to get to the next. To an extent, in hierarchical subjects, at least parts of this sequence are settled and common between schools because of the progression students *must* make. Maths is often used as an example of a hierarchical subject, where students require mastery of one step before they reach the next.

Cumulative subjects tend to allow more curricula decisions: *What shall we teach Year 7 in term one?* has a range of possible answers. In English, one secondary school might choose one structure – a chronological study of literature, say, with lots of grammar and writing practice built in – whilst another could structure the curriculum completely differently – perhaps around thematic episodes like Outsiders or Power, where tasks and texts are selected based on their link to the theme. In both models, students will develop knowledge of genre and theme as well as writing ability cumulatively as they revisit topics, adding layers of complexity to their understanding.

Bruner's spiral, like the terms hierarchical and cumulative, may be a useful guide or way of seeing. A problem with strict belief in the cumulative/hierarchical divide is that it doesn't quite work. At best, it can be an illuminating starting point. 'Cumulative' subjects might lend themselves to Bruner's spiral metaphor because the teaching of them allows for this gradual repetition. Teachers of 'hierarchical' subjects would rightly resist a spiral structure that doesn't respect the structure of their subject. The deeper you go into subject structure, the more you realise these terms can only ever apply to *parts* of a subject. At times within the same subject, you'll encounter hierarchical elements alongside cumulative.

How useful Bruner's curriculum metaphor is might depend on the subject you teach. To the history or English teacher, the idea that we can return to the complexity of Shakespeare or the Anglo-Saxons is a comforting reminder that there is always more to get from these subjects. To the languages or Maths teacher, the idea of leaving mastery of a topic to another year might feel woefully inadequate as a way of ensuring students progress within the subject and the curriculum. That said, Bruner recognised the importance of the knowledge of the teacher, exhorting us to attain 'the most fundamental understanding' of the subjects we teach.

Narrative

Christine Counsell gives us one of the pithiest definitions (and metaphors) of curriculum when she describes it as 'content structured *as narrative* over time'[3] [her emphasis]. Narrative, Counsell reminds us, 'is full of internal dynamics and relationships that operate across varying stretches of time. Those dynamics and relationships realise the function of every bit of content'. Or, more succinctly, 'every bit of content has a function'.

Once we understand this, the importance of each bit of what we teach becomes more apparent, whether we're teaching a physical skill or activity or a body of knowledge full of complex, interconnected facts. Knowledge and skill snowball as new connections are made and new abilities are harnessed.

When the narrative is working, every element joins together in a marvellous coherence of subject matter. Occasionally, a student will come along to shatter the illusion that this narrative is working perfectly. *Why are we doing this now? You never taught us that. Shouldn't we spend more time on…* Whilst the narrative is the aim, narratives vary in success and clarity. If there are incongruous bits of content that don't seem to fit the narrative, ask about them. Become a curriculum thinker early by considering how the narrative fits together well and where perhaps it feels disjointed.

New teachers are rightly taught to plan their lessons, sometimes having to fill in cumbersome proforma to evidence the work of planning. What is often missed in this focus on planning is the understanding of the bigger picture. Lesson length is arbitrary and variable. If you're constantly overrunning, you may need to look at your planning, but extending the study of a topic over two lessons or five and a half lessons or anything else is perfectly acceptable. Keep an eye on your place in the narrative as well as on the clock in your classroom.

Curriculum metaphors, and I've shared only a small number with you, will only ever convey part of what we need to know about the curriculum. As you approach the curriculum – in examining resources, in planning, in teaching – such metaphors and characterisations can begin to feel detached or incomplete. It's worth spending some time understanding the big picture, the overarching narrative of your curriculum, but more time, for the new teacher at least, should be spent on the granular level of what your curriculum requires you to teach. That is what we will turn to now.

Get to know your curriculum

Alice, a Year 5 teacher in her third year, talks about getting to know the Science curriculum at her school.

In training, when learning about Science, we were focused on activities, not curriculum. When we were learning about the human body, we went outside and got some sticks to build this skeleton. What was the outcome of that? I must have been about 20 and I was playing with sticks. I remember coming to my placement here and explained what we did and the teacher just said, 'We don't do that here'.

We have our own curriculum at my school. We know what we need to teach. That gives us an idea of what will go in the classroom. A lot of my knowledge has come from my personal learning. Our curriculum might say students are learning about skeletons in Science and will tell us what students need to know, what vocabulary they will learn, what will go on in the lesson.

Our curriculum is also planned out so that we know from the year before what students have learned so that it all weaves in. I think this is good to know because recently we've had a big focus on retrieval and I've been able to work out what they've remembered from Year 4. Other schools might have an idea but not know how well students understand something. Our curriculum is so specific that we can check what they should know and whether they still know it.

To get to know your curriculum, there are some questions you need to seek answers for. In some schools, these will be provided for you, possibly in painstaking detail on your first visit. In others, the curriculum will be barely held together by a single disused document that vaguely outlines what is taught and when. Either way, our job is to know enough to plan, teach and assess our students.

Once you are teaching extended sequences of lessons, it is worth asking the following.

What type of knowledge am I teaching?

Substantive knowledge is described by Christine Counsell as 'the content that teachers teach as established fact – whether common convention, concept or warranted account of reality'.[4] Facts, terminology, understanding of concepts all fit into the substantive knowledge within a domain. Easy to dismiss, knowledge like this is essential for students to build schema and tackle complex tasks within a domain.

Counsell describes **disciplinary knowledge** as 'what pupils learn about how that knowledge was established, its degree of certainty and how it continues to be revised by scholars, artists or professional practice'.[5] Disciplinary knowledge includes understanding of how discoveries are made and theories are established in science, how sources are used as the basis of an argument for truth in history, and how art is assessed as effective (or beautiful) in art.

Procedural knowledge is the skill or know-how of a subject. All subjects have some skill to practice and embed, from the lay-up shot in basketball through to the introductory sentence of an analytical essay. Too often, skill is framed broadly to the point of uselessness. Critical thinking, analysis, creativity are not really skills you can teach, at least not in one go. Not only will these big 'skills' look different from subject to subject, but they are also made up of component parts which can and should be defined and taught. And these component parts can probably be broken down further until we have defined behaviours students can rehearse to the point of automaticity before stringing them together in order to tackle the larger, more complex tasks of the curriculum.

It would be strange for a curriculum to only dwell on one of these. most visit each in turn, or more often, intertwine the different elements of them. Ask how these types of knowledge are defined in your subject at your school. A follow up question would be *How well defined are these areas of knowledge?* which leads us to our next set of questions.

What is essential? What is desirable?

Whilst the curriculum is in the spotlight because of fresh reading of evidence around learning, because of renewed belief in curriculum entitlements for all and, cynically, because Ofsted have become more interested in it, what you encounter in curricula in different schools and subjects will vary massively. Nowhere is this variety between schools and subjects likely to be felt more keenly than in the level of specificity with which content is defined in the curriculum. Some curricula define everything that should be taught and learned. Others give a vague set of directions. Check with whoever has developed or leads on the curriculum. Is there a set of essentials which must be covered? Are they listed? Must some content be mastered before students progress to something else?

Asking what's essential only gives partial understanding when it comes to considering *what to teach*. Ask teachers what they like to include, what they include if they have time, which stories and examples they use to illustrate the points they make. Christine Counsell calls this hinterland, a 'supporter and feeder' of the essential content of the curriculum.[6] To Counsell, this is not just an added extra; it is an essential way we enrich and elucidate the curriculum. Where suggestions or guidance aren't forthcoming, this hinterland is hard to come by for new teachers because it is won through experience. You might find just the right explanation, story, video or activity which is not essential but does clarify and embed the essential knowledge in a way that wouldn't have been possible without such hinterland. A catalogue of such things is likely to be developed over time. Where you can, plan with others and ask for their examples.

How is the curriculum codified? And why?

It would be foolish to think that curricula simply exist in the heads of those who write them. Equally foolish is the idea that the resources, materials or curriculum paperwork *are* the curriculum. A useful contrast is found in the terms 'intended curriculum' – what those devising the curriculum hope and plan to see – and the 'enacted curriculum' – what actually happens in the classroom.

Curriculum codification is the springboard from which the intended curriculum can begin to be enacted. As Ruth Ashbee explains, codifying the curriculum is the process of bringing together – at times 'writing down' – 'into maps, booklets and other working documents'.[7] In turn, teacher time is freed up to spend on 'subject knowledge and pedagogy planning'. Unfortunately, as a new teacher, you don't have much control over whether this time has been freed up for you. Arriving in your school, you may find clarity and precision, or their opposites.

To gain the necessary knowledge of the curriculum you are teaching you should ask:

- How are knowledge and skill defined in the curriculum? Are there lists or maps that students need to have covered by certain points? Does this definition exist in a document, in resources, a textbook, somewhere else or nowhere?

- What are the relationships between the knowledge and skill taught? Does the curriculum mandate the links that should be made between different facets of the content taught?

- How do students progress through the curriculum?

I recognise the previous questions are theoretical, focusing on the thought underpinning the curriculum (or very much hoping such thought has taken place). It's important to understand those things but it's also important to understand answers to:

- What resources are available? How do these resources link to other curriculum documentation – maps, schemes of work, plans etc.?

● What is the expectation to use (or deviate from) such resources? Are teachers allowed to teach however they like as long as certain content is covered? Or are the resources essential?

● How are these resources updated and what is the process for updating?

Ruth Ashbee reminds us that the codification of the curriculum is in a constant state of 'flux'. Not because it is not good enough but because review, refinement and updating are expected features of curriculum maintenance.

What are the destinations, assessments and aims of the curriculum?

A six-week block is an arbitrary length of time. In an ideal world, getting through a unit of work or the teaching of a topic would take as long as it takes. It is right for departments to consider how best to use time without being constrained unnecessarily by the structure of the school year. However, time constraints also mean that we can't spend forever on a single topic. Calendars dictate moving on points or assessment windows we must be aware of.

In summary

Curriculum knowledge prepares us to tackle a whole host of challenges thrown at us. How students will learn and connect what they learn is sequenced clearly and overtly signalled in the best curricula. Mary Kennedy describes 'Portraying the curriculum' and 'making it comprehensible to naïve minds' as a persistent challenge of teaching.[8] Hundreds of decisions about what to teach – which activities, explanations, demonstrations – assault us before we've even considered how we'll ascertain what students have learned. Knowledge of the curriculum doesn't exist in a vacuum. We know it to plan with it. The subject of the next chapter, planning is a challenge made simpler by deep knowledge of the curriculum.

Possible next steps

Ask curricula questions. Ask what is essential and desirable. Ask about the expectation to follow resources and the conditions in which we can deviate from them. Ask how knowledge is assessed and why. It's best to have this conversation when you start at a new school or before you start teaching a new unit but, if you've been teaching somewhere for a while and don't know the answers, you can ask whenever you need to.

Notes

1 Tharby, A. (2018). *A 'Mastery Light' Subject Curriculum Model.* https://classteaching.word-press.com/2018/03/12/a-mastery-light-subject-curriculum-model/ (accessed 26/02/2022).

2 Bruner, J. (1977). *The Process of Education*. Harvard University Press.

3 Counsell, C. (2018). *Senior Curriculum Leadership 1: The Indirect Manifestation Of Knowledge: (A) Curriculum as Narrative*. https://thedignityofthethingblog.wordpress.com/2018/04/07/senior-curriculum-leadership-1-the-indirect-manifestation-of-knowledge-a-curriculum-as-narrative/ (accessed on 28/02/2022).

4 Counsell, C. (2018). *Taking Curriculum Seriously*. Impact Issue 4. https://my.chartered.college/impact_article/taking-curriculum-seriously/ (accessed on 07/03/2022).

5 Ibid.

6 Counsell, C. (2018). *Senior Curriculum Leadership 1: The Indirect Manifestation Of Knowledge: (A) Curriculum as Narrative*. https://thedignityofthethingblog.wordpress.com/2018/04/07/senior-curriculum-leadership-1-the-indirect-manifestation-of-knowledge-a-curriculum-as-narrative/ (accessed on 28/02/2022).

7 Ashbee, R. (2021). *Curriculum*. Routledge.

8 Kennedy, M. (2016). Parsing the practice of teaching. *Journal of Teacher Education*, 67(1), 6–17.

How does knowledge of the curriculum affect our planning?

At the end of my university-based training year, they got a newly qualified teacher in to talk to us about her first year teaching. I enjoyed listening to her experiences and was encouraged by her struggles which were not unlike my own. But towards the end of her talk, she said something jarring. Each week, this teacher set aside time to plan one or two 'really good' lessons. 'Really good' meant engaging, resource-heavy and, dare I say, fun. I was most troubled by the admission that the best she could do was one or two lessons a week that she considered 'really good'. This teacher's headteacher was sitting on the stage, having just given a talk herself, and I looked across to gauge the reaction there. The headteacher smiled and nodded through the talk, clearly proud. And I'm sure there was much to be proud of, but I was left baffled that we were about to enter a profession where 'really good' could only be expected a fraction of the time.

In the previous chapter, we explored the things we need to know about the curriculum to be ready to teach it well. You don't need these things so that you can write your own curriculum from scratch. Rather, we know the curriculum so that our planning of lessons is effective; effectiveness is based on an understanding of how students learn and a faithfulness to the curriculum being taught.

In this chapter, we'll look at planning. Usually, this starts with a focus on individual lessons and progresses to thinking about sequences of lessons. This is fine as long as an individual lesson's place in the curriculum is considered as it is put together.

Teaching an individual lesson

Sarah, a Year 4 teacher, describes her experience planning using resources from the school's curriculum.

Sometimes when I open someone else's resource, I don't have a clue. I have to change things around and make sure it makes sense to me and to my children as well. I remember there being a lot on the slides and thinking, That's not going to work for my class.

DOI: 10.4324/9781003281306-19

Lots of them are quite low ability so I had to chunk the work out into smaller steps. There was too much to do as well so feeling alright about not doing everything in a single lesson.

We had to have a lesson on switches. There was no lesson on switches in the curriculum. Children didn't understand when I said, *You don't need a switch to work a circuit.* We had to have that lesson because the children just weren't understanding it. Then I had to do a demonstration to show them and get them involved, hopefully a bit of sticky knowledge for them. We had different resources and I got the children to try the circuit with a spoon or a coin or something else so they could see circuits without a switch.

In some training schemes, lesson planning is adherence to a particular form, a Word document segmented into boxes which focus your attention on different aspects of the lesson. Structure can be helpful when you're starting out. A scaffold to your thinking, the form gradually creates for you a mental model of lesson planning. Or it should.

Unfortunately, lesson planning forms can construct faulty scaffolding where prominence is attached to a minor part of your thinking. Forms also tend to make new teachers a slave to timing, forcing them to predict timings before accuracy is likely and making them feel guilty when these timings aren't followed. Possibly the greatest problem with lesson planning proformas is that they exist in a vacuum, with no apparent connection to the curriculum or to your subject knowledge. Thinking is funnelled towards activity rather than content and skill.

A set of principles or questions, outlined below, can direct our thinking both as we use a planning form and when we need to shed it. All too quickly, planning can move from a process constrained and restricted to one with too much freedom. Do you plan in your teacher planner, or in Word, or PowerPoint? There are benefits and drawbacks to each of these, some significant, but the principles providing foundation to your planning should remain the same.

Where does this lesson fit?

The narrative tendrils of the individual lesson stretch back into what has already been taught and they stretch forward, foreshadowing what is yet to come. If it is possible to completely disentangle the lesson from the curriculum then either the lesson or the curriculum must be at fault. A moment in the curriculum, the individual lesson is the culmination of much and the preparation for more. How then does the individual lesson look back? How does it look forward?

What is the purpose of this lesson?

For a long time after I trained, it was the fashion to get students to write down a learning objective. They'd spend the first few minutes of each lesson jotting it down, with those students who might struggle to write and copy quickly failing to keep up. The act of copying was largely an act of fear on the part of the teacher, fear that someone – a senior leader or inspector – would come into a room and ask students what they were learning or why they were learning it. If this happened, and it was rare, students dutifully recited the lesson objective. Job done – they knew what they were learning.

Thinking about *purpose* of the lesson buckled under the weight of this act of objective writing, where every kind of learning had to fit into a *To understand…* or *To be able to…* sentence structure. If someone asks you to get students to write down the lesson objective into their book each lesson, politely ask if 2010 wants its bad idea back.

A lesson's purpose or objective ties it to the curriculum. Substantive or disciplinary knowledge is introduced, revisited or connected to what has come before. A piece of the narrative jigsaw is added. Purpose must be tied to the place in the curriculum we find ourselves. Don't look beyond the curriculum for another purpose. Trends come and go; one trend that won't die is to give your lesson an aim outside of the content. Creativity, critical thinking as well as social and emotional 'skills' have all had their day in the sun as aims of individual lessons. All are worthy aims for education but when we make them central to our planning we step too far from the content of the curriculum.

Instead, we focus on the ultimate aims of the curriculum. To borrow Stephen Covey's phrase, we 'begin with the end in mind'. More than just a principle, this should direct the planning process. To get to 'the end', what will students need to draw on? What is 'the end' made up of and therefore what should be broken down and practised? What vocabulary, concepts, dates and ideas is 'the end' made up of? This is the content of your lesson.

Plan thinking, not activities

Beginning with the end doesn't work if we're labouring under the illusion that students need to repeat the end product endlessly to reach mastery. We get them to write essays to get good at essays, play basketball matches to get good at basketball, draw scatter graphs to get good at scatter graphs. There's a problem: you don't *get good* at something by repeating the end result. The end result comprises a tangle of skill and knowledge. Planning involves untangling the content and sequencing it into manageable chunks, a process that gets easier with time and experience.

Remember Rob Coe's encouragement to see learning as the result of *thinking hard*.[1] Remember too Daniel Willingham's maxim that 'memory is the residue of thought'.[2] A series of resourced activities give the appearance of a well-planned lesson, and it's true that lessons will need activities. The vital distinction for the lesson planner is between filling time with activities and planning activities that will prompt the right thought, about the right content, in the right order.

Beware of tasks that mask content rather than shine a light on it. If students have to juggle a complex process with new content, they're likely to struggle with both. Once, when being observed, I was teaching students about imperative verbs, a rather dry topic that I felt needed to be made more engaging. I got the class to write a scripted argument between a downtrodden teacher and a recalcitrant student, a situation they were more than familiar with. Students enjoyed deciding what their badly behaved character would do but they loved writing the teacher, a draconian but ultimately ineffectual figure. A script posed problems though: how was it laid out, were speech marks necessary, what were stage directions for? More than this, imperative verbs were entirely absent from some of their work. My observer gently suggested that it was, unsurprisingly, quite hard to write a good script with no direct teaching on scriptwriting.

Students hadn't thought about imperatives whilst they were writing but the same is true about so many activities. If memory is the residue of thought, then the teacher's responsibility is to carefully direct thought, a difficult task when thinking is invisible. Directing thought becomes easier when we shed the complexity, the frills and the distraction from our lessons. Content should drive activity, not the other way around.

Teaching a sequence of lessons

Kate, a secondary Maths trainee, describes how she is starting to think ahead in the curriculum.

I'm at the stage of thinking topic by topic. Our topics are eight or nine individual lessons. I started by thinking lesson by lesson. Then I started thinking ahead: *In three lessons' time, it will be really useful if I make* that *clear now.* I want to move towards, *How does this topic help in five months and then in three years?*

Learning happens in the extended periods we spend with a class, as we work our way through the narrative of the curriculum. Starting out, planning individual lessons and assessing success of individual lessons are all valid and useful activities. New teachers should celebrate individual lessons when they go right; new teachers should reflect on what's happened when they don't. You should dwell in the individual lesson until the slog of planning these wanes. As you reach the point that lesson planning uses less mental effort, a new horizon opens up, one focused on the sequences of lessons rather than the one-off. A sequence of lessons better reflects how learning happens. Learning accumulates, built from connection between past content and present study. A sequence allows us to tell the story of the curriculum rather than take an episodic cruise around the archipelago.

Beneath the lofty aim of *doing the curriculum justice* lies a more pragmatic goal: *making your life easier.* Planning in sequence reduces workload because tasks will fill the time we give them. As soon as a teacher can plan two or three lessons for one class in one sitting, life becomes easier. Let's turn to some questions we can ask as we plan our first sequences.

What am I heading towards? What part of the narrative is this?

Natalia, a new secondary history teacher, describes planning a sequence of lessons in a scheme of work.

By far what I've enjoyed the most about teaching so far was [planning sequences of lessons]. It was just really fun. I like thinking in terms of the question *What is my end goal with this? What do I want them to have at the end? And then how do I kind of get there?*

Recently, I planned a sequence around the British Empire. So I spent a Saturday morning with the curriculum working out what questions I needed them to answer: *Why did Britain want an empire? How did they get an empire? What changed for Native Americans?*

Teaching a sequence requires understanding of the narrative. Even a small segment of the narrative has a point we're working *from* and a point we're working *towards*. As we do with individual lessons, we begin with the end in mind. The end, in this case, is just a more distant and complex goal.

Often the codified curriculum will dictate the sequence so responsibility for narrative design won't be yours. As you start to plan sequences of lessons, select a series and a goal that makes sense to you. This might be two lessons to begin with, extending into longer chains with time. Whatever number of lessons you're working with, work hard to make clear – to yourself first of all – what part this sequence plays in the wider curriculum.

A good way to see how well *you* understand this is to plan an explanation of the sequence for your students. Identify the way you want them to understand the target, learning or end result. Check the clarity of this explanation with a colleague. Use this explanation at the start of the sequence and return to it in every subsequent lesson.

How does each part of the sequence link to past and future learning?

Annalise, a Science trainee, describes her basing her planning on what students already know and can do.

The Year 10 Physics material builds upon their Maths knowledge but uses the application of the Maths to explain laws of Physics. Starting on *I do, We do, You do* in teaching calculations such as weight, then moving into changing the concept slightly.

I have repeated 'drilling' an idea [before] giving students extended practice. The heavy scaffold early on, and the repetition in drilling, means I can give feedback on the go which is applicable to students at all different points in the task.

Our aim is a memorable curriculum. To retain more, evidence from neuroscience and cognitive psychology makes clear that students need to activate relevant prior learning in advance of new, related content.[3] A reasonable question is then *What does activation look like?*

- **Explanation.** At its simplest, activation of prior learning is making explicit the implicit links between content. *Last time, we learned how to use technical drawing to create three dimensional images. This lesson we're going to use technical drawing to design packaging.* Or *In yesterday's lesson we learned what the Blitz was and when it was. Today we're going to read about what life was specifically like for children.* Activation by way of explanation starts simply (like the examples above) but we can make it more effective by using retrieval practice.

- **Retrieval practice.** The Forward-Testing Effect is the phenomenon where testing on previously learned content supports retention of new learning.[4] A quiz or other retrieval activity requires students to bring back prior learning. Writing down everything they can remember about a topic or answering five questions on the screen or explaining a diagram relevant to today's lesson – all these retrieval activities can do more than strengthen memory.

Activation prompts links and connections but so does the clear connection between past and present content. Findings from neuroscience research show that when new learning is 'congruent' with past learning, new memories and connections are more likely to form.[5] Congruent shares some meaning with *harmony*: past learning reaches harmony with the present when we make links explicit.

What might students get wrong?

A study into teacher knowledge of student misconceptions revealed the power of knowing how students will approach a subject. Science teachers were tested on what they thought were the most likely student misconceptions in an upcoming topic. Teachers who accurately identified student misconceptions in advance achieved better results than those who couldn't.[6]

Effective teachers do three things with student misconceptions: know them, pre-empt them, adapt to them. One subject's misconceptions will not look like another's and, depending on your subject, misconceptions might be easy to spot but they might not. Get to know your misconceptions by talking to experienced staff about what students regularly struggle with. A trainee Maths teacher I worked with completed every assessment students had to, including GCSE papers. This kept her knowledge sharp but it also allowed her to view topics from the students' perspective, searching for possible pitfalls. Your first time teaching a topic might throw up mistakes you hadn't expected; make a note of them for the second teaching.

Once we have an idea of some misconceptions of students, we plan accordingly. We don't plan to react to mistakes when they arrive. Plans pre-empt mistakes, stopping them from happening in the first place. If we know students are likely to comma splice, we show them how and why this is wrong and give them practice getting it right. If students regularly miss a step in their calculation, we model that carefully in advance and tell them what others have missed.

A slew of inspirational posters tells us that making mistakes is how we learn. It's true that we can learn from mistakes. Proactively trying to stop mistakes from happening might feel desperate and futile. Not every mistake can be caught. And aren't we withholding a powerful learning experience from the students? Even if we do some serious preventative work, students are going to make mistakes and hopefully learn from them. Learning and retention are more likely when we minimise what it is possible to minimise.

How will pre-empting misconceptions manifest in your planning? Write down a topic or a process as your heading. List everything it is possible to get wrong under that heading. Planning for misconceptions is also difficult as a new teacher because you are an expert, or at least probably haven't struggled as some students will. Examine resources. Ask other teachers. Use what you find to create that list. Plan your tasks and explanations to deter these errors by getting out in front of them. Your explanation includes, *Students often get this wrong by...* Your resources highlight steps in minute detail. You monitor purposefully during a task fraught with misconception and share correct answers early or intervene the moment you see someone going wrong. Planning in this way will be time consuming and is not necessarily possible for every lesson but you can think about it for each new topic you teach.

A well-planned sequence anticipates student error. In part, the sequence pre-empts the error through practising the specific processes and retrieving the knowledge necessary to avoid future error. Not every mistake can be caught. Sequences must be adjusted where students aren't getting what we're teaching. As with an individual lesson, a plan must be adapted when it becomes clear that more time or different activity is required for student learning.

What retrieval practice or spaced practice do I need to embed?

As we saw in Chapter 10, retrieval and spaced practice both help students to retain the knowledge and skills you teach them. Across a sequence, the choice about what to retrieve and what to practice becomes about which parts of the whole do students need to automate. When writing that essay, playing that match, writing up that experiment, or doing any number of other activities, students call on a range of prior knowledge. As with the curriculum, retrieval and spacing should increase in complexity, working cumulatively the more students are taught and forging links between content.

As well as increasing in complexity, when planning a sequence we should consider how we slowly remove supports, prompts and aids from students. If students are using vocabulary or formula sheets or sentence starters at the start of a unit, that's fine. But should they still be using them at the end? Students will need support to practice initially but they shouldn't always. At the start of a term, your retrieval quiz might give students everything but the answer. By the end, more should be expected of them.

A practical note about planning

How you plan – physical planner, PowerPoint, using booklets and textbooks – doesn't really matter. Those things aren't the curriculum; they are your intention for how to implement the curriculum. Your planning should work for you. Good planning isn't leaving a big chunk of your job to a set of shared resources. Teachers lucky enough to have workbooks, PowerPoints or textbooks with ready-prepared lessons can plan lessons with those resources by annotating, editing or making notes on resources available. This is still far quicker than making those resources from scratch!

When I was training, the schools I worked in used PowerPoint for lesson resources so my first sequences were single PowerPoints acting as one part of the curriculum narrative. I was able to pick up a PowerPoint where I'd left it and continue in the sequence. The problem with this approach is the possibility that the PowerPoint puts you on a track which is difficult to get off when you need to. A PowerPoint's focus tends to be on activity and often the slides exist to remind the teacher of something as much as the students. PowerPoint is easy to overfill. Whilst I wouldn't tell you to never use PowerPoint, it's worth learning to teach on the board and under a visualiser as well. Overreliance on one medium is likely to embed the drawbacks of that medium into your teaching. As Head of Department, I introduced booklets we all used containing content and some ideas for activities. Perhaps less activity-driven, booklets still need careful thought from the teacher.

Remember that having resources isn't the same as having a plan. Resources may be vital to your plan but they aren't everything. Often resources provide an idea of what *students will do* but you still need to consider *what you will do*: How will you explain and introduce a task? Where will you stop and ask questions or get feedback? What questions will you ask? What answers are you expecting? How will you know if students have 'got it'? The next chapters will examine some of the answers to these questions.

Georgia, a trainee PE teacher, describes planning a sequence of lessons in the PE curriculum and thinking about her end goal.

You see them all the time in PE, blocks of ten lessons on the trot, seeing the same group. So it's really nice to see progress. That makes your planning cycle work much better 'cause you see progress and can plan for progress.

In the last week of a block, in the last two lessons, I want to see them setting up a match. They can do their own warm-up. They can get into a game. Somebody's able to referee. And I'm literally there to manage what's going on. To get to that point, there's loads of repetition.

In summary

Planning a sequence means you don't have to rush to finish everything in a single lesson. Links become overt and clear when they are natural: where we left off last time is where we begin this time. Be wary of never getting through the content, though, and ask where you're unsure if you're covering things in the expected time. Doing less but doing it better, doing it in more depth is good advice for planning. Each new activity adds to students' cognitive load. So include fewer activities where students have more time to think about the content without being moved on.

When the lesson is elevated above learning, we send our thinking down a blind alley, one fixated on activity and engagement. If you find yourself scouring the internet for a more 'engaging' way of doing a task, stop it. If you spend your weekends cutting up pieces of paper into smaller pieces of paper or marshalling friends and family to help you organise resources, stop it. To return to the concept of progressive problem solving, planning the individual lesson is a problem we should aim to pass through. Our intended destination? Planning sequences of lessons with fidelity to the curriculum. A career can be spent facing the challenge of making content comprehensible for young people over the extended periods we spend with them.

One weekend, I got my wife, sister-in-law and her husband to help me organise the most complicated card-sort I could have devised. They dutifully helped me organise paper into envelopes when we should have been enjoying each other's company. I decided then I wouldn't do that sort of activity anymore. I'd be lying if I said this prompted an immediate change to well-planned sequences of lessons. Gradually, my planning turned to activities that weren't such a drain on time for so little reward. I became comfortable with teaching activities that were straightforward but focused on the right things. I stopped looking for the most engaging way of introducing a concept because engagement tended to mask rather than enhance the content. My planning sped up dramatically and, to my surprise, the quality of my teaching improved as well.

Shifting your perspective from teaching a lesson to teaching the curriculum reaps only benefits for you and your students. It may take some brave decisions when you start out as you ignore the short term in favour of the long, as you focus on thinking and not activity. Curriculum and sequence thinking reflects the nature of learning: it happens over time. Perhaps most importantly, students' experience of our subjects is all the richer for it.

Possible next steps

1. **Plan a sequence.** Set aside time to plan a short sequence of lessons. Anything from two to ten lessons and beyond. If you already do this, great. Plan retrieval, practice or review activities that link to and build upon a previous sequence.

2. **Take planning beyond resourcing.** As with all these steps, this may not apply to you. Increasingly, schools have curricula which are resourced. This is undeniably a Good Thing. Time is saved – wheels aren't reinvented. Resources aren't a plan though. As we'll see in Chapter 14, your subject knowledge is distilled into explanations and models, as well as feedback and questions. When privileged to have a resourced curriculum, your plan might be the notes on those resources: a scripted explanation, a set of questions, checks of student understanding, success criteria and many other things.

Notes

1 Coe, R. (2015). What will it take to develop great teaching? www.ibo.org/globalassets/events/aem/conferences/2015/robert-coe.pdf (accessed 21/01/2022).
2 Willingham, D. (2009). *Why Don't Students Like School?* Jossey-Bass.
3 For example, van Kesteren, M.T., Rignanese, P., Gianferrara, P.G., Krabbendam, L., and Meeter, M. (2020). Congruency and reactivation aid memory integration through reinstatement of prior knowledge. *Scientific Reports*, 10(1), 1–13.
4 Yang, C., Luo, L., Vadillo, M., and Shanks, D. (2020). Testing (quizzing) boosts classroom learning: A systemic and meta-analytic review. *Psychological Bulletin*, 147(4), 399–435.
5 van Kesteren, M.T., Rignanese, P., Gianferrara, P.G., Krabbendam, L., and Meeter, M. (2020). Congruency and reactivation aid memory integration through reinstatement of prior knowledge. *Scientific Reports*, 10(1), 1–13.
6 Sadler, P., and Sonnert, G. (2016). Understanding misconceptions. *American Educator*, Spring.

How do we use all that subject knowledge in the classroom?

For most of my career, I've not planned my explanations or models or questions. I've just talked. Even when I realised how important what I said could be, I just turned up and said some things to classes or did the task in front of them. I'd plan other parts of lessons in detail but leave explanations and models to chance, perhaps because they feel ephemeral or *of the moment*.

I realised, more recently, that I hadn't really differentiated between planning and resourcing a lesson. With resourcing, we make sure students will have something to do, something to look at: there's a PowerPoint slide or worksheet for every moment of the lesson. Planning, of course, cares about the resources but it cares far more about student thinking.

Thus far, the subject knowledge we've been talking about has been one step removed from what you do in the classroom. Subject knowledge development is not some abstract process though; it is about the classroom. If we're unable to pull the subject knowledge developed in the background into the foreground, our work has been in vain.

Teachers, like students, are susceptible to cognitive overload. Amongst other things, this means that new teachers need to prepare for lessons differently to their more experienced colleagues. An experienced teacher might have a set of polished explanations banked in long-term memory. These explanations may not have been scripted and practised diligently. Steady accumulation of remembered process is an effective but inefficient way of developing. And just because time and experience have led to automaticity for those teachers, there's no guarantee that time and experience will develop *effective* explanations.

Real planning should attend far more to those moments in between activities. Real development for new teachers, too, will focus on exercising the often ignored muscles used for teacher activity in lessons. This is true as we manage the practical transitions and routines of our classrooms. It is all the more true and all the more important, however, as we plan the way we will communicate the subject to our students.

For Lee Shulman, pedagogical content knowledge, including analogy, explanation, illustration and demonstration, is the missing link between content and the

DOI: 10.4324/9781003281306-20

classroom.[1] For many teachers, myself included, pedagogical content knowledge has been a muscle in constant atrophy. The activity of the student, perhaps rightly, is seen as more important than the activity of the teacher. Reality, however, is not either/or. Both are vital. Both require careful planning. The final step between content knowledge and classroom is not simply resource creation or activity planning. It is the careful craft of any in-lesson behaviour that brings your subject expertise into focus for the students.

Explanation

What counts as an explanation? A ten-minute scripted explanation about sweatshops in Geography? A 30 second reminder? A one-on-one conversation? So much, in fact, that it's easy to just do these things without really thinking about how we do them or how to get better at them. When you think about it, this is bizarre. Explanation and modelling pose a particular problem to those with subject expertise because that expertise needs to be distilled, filtered through the curriculum or scheme of work and ultimately communicated effectively.

When I trained to teach, I was mainly told not to speak too much to my classes and praised when I didn't. It's true that spending half an hour to explain a concept you could have spent five minutes on (or broken down into more manageable segments) is not a good use of time. But there's no escaping the fact that you have expertise, knowledge and skill that students don't yet have. To sit in the same room with them and never communicate these things is a dereliction of duty. We need to be able to take what we know and make it accessible and understandable for our students. That's what we'll think about as we look at explanation and modelling.

Principles for explanation

As we examine the principles for explanation, we're drawing on our knowledge of the curriculum. What we decide to explain and when is directed or driven by the curriculum, the sequence that best guides students through the content they are learning.

The principles outlined here demonstrate where your knowledge, and what type of knowledge, will be needed. Good grounding in a subject is important but understanding how to make that subject clear, how to join links to a great chain of understanding, that is the challenge. That is the essence of Lee Shulman's pedagogical content knowledge, the combination of pedagogy and content.

Build on prior knowledge and skill

A simple but powerful question is *What previously taught knowledge will students need to understand what they will learn in this lesson?* As one study explains, 'reactivation of previous memories while learning new information [can help to] integrate them with an existing schema'.[2] Remember, schema are the interconnected webs of knowledge we're trying to build in students' minds.

We connect what we want them to know with what they know already. If you have the chance before your explanation, quizzing students on this knowledge primes them to cope with what's coming. This could take the form of a few questions to answer, a whole class mini-whiteboard session or any other task where they must retrieve relevant details from what they already know.

Prior knowledge includes what you've taught them, what they learned last year, what they've been studying in other subjects, but it also includes what the students are likely to know from their lives and experiences. Finding the sweet spot between familiar and new, the research tells us, is the key to making learning stick.[3] So, as well as *linking* new learning to prior knowledge, we should show students that what we're teaching goes beyond, supplements or is significant in different ways to what has come before.

Alex, a secondary English trainee, describes linking an explanation about *A Christmas Carol* with students' knowledge.

I always try and apply it to something that they know first and foremost. Teaching *A Christmas Carol*, my students had little understanding of what Victorian England was like, what working conditions were, the nuances of the Industrial Revolution and the societal and economic situation at the time. But they know who Jeff Bezos is.

Let's say we take Jeff Bezos and we say, 'He runs a big company where he employs a lot of people quite cheaply and a lot of people criticise him for having a low standard for his workers. Scrooge is like that'. The students understood that.

Start with the concrete

Michaela School in Wembley is a veritable emporium of quality explanation, with teachers who are expert in being the expert. Explicit teaching is on offer in every classroom but such teaching is often characterised as dry and detached. When I visited, nothing could be further from the truth. I saw teacher after teacher explain their subjects to gripped rooms full of children. Delivery was powerful but so was the thinking underlying each explanation. It's worth considering how such teachers go about the business of explanation.

Pritesh Raichura, Head of Science at Michaela, describes how students need concrete, real world examples to understand complex definitions. Concrete examples 'give pupils something to think about when they encounter the generalised definition'.[4] Pritesh teaches homeostasis, the maintenance of a constant internal environment (a definition sure to initially confuse) by using concrete examples: body sweat in response to exercise, urination in response to drinking a lot, thirst in response to heat. Each concrete example gives texture and layer to student understanding of definitions. In this way, concrete examples work better than definitions for the introduction of an idea. Even the most student friendly definition is likely to be harder to grasp unless it links to what students already know or have just seen.

Examples can't always tap into a student's lived experience. Some concepts are too abstract or unknown. The definition of a comma splice is *joining two independent clauses with a comma*. Sounds straightforward but leaves lots of students stumped. Real sentences, either projected or written in front of the students, can better illustrate the principle than a simple definition, at least initially.

At times, the use of prior knowledge will be enough, particularly when students have already been introduced to at least the fringes of the topic. At times, concrete examples will feel elusive. Their power is in their ability to add layers of complexity, a deep richness, to the definitions and concepts we want students to understand.

Alex explains how he uses a concrete example.

Throughout my year here I think I've been good at turning abstract concepts into concrete examples. In preparation for *Animal Farm* I have been teaching my Year 7 students the various economic models by using a token system for students in class where they have to try and share their tokens equally in keeping with the models of Capitalism, Communism and Socialism.

Use examples and non-examples

In the process of introducing a concept to students, we'll often, intuitively, show them examples. Intuition doesn't lead as directly to showing students non-examples. A non-example is an incorrect example. Often non-examples look right or exemplify another, different principle. At best, as one guide to teaching explains, examples and non-examples should be 'similar to one another except in the critical feature and indicate that they are different'. We are then able to show the examples side by side, 'making the similarities and differences most obvious'.[5]

Georgia, a PE trainee, talks about managing misconceptions in PE.

In PE, we have to do things over and over again. You drill passes and moves. You have to plan demonstrations that show students what they can and can't do. In hockey, for example, you can't use the round side of the stick to push the ball so when students are trying to control the ball, they must use the flat side. But it's very natural to just start using both sides of your stick to control the ball, because it's easier. It takes lots of repetition and practice to show them how to control the ball with just the flat side of your stick.

In our comma splicing example, our aim is to show students examples of comma splicing and examples of comma usage which isn't spliced.

Examples of comma splicing:

> Jake ran after his friends, he couldn't keep up.
> I like English, I hate Maths.

Non-examples of comma splicing:

> At break, Jake ran after his friends.
> I like English, but I prefer Maths.

One example and one non-example won't be sufficient. Examples and non-examples serve to tease out the edges of the concept, to delineate the boundaries between right and wrong. For this reason, the boundaries of a concept come into focus when non-examples highlight a range of errors or differences with the examples.

Make use of Cognitive Load Theory

In Chapter 9, we saw how an understanding of Cognitive Load Theory helps us to plan in a way that will support learning. Our understanding of what students already know, of concrete examples and of non-examples marries well with what we know about cognitive load:

- Content should be broken down into manageable chunks. At times, this will mean breaking down your explanation into parts with tasks and interaction planned between.

- Extraneous load should be minimised. Whizzy animations, unnecessary pictures or content that you're not covering now can all be avoided. Student attention should be telescopic in its focus. Cut everything else away.

- Avoid splitting attention in your explanation. Diagrams with separate, and complex, annotations. Slides with text you're talking through as well. All of these things split student attention, making it harder for them focus on what you are saying.

Planning an explanation

Kate, a secondary Maths trainee, describes her reasoning behind planning explanations.

I definitely think about and plan explanations because if that part of the lesson crumbles, the activities you've planned aren't going to matter. I think about how I'd want to hear it as a student and how I'd want to hear it as a mathematician. Typically, I try to give both. You have the *Why* students and the *What* or *How* students. You have some students who say, 'I don't care why; I just want to know the process'. So I can bullet point the process for them. There are other students who, until I say mathematically *this is why*, they won't listen to me.

In solving equations, *Why do I take the plus three over before I divide?* With some of them, I can use a silly story that helps them remember to do that. But some want to know *Why, why do I have to do things in that order?* With them, we might plug in a number and try it and see what happens. We ask, *Does it work? No, it doesn't.*

Some want to know *Why*. Some want to know *How*. Either is fine. Mixed together has got the best results for me but I wouldn't be able to do that unless I thought about it before I taught it.

Principles are useful but they don't necessarily prepare you for a tricky concept and a trickier class last lesson tomorrow. How do those principles marry with your planning? The process of planning and delivering these explanations puts your subject knowledge under a type of pressure it is unlikely to otherwise experience. You, an expert, don't think like your students but to explain well you're going to have to try. Experts don't need help defining the boundaries of a concept. Experts don't usually need to refresh their understanding of examples and non-examples. Experts don't need concepts broken down for them.

This is the curse of knowledge: a bias built from the assumption that others have the knowledge we possess. Stephen Pinker explains, 'Anyone who wants to lift the curse of knowledge must first appreciate what a devilish curse it is. Like a drunk who is too impaired to realize that he is too impaired to drive, we do not notice the curse because the curse prevents us from noticing it'.[6] Because the curse means we're likely to underestimate the power of our own expertise, we need to put safeguards in place to mitigate the effects.

Tackle one thing at a time

Concepts we can swallow whole are likely to cause problems for our students. Our refrain in applying cognitive science must be to narrow our focus. For ourselves and our students, we focus on the component parts to create the whole in students' minds. The problem, of course, is what constitutes *one thing?*

To begin with, the curriculum, or your planning, dictates the content of the lesson. Which concepts, in the curriculum or your plan, are new or, as yet, without strong foundation in student thinking? These require explanation. Some concepts, however, are unwieldy when dealt with in one go.

A Religious Studies teacher is planning a lesson on Christian beliefs surrounding the resurrection of Jesus. A two-page textbook spread provides the basis for the lesson, and the teacher's planning. The two-page spread covers the biblical accounts of the resurrection, Christian views on the significance of the resurrection, and how this affects the Christian calendar or a Christian lifestyle. At the end of the two-page spread, a set of questions helps students to think about this content.

That different teachers would approach this content differently is not a problem. All lessons planned with this content in mind are aiming at a student understanding of the resurrection. A lesson where the teacher tries to explain *everything* about the resurrection in one go before students read and answer questions is likely to demand too much of their cognitive resources. We break tasks and content down; we should do the same with our explanations. The teacher decides to start by telling the story using a student-friendly account from the Bible.

Prepare them for your explanation

If learning works better after recap or retrieval of prior learning, you are responsible for the work of preparation. You are responsible for checking students are ready for your explanation. Firing off hands-down questions around the room doesn't just retrieve what students need to know. Questions check if students are ready for your explanation. A multiple choice or mini-whiteboard task can check the understanding of all *very* quickly.

A Spanish teacher might be about to explain how students say what they *plan to do* at the weekend. To start the lesson, the students go through their embedded mini-whiteboards routine. Boards, pens and rubbers are passed down by students at the end of each row. The teacher says:

> Today, we're going to look at how we can share a plan of activities we *plan* to do in the future and why we plan to do those things. This is different to what we've done before where we talked about and asked each other what we'd done at the weekend – in the past. Before I explain the difference, I want to check you still understand the vocabulary we'll need and the way we've talked about activities in the past.

The teacher projects one sentence in Spanish at a time onto the screen. Each sentence is from an imagined Spanish student, explaining what they did at the weekend and why. The class have to write the activity the Spanish students did and the reason why they chose that activity. The teacher is checking students understand what they've studied previously; students are retrieving lots of vocabulary knowledge to complete the task. But the teacher is also preparing students for the next task, drawing on required memory and preparing to highlight a division between *past* and *future* activities.

The teacher must, of course, be awake and alert to the information received in this preparation phase. We're both bringing our subject knowledge down to the level of our novice students and checking they are ready to make a small step (or at times, a giant leap) to the next bit of content. Deep understanding of curriculum, of subject and pedagogy, will be lost if we don't adequately prepare and check.

If, at this stage, students reveal that they don't understand the prerequisites for the current lesson, taking a step back is better than stumbling forward. Teaching, even the most teacher-led teaching, is never just delivery.

Script and practise the essentials

As a teacher of English, I have become used to students telling me that *they* don't need to plan and the reasons for this. Whether it's a story or an essay, students often tell me that they plan in their heads. Planning gets in the way of their process. And anyway, they've done okay so far without it (they haven't). Teachers can reject scripting with similar romantic but misguided arguments: scripting undermines or even ignores the teacher's expertise; scripting removes the spontaneity from my lessons; scripting isn't my style.

Later in your career, you'll reach the point where each year's explanations are habitual repetitions of the explanations that have come before them. Be careful of assuming these future explanations will be any good without careful planning. And be careful, when they become automatic, of assuming automatic explanations are good explanations. A script can be on a post-it note, in your planner, annotations on a resource, or on a screen in front of you. It shouldn't be, for reasons of split attention, something projected so that the students can see it. If you're explaining it, they don't need to read it too.

What could your notes include?

- A complete script of *everything* you want to say to students.

- A scripted definition or other key sentence with notes for the rest.

- A list of words, events, concepts or examples you will include.

A script without practice is likely to become an unhelpful crutch in lessons. Heavily relying upon, or simply trying to find, your notes in lessons can disrupt the flow of learning and activity. Practise with your notes, considering emphasis and delivery, pause and projection. Practise until you don't need to look at your notes all the way through your explanation.

Feedback is a core element of *deliberate* practice. Our aim should be to improve and refine *before* we need to deliver our explanation. A coach can help with each step of scripting and practice. Present it to them. Let them question and unpick it. Set your sights on improvement and excellence, on the best and clearest version of an explanation. When you do this, acknowledge that feedback from a coach is an important refining fire.

Enrich but don't distract

When Christine Counsell talks about core and hinterland, she reminds us of the delicate balance we must strike in explaining anything to students. Students who walk a curriculum road lined with only the essential may come to see the journey as purely utilitarian, about getting from A to B. As teachers we need to be careful of rushing through the curriculum or the content. We need to be careful of turning the curriculum, or our explanations, into a list of things students must know *for the test*.

If hinterland becomes part of your explanation, it should be planned and scripted. Some of my favourite teachers at school seemed to revel in the tangential, the question asked, the illuminating diversion. Underlying the ability to pursue these threads on a whim is the unseen expertise, built from expansive knowledge and experience. Trying to be that teacher without the same knowledge and experience is likely to lead to disappointment and confusion. I'm also not sure that we should aim to be the teacher who jumps around from one thing to another, at least not as the norm.

Hinterland should enrich and expand a student's understanding more than it should divert. Counsell describes it as a 'supporter or feeder' of the core.[7] Hinterland is the story that illustrates the scientific concept or moment in history, the biographical detail, the quirk in a case study.

Plan to embed

I was going to say *Plan your check* but check might be the wrong word. Or, at least, it's incomplete. We don't explain, check and repeat *ad nauseam* until the end of the year. Once something has been explained, it's right to check that students have understood the explanation. But the activity after the explanation is doing more than checking; it is embedding the content of that explanation, allowing students to enrich their understanding of if through deliberate and directed thought. Assuming that students have got it because we have explained it is a risky strategy. If we've chunked learning down into manageable pieces, the explanation is likely followed by practice or activity.

Explanation is the realised power of your subject and curriculum knowledge to make content accessible for students. It is not an add-on or off-the-cuff possibility for your lessons. What's more, explanation is going to happen whether you think about it or not. You will stand in front of classes and tell them things. Don't, as I did for much of my career, stand in front of them with nothing planned but an over-confidence in your ability. Instead, grapple with the content, with its challenges and pitfalls. Grapple with the connections between what your students know and what you want them to.

Modelling

Is modelling simply about doing the tasks we expect of students before they are attempted by students? Or is modelling any demonstration? So much of what we do is modelling that we can be unaware of it. Equally, modelling feels at times like something we'll just come up with in the moment. Modelling, in this way, occupies the blank spaces, the gaps, in our planning proformas between activities.

Tasks *are* planned. Models less so. Thinking about modelling pushes our pedagogical content knowledge to its limits. This is both a planning and a development activity because we are confronted with our abilities and inabilities, our capacities or lack thereof, to adequately communicate how students should progress through a task.

Competent modelling rests on our knowledge of the subject matter but, more crucially, an ability to condense and communicate that subject matter in a way that makes sense for children. More than simply saying how something is done, modelling offers students the ways they may get things wrong (and the ways we get things wrong), the ways they can get unstuck and, ultimately, the ways they can apply their subject knowledge. Modelling is, therefore, our way of trying to solve the problem of young, undeveloped knowledge which must be applied.

Principles for modelling

Modelling is for anything (but not everything)

Our focus is the subject but modelling can and should be for anything. How the books are handed out, how students come into the room, how they answer questions can all be modelled. In the realm of the subject, we model anything that will help students to access, progress through and succeed in the curriculum. Modelling isn't just reserved for the big tasks, the extended writes, the 12-mark questions, the complex problem solving. The steps of those processes and activities can be modelled and unpicked. Students often answer short questions following the introduction of content across subjects and across phases. Modelling how students take a question and form a sentence can be usefully modelled. Modelling how students answer questions verbally is an investment in your whole class discussion.

A counterpoint to the model *anything* argument is that we can't model *everything*. Deep understanding of a well-planned curriculum should direct some of the subject-specific modelling we do but decisions in this area should be based on our classes. Ascertaining what students know and can do is vital for our ability to model the right things, the things they need direct guidance through.

After you've planned a lesson go back through the plan and consider the tasks with the most demanding subject content, processes or both. Cast your mind back to *element interactivity* – the number of components a student will have to juggle in a task. Tasks with high element interactivity will benefit from a model.

Narrate the steps and pitfalls

Cognitive Load Theory and *element interactivity* might prompt our modelling but subject knowledge and pedagogical content knowledge offer direction of what and how to model. The subject domain we inhabit may feel alive and colourful to us but gloomy and dark to our students. Our job is to find those items, those nuggets, tasks and processes, that brighten a student's understanding of that domain and enable them to navigate it without our future support.

Ask, *What do I, as an expert, know that my students won't?* Models both provide strategies for using subject content and strategies for coping when students aren't sure how to use that content. Students should witness the struggle even if such struggle, for you, is a bit of a performance. Students are likely to be more successful when they see the struggle than when they see effortless perfection.[8]

As we model, we can narrate what we're thinking (or possibly what students should be thinking) and where mistakes can be made and how to avoid them. We may find it easy, as experts, to model and talk at the same time but we should be cautious of seeing this multi-tasking as evidence of effective narration.

Script your narration with your planning, resources and curriculum in mind. Make it succinct and direct. As with the scripts for our explanations, key vocabulary or points you're likely to forget are both worth including. Practise it in your classroom without any students. To reduce your cognitive load, decide early how you will model. Under a visualiser on a piece of paper or in an exercise book have the benefit of mirroring what the students will be doing and can feel natural. For models you're concerned about or haven't quite 'got' yet, practising with a coach or mentor first can be invaluable.

You can't practise every model for every class. Content you don't know well or are teaching for the first time is worth practising and scripting.

But don't overload them

A further reason to script a model, or at least the narrated thought process, is to check that it isn't likely to overload your students. Talking too much over your model is likely just as ineffective as not talking at all. Students can't hold onto every tangential thought your brain forces from your mouth. A script is a limiting safeguard on what you say. Of course, you can deviate from it where unforeseen problems arise; you can still respond to the needs in your class. A script is simply your attempt to distil the necessary knowledge of curriculum, content and process. We only tackle the curse of expertise when we distil that expertise into something manageable for students.

Unpick the model with questions

Completing the model isn't the end of the story. Questions allow us to tease out what makes the model successful. Go for hands-down questions and hold your perception of the model up against their understanding. Questions like these aren't just to check if students understand; we also check which bits students understood or how well. If you've spoken about mistakes to avoid, ask about them. If you've offered two methods, compare them. If there's something students *must* remember at a certain point, see if they remember it.

Paradoxically, much of this chapter offers you generic advice in that you can apply it to some degree no matter what subject you're teaching. A distinction between generic teaching and learning strategies and a deep knowledge of what you teach depends on what you bring to these activities and how you apply knowledge to classroom practice. Your schema or mental models for your subject merge with principles about explanation and modelling.

Clearly, a teacher's activity isn't limited to explanation and modelling. Questions and feedback, and much more besides, use our subject knowledge to shape student knowledge in a lesson. Explanation, modelling, questioning and feedback are often things we don't plan; we just do. Pressing into these unexplored areas, areas often ignored in the planning process, forces us to confront the capacity of our subject knowledge to meet the needs of our classes.

In summary

Subject knowledge goes on quite a journey from what you have when you start out to what can be useful in facing the challenges of the classroom. Subject knowledge developed at distance from the classroom – reading a book about our subject or attending a talk, say – can definitely improve our knowledge but these things are long-term strategies, unlikely to improve our teaching this week or next.

More likely to improve our teaching now is a growing knowledge of the curriculum, both zoomed out in its understanding of the narrative our curriculum tells and zoomed in on the lessons we plan within it. Within those lessons, the subject knowledge that will really matter is the knowledge of how to make clear what is unclear, how to contain key elements of it in a task, how to chip away at it until something comprehensible is left.

Possible next steps

1. **Prepare to explain.** Consider the prior knowledge that will be useful or essential for students to grasp your explanation. With brand new topics, this might include students' general or everyday knowledge. In most cases, there will be previous topics, lessons, content or skill to be reviewed in preparation for the explanation. Plan a short quiz that lays the groundwork for your explanation.

2. **Script and rehearse an explanation or model.** It's not possible to script everything. No doubt there will be times when you find yourself explaining a complicated topic that would have benefited from a bit more careful planning. Don't beat yourself up about it. When you do script an explanation or model make sure you rehearse it, if only briefly, as well.

Notes

1 Shulman, L. (1986). Those who understand: Knowledge growth in teaching. *Educational Research*, 15(2), 4–14.
2 Van Kesteren, M. and Meeter, M. (2020). How to optimize knowledge construction in the brain. *Science of Learning*, 5, 5.
3 Ibid.
4 Raichura, P. (2019). Clear teacher explanations. https://bunsenblue.wordpress.com/2019/10/20/clear-teacher-explanations-i-examples-non-examples/ (accessed on 25/05/2022).
5 Watkins, C., and Slocum, T. (2004). The components of direct instruction. *Journal of Direct Instruction*, 3(2), 75–110.
6 Pinker, S. (2014). The source of bad writing. *Wall Street Journal*. www.wsj.com/articles/the-cause-of-bad-writing-1411660188 (accessed on 25/5/2022).
7 Counsell, C. (2018). *Senior Curriculum Leadership 1: The Indirect Manifestation of Knowledge:(A)CurriculumasNarrative.* https://thedignityofthethingblog.wordpress.com/2018/04/07/senior-curriculum-leadership-1-the-indirect-manifestation-of-knowledge-a-curriculum-as-narrative/ (accessed on 28/02/2022).
8 Schunk, D.H., Hanson, A.R., and Cox, P.D. (1987). Strategy self-verbalisation during remedial listening comprehension instruction. *Journal of Educational Psychology*, 75, 93–105.

Further reading

Something about your subject(s).

PART 6
Knowledge of students

Conspicuous in their absence thus far, students pose a difficult question when it comes to teacher knowledge. What do we need to know about our students to be effective teachers? Knowledge of subject and pedagogy would be incomplete without turning our attention to those who are meant to benefit from such knowledge.

I was presenting on knowledge of students at a training day for teachers. As I started, I made a flippant comment about how knowing students' birthdays or pets' names might make you a nice person but it wouldn't make you a better a teacher. In the discussion that followed, various members of the audience (and other presenters) made it clear that this kind of unfeeling attitude was exactly what is wrong with the profession. And they were right: there is a sense that our knowledge of these human beings we teach will shape our time in the classroom.

Like every area of teacher knowledge we've examined, the sheer quantity of what we could know about our students is a daunting prospect. Child development, adolescence, youth culture could all be worthy of our time. As I was corrected on that training day, there's much to learn about the students in front of us. Reducing this to trivia about them ignores the importance of knowing who we teach and how they respond to the classroom and our subjects. Whilst there is no chapter in this section on how to find out the name of a student's pet, knowing students' interests, being able to talk to them about what they like and dislike and understanding something about their temperament can all be incredibly helpful.

Especially important in knowing our students is knowing any special educational needs they have which we may need to consider in our teaching. This book has no section on teaching children with dyslexia or ADHD or Asperger's syndrome. In each case, our teaching will take into account such needs but we shouldn't confuse knowledge of a need with knowledge of a child. Each need presents differently in each child.

DOI: 10.4324/9781003281306-21

> **Kate, a secondary Maths teacher, describes how she's tried to get to know students beyond her lessons.**
>
> In my experience, it's out of the classroom that I make best connections with my most difficult or challenging students because they sort of see you as a human. So I made an intentional decision to help with a sports club after school and to help with D of E to see them in environments that aren't Maths because some students walk into the room hating my subject before they've even met me. It's the conversation in the corridor too – *How's your day going?* – and then being able to bring that into the lesson later.

One type of knowledge requires daily updates: knowledge of what students can and can't do, as well as what they do and don't know. We must update this knowledge constantly because:

● It is difficult to ascertain in the first place.

● It's easy to misdiagnose struggling or successful students.

● It will inform short, medium and long-term adaptations to our teaching.

Mary Kennedy describes this as the problem of 'Exposing student thinking', highlighting that 'the most useful knowledge for teachers is the knowledge they have in the moment, for this knowledge can guide their actions in the moment'.[1] This is the reason why we've left knowledge of students until last: it's probably the most complex and challenging to develop.

If these are the problems, the solutions will take us into a set of strategies sometimes called *assessment for learning* or *responsive teaching*. Having examined these solutions, this section will then put a dampener on proceedings by warning against trusting too much in our intuitions, expectations or other types of knowledge of students.

With that in mind, Part 6 will answer the questions:

● How do we figure out what students know and what do we do about it?

● What are the limits of what we can know about students?

Note

1 Kennedy, M. (2016). Parsing the practice of teaching. *Journal of Teacher Education*, 67(1), 6–17.

How do we figure out what students know and what do we do about it?

In *The Matrix*, a film I imagine is depressingly out of date for the young new teacher, Neo, the main character, learns new things by having a plug shoved in the back of his neck and downloading information straight into his brain. Unfortunately, as Neo is the hero in a dystopian world, he can't spend time learning the complete works of Shakespeare, a new language or classical piano (and in my mind the film is the lesser for it). No, he must learn how to fly a helicopter, how to shoot and, of course, kung-fu. In the world of *The Matrix*, there is no gap between being taught – having a wire shoved in your neck – and having learned. One naturally leads to the other. Real life and real teaching are more complicated.

Dylan Wiliam and Paul Black use a metaphor to sum up this complexity. In their seminal work on formative assessment from 1998, *Inside the Black Box*, Black and Wiliam describe the classroom as the black box. Pupils, resources and teachers provide inputs to the box. Outputs include knowledge, test results and feelings of satisfaction and achievement.[1] The problem, as Wiliam and Black put it, is that we can't really be clear on the specific inputs resulting in certain outputs.

Formative assessment, any type of assessment where evidence gathered is used to 'adapt the teaching to meet student needs',[2] is offered by Black and Wiliam as a method of breaking open the black box, the classroom, and understanding what is going on inside. Not only is there evidence that formative assessment strategies raise achievement of our students, but these strategies are also more likely to raise achievement for the lowest achievers in our classrooms. So, we must introduce a new type of knowledge the new teacher will require: the knowledge of what students know and can do.

When we question, when we examine work, when we look over their shoulders, we see and know in part. Where our knowledge of subject and pedagogy are brightening expansive landscapes, knowledge of student learning is viewed through a glass, darkly. Variously labelled *formative assessment, assessment for learning, responsive teaching* or *checking for understanding*, activities that seek

DOI: 10.4324/9781003281306-22

to understand what students have learned are vitally important. The names here reveal the dual function of such activities: *assessing* what students know and *responding* to this information. The concept of *assessment*, however, can confuse teachers and students. Assessment for learning happens whilst students are learning and whilst you are teaching. Assessment here is not after the fact nor is it assessment to grade, mark or define ability. Dylan Wiliam reportedly regrets the naming of *assessment for learning*, wishing he had used the phrase *responsive teaching* instead.

Hang on a minute, you cry. *Learning takes place over time. Can we really assess learning in the lesson? Or are we just assessing performance?* There is, admittedly, a paradox at the heart of assessment for learning. Learning as assessed in a single lesson is not guaranteed. If a student shows us perfection in one lesson, don't assume it's permanent. If they know in the lesson, great – there's at least a small likelihood they'll know next lesson. If, however, they don't understand in *this* lesson, there's a strong to certain chance they won't know in the next. Anyway, we assess not just to know but to respond.

Teachers, particularly new teachers, struggle with the response. A student gives a wrong answer but the rest of the class seem fine – do we just leave it? Some students are using the sentence construction we've taught incorrectly but it'll come up again soon – do we just wait and see? Even if we want to act, what should we do? Options abound, from seeing an individual later right through to stopping the whole class and re-teaching something.

To gather and respond to this knowledge, use a three-part process: *plan* the assessment in advance, *do* it in lesson, *respond* to the information.

Plan

Before we ask *What do they know?* we need to be clear about what we want students to know. Teachers who get into the minutiae of their curriculum plan better assessment. Clear objectives and success criteria provide something to work towards and therefore to check.

Objectives are too often nebulous. Explaining to a class that *We're learning to synthesise our ideas* or *construct a powerful argument* doesn't give students or you a clear idea of what you'll need to check at the end of the lesson. As with planning though, thinking about purpose and here more deeply about success criteria is an important part of being able to check that students have learned. Checks don't work in general. An in-lesson check isn't a review of *everything* students know. Precision about what we're looking for is important because we can't look for everything. That said, checks struggle to work in binary too. It's not that students *do* understand or *don't*. They understand in part. They misunderstand slightly.

A success criteria might precisely define the vocabulary students should know and use; it might set a goal of competence in a process. More broadly, it should define what students should know or be able to do. Expecting students to *Write a range of sentences* or *Simplify fractions* can mean wildly different things. Such objectives don't meet the demands for clarity and precision that we're after. *Write a range of sentences* can become a sequence of lessons including, *Use a comma to separate adverbs, subordinate clauses or prepositional phrases from the main clause* and *Use semi-colons accurately* before students are expected to combine these different techniques.

A success criteria like this can exist in your mind – but there is a danger you forget it – in your planner, in a planning proforma, or in the resources you share with students. Some curricula will provide this for you. Others will leave at least some of that decision to you.

Even when we've fixed on what we're checking, learning happens over time. In a single lesson, there's no watertight task you can plan that will guarantee long-term learning. All you can do is check that students understand what you explain and practice in lessons.

Planning then needs to make two things clear in your mind:

- What do students need to know?

- How will you check?

We'll turn to that second question now.

Do

What we do is a result of what we've planned. Most of the activities listed require careful preparation so that questions or resources are ready. Every activity is about gathering knowledge you can act on. None of them are about catching students out.

Hands down

Picture the scene: you're being observed with a tricky Year 9 class. You've just finished an explanation of a challenging concept. Students need to do some independent practice but first you want to check they understand and, looking round the room, it's not clear they understand. One student is picking crumbs from his tie; two girls are having a whispered conversation at the back of the room. Tentatively, hopefully, you ask a question of the class. One hand shoots up. Another far less confident hand follows. The rest of the class sit in sullen disengagement. What's your next step?

The easy way out is to ask the confident hand. This student knows. You know they know. They know they know. The class knows too. Perhaps, at times, there's wisdom in students hearing the right answer from a peer rather than their teacher. But as a method of figuring out what the class know, confirming the most able child in the room understands you is useless information. They understood before you started speaking.

If questions like this exist to check student understanding, the questions them-selves are incredibly important. Most teachers don't tend to plan questions. Questions just emerge, unformed and unplanned, from our mouths. Planning *all* questions you ask in a day is impossible. Planning *some* is essential.

Some practical points about hands down:

- Tell the students you're going to do it: 'Keep your hands down for these ques-tions. I want to see what you know'.

- Put the name at the end of the question, after a pause. That way, students will have to listen and get used to thinking about each question asked.

- If you have a particularly reluctant class, get them to talk to their partner or write down their thoughts first, just for 30 seconds. Your first question can then be, 'What did you talk about?' or 'What have you written?'

- Don't accept 'I don't know'. Ask a follow up. Ask another student or students and then return to 'I don't know'. Ask them to sum up what they've heard or choose the most likely answer or, at a minimum, just repeat the correct answer they've heard.

- Allow students to demonstrate enthusiasm and interest by offering answers with hands up. Be clear with yourself and your students about *when* it is important to gather responses with hands down.

We ask hands-down questions to elicit responses from students who may not have got it. In fact, we go directly to those students. Which student can act as a barom-eter of class understanding? If *they* know, most will. This approach may cause some awkwardness in that observation, producing situations where the class hav-en't understood and you have to return to the board, to your examples, to your resources to try again. We'll look at what to do in these situations when we get to *Respond*, but for now, it's vital you're able to stare down the awkward revelation that you've taught something the class haven't understood.

Mini-whiteboards

Alice, a Year 5 teacher in her third year, explains how she uses mini-whiteboards.

We do retrieval activities with whiteboards. Sometimes it may be a diagnostic question – A, B, C or D. By simply putting it on their boards, I can see. They think it's a bit of a game. They love it. If I've asked something, when I say *Go*, say what this means, they write it on the board and it helps with assessment. It helps me know if they're ready to start the lesson.

I might say 'What is a comma splice?' and they write it on their whiteboards. At first, if they didn't know, I wasn't sure what to do. Now, I go to someone who does know and ask for their explanation of the answer. Then I go to the person who doesn't know and say 'So what's the answer?' Basically, they'll have heard the correct answer. I've got a boy in my class who, if I say it, he doesn't remember it, but if one of his peers says it, he remembers it.

Before we become too enamoured with, too proud of, our new hands-down habit, we need to realise something. Trying to ask your way to understanding, one child at a time, is an incredibly inefficient way of grasping for knowledge. Particularly if the kind of questions we're asking can be directed towards the whole class. The ephemeral nature of the whiteboard also means students sometimes feel more able to *have a go* because answers will always be rubbed away.

I've heard history and English teachers say that mini-whiteboards don't work in *their* subjects. It's true that certain tasks don't transfer well: writing an essay or even an introduction won't fit into a relatively small white rectangle. But lots will.

Some practical points about whiteboard use:

- As with hands-down questions, planning the questions you ask is essential.

- Ask a question, give a clear time limit and train students not to lift their board until you want. Students can hold them horizontally so you know they're ready but others can't see their answer. Countdown and give a clear 'Go'.

- Don't worry too much about seeing every answer. Unless students are writing a single letter or number, checking every board will be very difficult. First check the students who you're worried have got it wrong. Arrange a seating plan so their boards are easy to see.

- Logistically, there's a lot to think about. Storage should enable ease of distribution and tidying away. Each row could have its own box with the necessary boards, pens and rubbers. You need to train students to unpack and pack them away but also just to use them well. Devote time to this when first working with a class.

Not every task can be done on mini-whiteboards but do consider the challenge when not using them: *Could I gather this information from more children, more quickly?* Other strategies can similarly be used to get information from the whole class. Students can offer answers to multiple choice questions on their fingers. Principles of mini-whiteboards apply. Call and response can be used to check confidence on definitions, vocabulary and factual recall. Shallow though this information might be, observing the room can show you who knows and who doesn't.

Hinge questions

> **Sarah, a Year 4 teacher in her first year, describes responding to student misconceptions.**
>
> It's important to give children a chance to show you what they don't understand in the lesson. I don't just ask them to tell me they if they understand. I test their knowledge by asking diagnostic questioning. I use whiteboards a lot for this. The children might know the answer but struggle to articulate it. The whiteboard gives them an opportunity to think and get it down before they're asked about it.
>
> When we're teaching, we can assume that children understand things but they don't. I've got to know them. I've got to know them in that way but also through looking at their work. We have a feedback book where we write everything they're doing, everything they're struggling with. I like writing specific names of children and what they're not getting in the lesson. That helps me when I'm planning the next lesson.

Lessons are full of transitions. Students enter and start working. One task draws to a close and another begins. The process is repeated until the lesson ends. We'll do the same again tomorrow. Chapter 6 talked about the practicalities of managing transitions to maximise positive behaviour.

Teachers are not on a track, inescapably moving through the curriculum. Even when we feel that we must get through the content – the curriculum is so full – we must remember our responsibility for learning, not coverage. Teachers build learning by ensuring students understand, by getting students to practice well and by linking that understanding and practice to what comes next. As well as attending to the practicalities of transitioning from one part of the lesson to the next, we must consider how we move from one part of the learning to the next.

Dylan Wiliam describes a lesson's hinge as the 'point at which the teacher checks whether the class is ready to move on by asking a diagnostic question'. This is a hinge because 'how the lesson proceeds depends on the understanding shown by the students'.[3] A hinge question, therefore, is one we ask at the point where the lesson should move on if, and only if, enough students demonstrate the required understanding. Diagnostic insofar as they offer right answers and reveal misconceptions, hinge questions check student understanding.

A teacher writes a hinge question for finding the area of a rectangle. The teacher shows a diagram where the sides of the rectangle are 5 centimetres and 3 centimetres. The teacher offers the following multiple choice answers:

a. 8 cm^2

b. 15 cm^2

c. 16 cm^2

Students who choose a. see two numbers on the diagram and add them together. Students who choose c. have added all the sides, confusing area with perimeter. b. is the correct answer; it is the area. Note, this question works well when finding the area has recently been explained and modelled. A teacher uses such a question to check if students are ready to practice independently. Students who have already practised finding the area of a rectangle will not find this a challenge. The principles described above apply: this question can be answered on mini-whiteboards or by holding up the fingers on one hand. Alternatively, hands-down can be used for the initial answer with lots of further questions to unpick why each answer is right or wrong. Two or three questions like this confirm that students are or aren't ready for some independent practice.

Multiple choice questions are effective where misconceptions are obvious, easily selected as possible right answers. Poor multiple choice questions include one right answer and several others which students immediately know aren't correct. These don't check understanding; they prompt and remind. Because planning time is important and you don't want to waste it, spending hours conjuring close but wrong answers isn't worth it. When you can't think of important misconceptions you want to check, plan some questions that all students can answer or a task that helps you to check understanding before moving on.

Monitoring

James is in his first year as a secondary science teacher. He's doing well but his classes can be a bit chatty, particularly in the freer, more independent sections of his lessons. He models and explains concepts clearly and concisely. He explains tasks with precision. He starts his tasks with a clear 'Off you go'. Students start putting their hands up. First one and then a small flurry. James dutifully begins his way around the room. He does what most teachers do as they move around the room: he helps where he needs to, he manages behaviour, and he cajoles students into working when they lose the energy for it.

There are two problems. Firstly, something has gone wrong in the set-up of the task. Either students weren't ready for it – and a hinge question or mini-whiteboards could have been used to better effect – or students have learned helplessness: they know they can switch off in the explanation because James will be there to help them. Secondly, James isn't checking for understanding. He isn't really gathering knowledge. He's firefighting.

What does James need to do? Firstly, he needs to sort out that transition into the task, embedding a clear check that shows students are ready. Secondly, he needs to make clear what support is available to students. Can they use a textbook or another resource in the room? Can they turn back in their exercise books or talk to their partners? Can they move on if they're stuck? Students need to be told. Finally, James can tell the class that no student will put their hand up in the first five minutes of the task (other timeframes are available). This might feel brave or cruel or stupid but hands up after you've explained a task, checked they've understood and signposted support suggest overreliance on the teacher.

To start with, James will stand at a point in the room where he can see the class well.[4] He'll stay there, watching, gently gesturing for students to lower their hands when raised. If students aren't following instructions, James will stop the class and bring their attention back to the front. For example, if he's asked for silence but isn't getting it, that's an opportunity to reiterate expectations to the whole class. Alternatively, if students aren't using one of the sources of help available and this is causing lots to struggle, it might be time to bring the class back together to remind them how to get unstuck.

After the class are clearly settled – possibly after a long couple of minutes – James can set out into the room. No longer is James setting off to sort out all the issues that need to be resolved. Now, he's looking for something precise – whatever content or skill the students are using, practising or describing. Doug Lemov describes this as *naming the lap*[5] because we're doing a lap of the classroom with a specific purpose.

I find it helpful to step out into the classroom saying, 'When I come round, I'm looking for...' and sticking rigidly to this. End the sentence with something specific. *I'm looking for finger spaces. I want to see answers to one decimal place. I want to see the word 'significant' in your first two sentences.* Getting sucked into a conversation about something else, correcting every mistake you see, or debating how soon after break it is acceptable to need the toilet will stop you gathering any useful information.

Some practical tips about monitoring:

- When planning, note down specifically what you're monitoring for in all independent activities. Link these moments in your lesson to the success criteria, curriculum content or objective of your lesson.

- If you see a mistake across several students' work, don't make a note to deal with it later. Deal with it now. Stop the class and explain, *A few students are... I've seen the answer... There's some confusion over what to do when...* Or take a book to the visualiser and ask what's wrong. Go through the example.

- Take round a notebook or a mini-whiteboard (or something to take photos with) and capture the best answers, the common errors, and the students who are struggling. This process can work without recording what you see but you're liable to forget something important or someone who needs your help.

Exit tickets

An exit ticket is what it sounds like: a task students do before they go to show you they understand. Generally, these are done on paper so that they can be gathered, checked and organised efficiently. In *Responsive Teaching*, Harry Fletcher-Wood describes three qualities of effective exit tickets. Firstly, they should 'permit valid inferences about students' learning'. Whatever the task, it should allow you to 'differentiate accurately between levels of understanding' whilst throwing out potential misconceptions. Secondly, exit tickets 'provide useful data'. Too often, teachers design tasks that provide too much data. If a lesson should have a clear focus so should the exit ticket. Thirdly, exit tickets should 'be focused'. They should be 'swift to answer' and 'swift to mark'.[6] Paragraphs and 12-mark questions don't make good exit tickets because they don't quickly demonstrate knowledge that can be quickly assessed.

Exit tickets then should act like hinge questions at the end of the lesson. We might have been adding fractions, describing circuits, explaining why sweatshops exist or evaluating the key features of a particular artwork. For any topic, the exit ticket should bring to the fore the key element we hope students will take away. They can be open – *list three features of...* – or multiple choice – *which of the following is correct...* – or complete the sentence activities. Have the students – as best as you can tell from a short task or small number of questions – got what you wanted them to? Remember, that students can do something at the end of the lesson is not a guarantee that they will be able to do it next lesson. However, when students *can't* do (or don't understand) something at the end of the lesson, we can be fairly sure that they won't be able to do it next time. As we pore over the exit tickets, we see the success and the failure of our teaching. Just knowing about this is not enough. We have to do something. We have to respond.

Respond

Sarah describes responding to student misconceptions.

I'm teaching electricity. I had to brush up on it and do my own research. Our curriculum gives us specific objectives to meet and some slides from previous teachers. And you still have to adapt that curriculum to your children and your class. I had to brush up on potential misconceptions students have about electricity. For example, you don't need a switch to work a circuit. A lot of children, when we started the unit, thought you had to have a switch to work a circuit but you don't. It's about finding their misconceptions and addressing them as you teach.

Adaptation is hard because it requires in the moment changes to what we had planned. Teaching, as we've seen, is a chain of intentionally or unintentionally automated processes. To check students' understanding, the chain must be broken. Intending to respond is unlikely to yield results. Instead, to begin with at least, we should have some additional tasks, questions or activities ready where we think students might need them.

Knowing that some haven't got it, knowing that we need to respond – even these aren't enough. What form should our response take? Options include everything from stopping the class and re-teaching a topic right down to catching up with a single student when you have a moment.

Individual or small group support

Sarah describes how she works with small groups of students to support them.

I tend to work with the lowest of ability and EAL children at the front of my classroom. I know everyone doesn't do that but I like to do that because I was a TA and I know those children need the most support from the teacher. I'll be honest, it can be draining sometimes. With a lot of the children, it's vocabulary that they're really struggling with. It's not that they don't understand all the work. It's that they don't understand the words and the sentences and the phrases we use – the language that goes with the work.

All students start off on the same thing but some children might need scaffolds, some need extra discussion. The four children sat with me just need some extra support, sometimes re-teaching or covering content in more detail.

If only a handful of students haven't got it in the hinge question or exit ticket, stopping the class or re-teaching may not be an option. Instead offer individual or small group support.

Think about the practicalities:

- If there are students you regularly need to support, seat them somewhere that is accessible for you. This may not be the front. At the back, you can watch the class and work quietly with a small group.

- Keep checking, even with one or two students. Ask them questions or use the mini-whiteboard. Don't just re-explain and ask if they've got it. Eventually, they'll say they've got it just to get rid of you.

At times, students will need to see the same principles borne out across different tasks. In Maths, do the same task but change the numbers. In English or History, change the question but focus on the same content. In Art or Design, keep the same process but change the purpose.

More questions or tasks

Perhaps just one more. In your planning, it's worth having a spare activity or set of questions at the hinge points in the lesson. If lots of the class don't get it when you're monitoring, explain or model once more and set the class off on some additional questions.

Future planning

Some errors can't be picked up in the moment because it's the end of the lesson, because they're big, or because they're subtle and need a bit more work to unpick. Use your planner, notebook or resources to track larger errors you want to come back to. It may be that the term is ending and you know they'll need *this* in the next topic. Figure out what *this* is; narrow it down.

A note on whole class feedback

There's no section on marking in this book. I don't want you to waste your time. When I was a new teacher, I basically ignored the school marking policy. I did mark my books but not with the frequency and detail that were expected. The policy itself felt cruel and unusual to me and I was surprised to watch teachers, all with more experience than me, bow thoughtlessly to its demands. No one checked the policy was being implemented and I was frequently told I was doing a good job. This is a cautionary tale rather than a recommendation. I could have got in trouble but perhaps we all knew – particularly leaders – that deep down the policy expected too much.

Marking in its most excessive forms seems to be on the way out. To be clear, it's not that marking doesn't have an impact. Of course, it can. When done effectively, you're basically offering one to one tuition. But this is far from an effective use of your time. Save it for assessments and mock exams or questions. Many schools have adapted marking policies into feedback policies, calling on whole class feedback to save them from workload and, hopefully, support learning. Because whole class feedback means different things to different schools, it's impossible to say what your school will mean when they say *whole class feedback*.

It might involve filling in a particular sheet or booklet. It might not. It might involve feedback lessons, where students write the title 'Feedback Lesson' so that everyone – particularly visitors – knows that 'Feedback Lessons' have taken place. It might not. It might involve purple polishers (other colours are available) or other editing. It might not.

What then are the common principles or activities of whole class feedback? First, we examine and record:

- Look at all or a sample of the books. Ask students to hand in books open on the page they've been working on. That way you can quickly go through them.

- Focus on and make note of the general – spelling errors, previously taught material – and the specific – what was being taught in that lesson.

● Make a note of specific students who need support.

● Make a note of students whose work can exemplify success.

Second, we plan:

● If lessons start regularly with review, plan questions that will practice weaker areas. Add words to spelling tests.

● If the task allows, plan some prompted editing of the work. You can set this up in different ways, telling students what to look for or modelling with a piece of work from the class.

● Plan your links to future content, making sure you properly prepare students by reviewing what they've got wrong or misunderstood.

● Plan in the medium and long term. Make a note or set a reminder to revisit a topic or aspects of it where your checks reveal potentially shaky understanding.

● Alternatively, you can plan a single lesson where students practise spelling, complete editing and any additional tasks. You can use these times to repeat models and explanations.

In summary

All that subject knowledge, all that knowledge of pedagogy and how students learn will have been for nothing unless we respond to what we're seeing in the moment, from our students. A well-planned curriculum, however we come by it, will be meaningless if we just plough on regardless of what students are understanding or misunderstanding, regardless of the mistakes and misconceptions they're embedding. Knowledge of students is dynamic because it requires constant attention. We don't just update this knowledge as we teach new students; we update it as our current students grow and develop.

Kate, a secondary Maths trainee, describes how she gathered and used information about what her classes know and can do.

It's checking in with them. It's checking their books. We use end of topic tests to say that's where we stood at the end of something. The results of those don't always feed into something immediately. Because Maths can be very topic focused, I find it hard to bring what I've found out about what they know and can do into the next half-term. Instead, I try and focus on their confidence. Because a student can think they don't like Maths anymore because we've done a few weeks on algebra.

Possible next steps

1. **Develop a checking habit.** To start with, you're just making sure not to breeze through a lesson without pausing to glance at the students and see if they're keeping up. Creating a hands-down habit here is positive and can be used in pretty much every lesson, phase or subject. If you arrive in a department where mini-whiteboards are embedded, using them yourself won't feel difficult. Write 'hands-down' on the whiteboard, on a wall at the back of your room. Or remove the friction from using mini-whiteboards by setting up boxes for each row with rubbers, pens and boards. The habit is not simply borne of a section in your plan or a check in your resources. It emerges from the way you force it into your practice with unmissable reminders and quick wins.

2. **Plan to respond in advance.** It's no good in the moment realising that students don't understand but having nothing for them to do. Have some extra tasks in the textbook ready. Change the numbers in a Maths question but keep the process. When you make this part of your plan, you make it more likely that you will actually respond to knowledge gained about student understanding. When good intentions are left to drive your in-lesson adaptation, it's more likely such adaptation won't happen.

Notes

1 Wiliam, D., and Black, P. (1998). *Inside the Black Box – Raising Standards through Classroom Assessment.* https://kappanonline.org/inside-the-black-box-raising-standards-through-classroom-assessment (accessed 22/11/2022).
2 Ibid.
3 Wiliam, D. (2018). *Embedding Formative Assessment.* Solution Tree Press.
4 Doug Lemov describes this technique as Pastore's Perch in Lemov, D. (2010). *Teach Like a Champion.* Jossey-Bass.
5 Lemov, D. (2010). *Teach Like a Champion.* Jossey-Bass.
6 Fletcher-Wood, H. (2018). *Responsive Teaching.* Routledge.

What are the limits of what we can know about students?

> **Kate, a secondary Maths trainee, describes how she started to put her students into categories.**
>
> I fell into a little bit of a habit of thinking, *The class (or the student) didn't really understand that so they won't really understand this.* It's really easy to categorise a student when you're meeting 80 of them in a day. I had to really check myself on the thought process that said, *they won't understand this because they didn't understand that.*

In Greek mythology, Pygmalion was a sculptor who fell in love with one of his statues and was blessed by Aphrodite when she brought the sculpture to life. Pygmalion's expectation became reality. There's more to the story: as you'd expect from Greek mythology Pygmalion's behaviour is strange to say the least. Pygmalion is important to us because of the effect named after him. The Pygmalion Effect is the phenomenon where high expectations of an individual lead to high performance. Its opposite is the Golem Effect where low expectations lead to low performance. Like a self-fulfilling prophecy, we get what we expect to get.

So far, we've looked at ways we can build knowledge to solve the problems of the classroom. That is still our aim. Now, however, we need to admit that our knowledge can be flawed; we need to admit that sometimes our assumptions, biases and expectations masquerade as knowledge. The knowledgeable teacher needs to be able to step back from what they believe to be true about their teaching and assess it dispassionately. Nowhere is this more true than in the judgements we make of our students.

What does the evidence say about our expectations of students?

In the mid-sixties, Rosenthal and Jacobson conducted a now famous experiment. They told a group of teachers that certain students in their classes were 'growth spurters', children who looked average now but would make rapid progress through

 DOI: 10.4324/9781003281306-23

the year. Those identified as 'growth spurters' were chosen at random. Rosenthal and Jacobson came back at the end of the year, keen to know whether a change in teacher expectation would lead to a change in outcome for students. They found that 'When teachers expected that certain children would show greater intellectual development, those children did show greater intellectual development'.[1]

There were caveats. The Pygmalion Effect was more pronounced with younger children. All students made progress and the gap between 'growth spurters' and 'non-growth spurters' was relatively small. These caveats have led one modern summary of the Pygmalion research to conclude that 'self-fulfilling prophecies in the classroom do exist, but they are generally small, fragile, and fleeting'.[2] Is Pygmalion or similar research worth our time if the effects of such expectations may be small or fragile?

To answer that question, we need to acknowledge Pygmalion isn't the end of the story, or the research. Various studies inform us that teachers form biases of students based on prior attainment, personal characteristics, socio-economic status, ethnicity, gender, SEND and even physical appearance.[3] When we read research like this, we mustn't think *This doesn't apply to me because I'm a good person*. We don't hold biased views because we're bad people. We hold biased views because we're human. I don't know which biases you'll hold and you might not either. The point of this chapter is not to fixate on the fact that we are biased individuals. The point is to ensure that neither bias nor assumption affect how we teach the different students we find in front of us. The point is to interrupt a cycle of behaviour that goes something like this:

1. We form or hold inaccurate judgements of students.

2. We behave differently with different students, for example in interactions in lessons.

3. Students notice different treatment of themselves or others. Students were able to observe the differing treatment of different students in a videotaped lesson, even when the lesson they were watching was in a different language.[4]

How do schools treat different groups of students?

None of this is ground-breaking. We're talking about research harking back to a study almost 70 years old. In England, schools have had to shoulder more and more of the responsibility for the gaps between groups of students – boys and the disadvantaged are perennially behind. Gap hysteria follows, a frenzied search for action to *do something* about the gap. In one meeting, a deputy head asked us to list our disadvantaged students from memory. We chanted the names to our partner like some hopeless prayer, all the more hopeless when we realised we'd forgotten several.

Schools try all manner of strange and desperate things to improve the outcomes for problem groups. Unthinkingly defining or perceiving a whole group of students to be a problem *is* a problem. Unfortunately, lots of schools have no idea what to do and a bizarre raft of unhelpful suggestions refuses to die. In the past – hopefully well into the past – teachers have been told to mark the books of their disadvantaged students first (or whoever's doing badly that term). Consider two assumptions this suggestion makes about marking: *number one*, marking potentially can have a huge impact on learning *and number two*, quality of marking dramatically deteriorates the longer you spend doing it. Unless you're playing some kind of marking drinking game neither assumption is true.

Other strategies for dealing with disadvantaged students in the classroom reach at something equally ephemeral: sit them at the front, ask them lots of questions, spend more time with them in lessons. Some of these might help but often they are suggested before we've assessed the particular challenges of *this* disadvantaged student, or whether the student is actually struggling to begin with.

By paying lip-service to groups of students and gaps between them, teachers and schools can entrench biases instead of toppling them. The teachers of the 'growth spurters' in the Pygmalion experiment didn't do things differently with their students, at least not consciously. They believed different things about these students and this shaped their actions. Until we can understand and alter our beliefs about students, we need to make sure that we treat students equitably in the classroom.

For the rest of this chapter, we'll examine three research-based areas[5] where these biases can affect our teaching and what we can practically do about it. As has been mentioned already, our aim is to build knowledge to improve our mental models of classroom practice. Our three areas are:

1. Explanations.

2. Questions.

3. Feedback.

For each area, we'll look at ways we can diagnose potential biases and what we can do to improve. We'll first diagnose whether this is an area to focus on for you before turning to how we can improve. As you work through the diagnosis activities, you might find these things are not a problem for you. If so, great – move on to the next section. Every child deserves equal treatment in our classrooms. Good intentions are not enough. We need to better understand our own classroom behaviour. Only then can we transform what we offer to all children.

Explanation

Recent research has shown that where teachers have low expectations of students, explanations of concepts are watered down or key ideas are ignored entirely.[6] If, over time, explanations are weakened because we believe – implicitly or explicitly – that students can't handle them, those students pass through a dog-eared curriculum, hollowed out by low expectation.

Diagnosis

How would we know if our explanations to students have been altered by our expectation of them? Unless you teach the same thing twice to two different groups, it's difficult to tell if your explanations change for different students. You might just know that with a particular group – because of your perception of their ability or behaviour or something else – you aren't giving them a full taste of the curriculum. Even then it can be hard to tell what changes about your explanation or why those changes take place. This is complicated further by the variety of explanations you give in a single lesson: from the front, to individuals, to groups or tables. Where you're unsure whether this is a problem, the following strategies give you a way of checking.

Measure your explanations against clear criteria

Often, these criteria will be found in the curriculum you're teaching from. It might be co-constructed across subject or phase teams. When introducing a new or significant concept, create a checklist or script for an explanation. A checklist is your way of ensuring your expertise and the expertise of those who've planned the curriculum makes its way into the classroom. You won't always need it but don't shirk it to begin with.

Record your explanations

If you have a checklist, you'll want to know it's working. You can do this yourself by recording an explanation and comparing. An observation works just as well as long as the observer knows what you're trying to achieve. A recording won't lie or misremember so, however awkward it might feel to listen back, you can check you cover what you intend to.

A problem with recording is that we'll often capture from-the-front explanations, potentially missing the one-to-one interactions around the room. You don't just explain to the whole class. So many of your interactions are you explaining and re-explaining content to children around the class.

Improvement

Improving our explanations is something we should be trying to do anyway. With our knowledge of subject, with our knowledge of pedagogy and cognitive load, we fine tune, clarify and foreground helpful detail in our explanations. To think back to progressive problem solving, the first problem we face is managing the class whilst we explain simple concepts. Once mastered, we can move on to explaining more complex material or we can more expertly use a combination of explanation and visual aid.

Plan together

Simply making explanations more complex it not our aim. Pitching an explanation at the right level is a vital part. Colleagues you work with have valuable knowledge of subject but also how students misunderstand the subject. Asking *What are these children capable of understanding?* is a difficult question for a new teacher (and one that takes us back to our knowledge of curriculum). Work with others – mentor, trainer, colleague – to seek to understand what should go into your explanation. At times, working with a teacher *just* ahead of you is more helpful as they will be able to point to recent mistakes and lessons learned.

Check they're ready for the explanation

When we *activate prior knowledge* we make it more likely that students will learn the new content. Knowledge connects; understanding builds. Skills link together, cumulatively creating a chain of processes that make up competent activity. Assumptions encourage us into ineffective practices, where we believe they know it because we taught it. Before you explain, check. Check they remember and understand what the explanation will build upon.

Ways to check include:

● Hands-down questioning – Who is the barometer for knowing if the majority of the class will have got something? Ask them. You don't need to ask the student who struggles and will need additional support. Give that afterwards. Ask the student who *might* get it but might not. Preferably, ask a few students like that. Hands-down questioning is a must for any classroom. You don't find out what they know without asking them. This can be done sensitively and carefully, never being used to catch a student who wasn't listening. But there is a problem with it: even at your most efficient, you can only ask a handful of students at a time.

● Mini-whiteboards – Remember, you're checking the students are ready for an explanation; this isn't practice or extended independence. You might check vocabulary, answers to quick questions, solutions to problems but you could also ask for sentences or Completion Problems. The point of mini-whiteboards is not that you must study every single answer. You can't. Mini-whiteboards force everyone to think and give you an opportunity to check a sample. Where students sit becomes important, with those you want to read necessarily sitting where you can see their board.

- Quiz – Like a set of mini-whiteboards a quiz involves everyone. It just takes a bit longer. To get to the kind of information we need, we have to step out into the class and observe students answering the questions. Pre-empt the slow process of back and forth feedback by looking at the answers as they appear. Visit students you expect much of and students you think might struggle. Observe without judgement. An alternative to quizzing for a practical subject is a process check. Set up the shooting drill the class seemed to master last time and see if they've retained what you taught.

Checks before and after the explanation should be followed by adapted or additional tasks. Return to Chapter 15 for more on gathering knowledge of what students know and can do and what to do when we find out.

Assess the success of your explanations

It's no good thinking, *I've explained it so they must understand it.* Immediate checks through task design help us to see whether students have got it. Returning to the content of the explanation a week or month later helps us to see whether they've retained it. Cultivate a set of strategies that can, as accurately as is possible, let you know what students have understood. The same strategies that helped you check students were ready for the explanation will help to check if they've understood it: hands-down questions, whiteboards, quizzes.

Practise

If we want an explanation to be pitch-perfect every time, it's worth practising it until it becomes automatic. Other steps have been taken: careful planning, collaboration with others, a prepped pre-explanation check. Practice ensures the explanation lands well. Say it out loud to your empty classroom, record and listen back on your phone or, perhaps preferably, share what you're planning with a mentor or colleague. Don't panic when it's not perfect but consider how to make it clearer.

Questions

Teachers are likely to ask more and more complex questions of those of whom they have high expectations.[7] This is unsurprising but troubling. If the students you expect great things for are the students who answer the bulk of the questions in your classroom, who benefits? Those we have lower expectations of won't become more knowledgeable by osmosis. They need to be held accountable for their learning, asked to articulate it and expected to retrieve what they've learned regularly.

Diagnosis

Diagnosing your questioning habits is about looking at who you ask questions to and what kinds of questions you ask. Legitimate choices can be made about using certain questions to challenge whilst using others to check knowledge. Closed questions aren't bad. Open questions aren't good. Both are needed and we will vary them depending on need. The purpose of this section is not to make sure you ask everyone similar questions.

Teachers are likely to ask more questions of the students they expect to know the answers. This is unlikely to be a conscious decision: sometimes we go to the ones with hands up or go to the student we know will answer correctly. We can't observe something, particularly one of our own behaviours, without changing it, perhaps subconsciously. If we decide to tally up who we ask questions to in a lesson and who gets to respond – either hands up or hands down – it's likely we'll start to change who we ask, no bad thing. The tally will poke holes in regular patterns of behaviour. A visitor to your lesson will spot these patterns too. A tally is just the start. Drill down into the process and a rich seam of self-knowledge emerges. Who is asked a follow up question? Who has to justify their ideas? Who is held to account when they say 'I don't know' and who is let off the hook?

Whilst you might start by getting someone in to tell you this, their job and yours is to bring this hidden knowledge into the light. Self-awareness is the aim.

Improvement

A tally doesn't tell you what kinds of questions you ask and to which students. *Who is asked* and *how much* are only the first questions in our reflective investigation. Teachers tend to ask more challenging questions to those students they expect more of, meaning certain students or types of students are in danger of being asked basic questions or none at all. Our questions communicate our expectations and students are likely to understand this better than us.

Now, there isn't a *good* type of question. Teachers are unhelpfully funnelled towards 'higher order'[8] thinking and 'higher order' questions, largely because 'higher order' sounds good. Lower order questions express what feels like a low expectation: to remember. Higher order questions demand students evaluate and synthesise and create. Reality, unfortunately, doesn't work like this. Students need the remembering to do the evaluating. They need the lower to achieve the higher. Furthermore, certain *What* questions are more challenging than some *How* questions. It's sometimes more difficult to explain than it is to create because it depends what you're explaining and what you're creating. Content should dictate questions. Questions, or types of questions, shouldn't be decided upon before we've pinned down what it is we're teaching.

My point, laboured thought it may be, is not that you have to ask a certain type of question to all students or even to the students you neglect to ask questions as revealed by a tally. Improving the questions you ask is not just about making them more difficult. Improving your questions is about asking the right people the right questions, an incredibly complex task you can spend a career perfecting.

Let's turn to three ways we can improve on what we've found in our questions.

Plan your questions

If you know you don't ask particular students, or if you know you don't ask particular students a particular kind of question, plan to ask them. Write it in your planner. Scribble their name on a post-it. Or take a seating plan and tick names as you ask the questions.

Improve pace by avoiding repetition

New teachers quickly stumble into a habit with questions that can linger for entire careers. A student answers a question; the teacher repeats and rephrases the answer. Sometimes we do this to praise what we're hearing. Often, we do what Doug Lemov calls 'rounding-up': adding what is lacking to a student's response in our summary of it. A student gives a partial answer. We complete it and praise them for giving it. They go away embedding incomplete or misconceived knowledge.

When a student answers a question, you have several options:

- Say *Thank you* and move on or ask someone else.

- Ask a follow up question. *Why do you say that? How do you know that?*

- Give specific praise: *Your use of our subject terminology was really strong in that answer. You explained that concept really clearly.*

Each of these options is dependent on the context and the question but each of them is better than repeating and rephrasing the answer.

Ask questions everyone answers

Mini-whiteboards are equitable because everyone answers every question. A powerful message is sent to the class: *You all can, and you all must engage with this.* Use them regularly and you stop seeing certain students as 'difficult to ask' or 'unlikely to know'. They both reveal who doesn't yet know whilst expecting everyone to attempt.

Mini-whiteboards might not always be available (ask your school if you want to use them but don't have any). Even without mini-whiteboards, you can and should plan questions that all students answer. These might be your hinge questions or a call and response involving everyone. Students can indicate an answer by holding up a number of fingers.

Feedback

Teachers tend to be quicker to reprimand low expectation students. Levels of detail in feedback also contrast between high and low expectation students. When a teacher has high expectations of a student, that student is more likely to be on the receiving end of feedback tied to content and skill. Where belief in the student's abilities is low, the student can expect minimal feedback on performance, with the attention focused on attitude and behaviour. This can be true even when a teacher is impressed with a low-expectation student. When we're surprised by a student's performance, there's a danger we hold back further developmental feedback because we're amazed they made it this far. They deserve some recognition… and then a break. In doing so, we put on hold the progress which is possible for them.

Diagnosis

If you've recently marked some assessments or books, you've got an insight into the kinds of comments students in your class get. Having done this with my classes in the past, I noticed some patterns emerging. Some students would get insight and questions, paragraphs and partial editing. Others got, 'WHY HAVE YOU LEFT THIS SPACE IN YOUR BOOK?' and 'Not enough completed'. The comments did nothing to help them and at times weren't remotely concerned with what they were learning. Consider the experience of those two sets of children. The former get a rich diet of correction, suggestion and encouragement. The latter get the message they aren't doing anything right.

Now, I do very little marking of books but the dangers are exactly the same. One student will have a totally different experience of your classroom to a different student sitting on the same row. You're walking around the room. At one student, Rheanne, you stop, congratulate her on recent homework or test result and check their work. Every question has been answered correctly. For the next questions, you give Rheanne the challenge to answer using some key words from the glossary that haven't been introduced yet. You keep walking and stop at another student, Ben. Ben finds your lessons challenging. He's picking at the corner of his page. The title has been scruffily written. The first task has been attempted but the ones after that are left blank. Ben gets a gentle lecture about making an effort and asking if he's stuck. You add some comments about presentation and move on.

As above, filming or recording your teaching might give you some insight into the differences in the way you talk to different students around the room. A supportive observer could create a record of this as well. The point is not so much to identify the students you only ever berate or chide. The point is to notice the differences in how you give feedback and what feedback is given. Of course, noticing is not enough. We have to do something about it.

Improvement

Set them up for success

If a student or several students regularly get reprimanded for effort or presentation rather than on the content they are learning, what have you done to pre-empt it? We set students up for success when there is absolute clarity of expectation and certainty of challenge when these expectations are not met. We set them up for success when support is readily available in whatever form will ensure students are on task and learning in our lessons.

Make expectations clear by:

- Explaining where a task will be completed. *Everyone will write on the sheet… This should be completed right underneath your title…*

- Explain the task as clearly and concisely as possible. *You will complete questions 1 to 5 and then close your book to show you're finished. Write the paragraph we've just planned on the board. Complete your technical drawing.*

- Explain the behaviour expectation for the task. *This will be completed in silence. You can talk only to the person next to you.*

Challenge students early by:

- Standing at the front and scanning the room. An observer once told me I was missing things around the room. As I got drawn into conversations and tried to help, even as I spoke to the whole class, I missed the fact students weren't listening or had drifted off task. Now, to check I've got attention or everyone on a task, I try to look at every face in the room deliberately. It's easy to wave your head around the room and believe students are *on task*. It's harder to look at every face and fail to notice when students are *off-task*. You shouldn't be surprised when a student isn't completing a task. You should know already.

- Where students clearly aren't engaging with the task, prompt either non-verbally – preferable at first – or verbally with a name. Point to the work, the task or the support available. The aim is that all students are working. We know this doesn't guarantee learning but it makes it more likely. Widespread work also means you'll have more to feedback on than a failure to engage with the task.

Offer support by:

- Signposting help given. *Remember you have the example we created in your books/on the board. Use the sentence starters as you work through your plan. Talk quietly to the person next to you if you have a question.*

● Remind them of these sources of help. *Some people look like they're stuck but I can't hear conversations about the questions we're stuck on. Some people have struggled on the third question but I'm not seeing students go back through their books to look at our notes on this topic.*

What's this got to do with feedback? Thinking about how you introduce a task can feel removed from feeding back. But setting it up right ensures feedback opportunities during the task. When you move around the room, you want to be able to give specific, learning-focused feedback. You can't do this if students have, wilfully or otherwise, misunderstood the task or aren't engaged with it.

Multiply learning feedback

We can't always escape telling Ben he needs to improve presentation or get on with things. What we must remember is that Ben *also* needs feedback on what he is learning. Stay with him and give two bits of feedback on what he has done already that are specifically and only about what he is learning. Or, particularly when the work is missing entirely, ask Ben questions to reveal what he does know. Give feedback specifically on the answers. The feedback should outweigh the reprimand.

At times, where students just don't want to engage, the behaviour system must be used to communicate that disengagement or opting out are not acceptable.

Blind marking

Ultimately, eliminating bias may require us to give feedback without knowing who the feedback is going to. Clearly, this is only possible for work we're taking in. For exams, essays and assessments, blind marking gives you insight into your expectations. Many students will live up or down to these expectations. The student you thought might struggle does. The student who knew it all before you taught them gets full marks.

Blind marking forces you to confront these assumptions and expectations. It works both ways: pleasant surprises from those you thought would struggle and reality checks for those you thought had already mastered it. Get students to write names on the back of assessments or exit tickets when you take them in. Or ask for books to be handed in to you open on the page you're looking at.

I expected nothing of one of the hardest GCSE classes I'd ever taught. I had been appointed Head of English and gave myself a class I knew would be difficult. There were only ten students. Half were impossible; the other half I just felt sorry for. I thought I could handle them but every lesson descended into chaos. A student took phone calls and texted from the back of the room. Others made crude jokes, watching eagerly for my reaction. They arrived late and left whenever they felt like it. To look at some students' books, you'd think we'd not had any lessons all year.

I gave so many lectures about how they would fail without work, without change. It's not that they disagreed; they just shrugged it off.

Unsurprisingly, on results day, those students who hadn't worked all year did quite badly. At least one of them expressed regret at how he'd behaved. The rest weren't bothered. But with the half of the class who turned up each lesson and quietly persevered, something strange had happened. They'd done quite well. Or, rather, they had done much better than I'd expected. And that's when I realised my expectations of the class had been so incredibly low. I'd checked out when I realised every lesson would be a struggle. Rather than seeing the positive results for some as a success, I wonder what they could have achieved if I'd expected anything of them. One quiet, diligent student who'd passed – a minor miracle – came up to me. He said 'thank you' which made me feel terrible and then offered the cliché, 'Hard work, sir. It pays off'.

Often students will meet your expectations. Although it does happen, it's rare to be totally surprised by what a student achieves. It's also hard to change your mind about a student. It takes time. Our aim *should* be high expectations of all. Until we change those expectations, the least we can do is to ensure the same behaviour towards all. This is an ongoing battle to achieve parity of curriculum and treatment for all students in every lesson.

Alex, a secondary English trainee, describes having his expectations of different classes challenged.

One of my Year 7 classes are a lower set and I was warned about the capability and behaviour of the group. But I've never had to give a consequence or had much trouble from them. But I have a top set Year 8 class, which had a reputation for being really good, and I often very much struggle with them. You have to be adaptive with your approach. There's no one size fits all solution.

In summary

Knowledge of what students know and can do is essential for the adaptation of our teaching. We adapt so that our lessons meet students where they actually are, rather than where we assume they are. Checks for understanding force information out of students. Learning happens over time; we can't guarantee students who demonstrate competence now will do so in the future. But students who *don't* understand now are unlikely to magic understanding from somewhere just in time for our next lesson. Checks are important but so is our response. Free yourself from limiting a check to a specific timeframe in the lesson. Prepare to spend time embedding or re-teaching what students haven't got.

All this talk of knowledge of students comes with a caveat. We know in part. Sometimes we don't know at all. We assume. Humans are biased by nature. I've not offered a way to get around that quirk in our humanity. Instead, I've offered some areas of your teaching that may be affected by bias and what we can do about it. We go upstream of a problem – perhaps watered down explanations – and make sure that doesn't happen in our lesson for *any* student. When we do that, we start to communicate that we have high expectations for all even when we don't.

Possible next steps

1. **Diagnose potential problems.** We aren't really diagnosing our biases. We're diagnosing the potential effects of those biases. Search out the knowledge of how your behaviour changes for different students or groups of students. Record a lesson. Ask an observer to look directly at your questions or the feedback you give to students. Accept the findings of these observations and consider the problems they throw up and the solutions at your disposal.

2. **Put one safeguard in place.** Mini-whiteboard tasks or questions to all communicate an expectation: everyone has to engage here. A tally of questions makes obvious that which we can ignore: I don't ask questions of everyone. A scripted and practised explanation makes it more likely all students have access to the same content. Do one thing that helps you to avoid the potential problems of your biases.

Notes

1 Rosenthal, R., and Jacobson, L. (1968). Pygmalion in the classroom. *The Urban Review*, 16–20.
2 Jussim, L., and Harber, K. (2005). Teacher expectations and self-fulfilling prophecies: Knowns and unknowns, resolved and unresolved controversies. *Personality and Social Psychology Review*, 9(2), 131–155.
3 The following studies note these biases in teachers:

De Boer, H., Timmermans, A., and Van Der Werf, M. (2018). The effects of teacher expectation interventions on teachers' expectations and student achievement: Narrative review and meta-analysis. *Educational Research and Evaluation*, 24, 3–5.
Gentrup, S., Lorenz, G., Kristen, C., and Kogan, I. (2020). Self-fulfilling prophecies in the classroom: Teacher expectations, teacher feedback and student achievement. *Learning and Instruction*, 66, 101296.
Wang, S., Rubie-Davies, C.M., and Meissel, K. (2018). A systematic review of the teacher expectation literature over the past 30 years. *Educational Research and Evaluation*, 24(3–5), 124–179.
4 Wang, S., Rubie-Davies, C.M., and Meissel, K. (2018). A systematic review of the teacher expectation literature over the past 30 years. *Educational Research and Evaluation*, 24(3–5), 124–179.
5 All are found in: Gentrup, S., Lorenz, G., Kristen, C., and Kogan, I. (2020). Self-fulfilling prophecies in the classroom: Teacher expectations, teacher feedback and student achievement. *Learning and Instruction*, 66, 101296.

6 Ibid.
7 Ibid.
8 Sometimes using Benjamin Bloom's taxonomy in a triangular version Bloom didn't create.

Further reading

Fletcher-Wood, H. (2018). *Responsive Teaching*. Routledge.

17 What do I do now?

Each section of this book ends with possible next steps. Let's be honest, it's not possible to implement all of those in one go. Even successfully implementing a handful will take time, effort and energy. One of the weird things about reading a teaching book is that the book doesn't make you a better teacher. Reading a book can give you a growing confidence that you know your stuff, that you understand what others don't, that you're grappling with the big ideas in your profession. It's not that those things aren't true. They probably are. But if nothing changes, no improvement has been made. Books which feel transformative often aren't because the feeling dissipates and leaves nothing tangible.

Teaching is a battle ranging between two sides. On one, your accumulated knowledge – your mental models of teaching and learning and subject and students. On the other, the challenges and problems of the classroom – students need to understand and behave, we need to elicit and evaluate thinking and learning. The battle exists for every teacher but how you approach it will be shaped by your personality and preferences. Mary Kennedy's final persistent challenge of teaching is to address all the challenges of teaching whilst accommodating your 'personal needs'.[1]

I don't know you. I don't know how you've arrived in teaching or what you've found difficult or straightforward. I don't know the challenges or problems that you currently face. There is a gap, then, between the book you're reading and the solutions you need, a gap that can only be filled by your thinking with the support of those around you.

In this final chapter, we'll look at some principles and strategies that can make sure that thinking takes place. These are:

1. Manage your time to make room for progressive problem solving.

2. Work with your coach to create mental models.

3. Develop a habit of identifying problems and searching for solutions.

4. But perfection is not possible.

 DOI: 10.4324/9781003281306-24

Everything listed here is attempting to marry the thinking we've done in the sections of this book with where you are right now.

Manage your time

> **Annalise, a trainee Science teacher, describes her experience of time management.**
>
> Time management has been very difficult, particularly the material to engage with outside of the 'job' of teaching. Having assignments and twilight sessions, while trying to engage with content to understand ideas to explain them, has been quite the juggle. I have adjusted to early mornings to set up my days. I stay in school to get work, such as planning, done. I have gained a new skill in using To Do lists, something I had not done previously. But, most importantly, leaving my work at the door when I leave as best as I can in the evening. Although I might work until 6 pm on a long day, if my laptop is left in school I cannot work on anything else at home, so I am not tempted to 'just pick up a few bits'.

Time management strategies are a bit of a con, particularly for teachers. You can't manage time you don't control, but we need to use the time we have to focus on those high-leverage activities that will help us to improve:

- Growing knowledge.

- Automating process.

- And out of these activities, creating mental models that help us to think, act and solve problems.

To manage your time, the following activities may help.

1. Make a list. Put everything on it.
   Everything means everything. Lessons to plan. Resource making. Phone calls home. Prep for meetings. Replying to emails. Practice of classroom behaviours. This could be a real, physical list or tech-based equivalent. Mine is a Word document with everything I need to do on it.
      Tasks on the To Do list should be as narrow as possible.
      If you write:

   ○ *Plan Science lessons for new unit.*
      Your list won't work. It isn't specific enough.
      What you really need is:

   ○ *Read up on the KS2 science curriculum.*

○ *Read an email from Lauren.*

○ *Talk to Becky about expectations about the curriculum.*

○ *Adapt resources for lesson one from shared drive.*

Often you realise a task is too broad when you put in work towards that thing and realise you still can't cross it off your list. Crucially, the next steps that you – or you and a mentor or coach – have decided will help you go onto the list. Or they get broken down further and go onto the list.

You can then prioritise tasks by importance and by deadline. If the science planning needs to be done by the end of the week, the preparation tasks you've listed are going to have to fit into the time you have on Monday and Tuesday. Larger, more intellectually challenging tasks work better in extended bits of time, your PPA or a day you know you're staying a bit later, whereas quick email tasks can fit in a short gap between lessons or the half-hour you have before a class arrives. With this in mind, it's worth reviewing your list at the start or end of each week. Slot those big tasks in the time you have for them and prioritise developmental, learning-focused activity over admin and email.

A list can give the illusion of productivity as you diligently work your way through it. The substance of your list needs to be right to enable the development and application of knowledge. If your list is all email and printing – things you have to do but aren't going to help you improve – then it will likely fix your attention on altogether the wrong things.

2. Ask *How?*

In one of my early teaching placements, I was unlucky enough to be present the afternoon of a circus skills workshop. Circus performers came in, wowed the children and taught them how to spin plates and juggle. Fire-breathing and sword-swallowing were sadly missing from their repertoire. I spent the day half watching and half frantically planning the next week's lessons. I was pulled from this productive reverie by the unexpected request for teachers to come to the front: 'Now, let's see what your teachers have learned this afternoon'. I may have learned to better attend to the expectations of me when visitors run a workshop but I hadn't learned to spin plates. Students watched pityingly as I repeatedly picked up and dropped a plastic plate after trying and failing to balance it on a long plastic stick.

Plate-spinning is the go-to metaphor to describe what you have to do as a new teacher. Or maybe it's juggling. Anyway, you're going to have to juggle a lot of plates. Lots of ideas from books and suggestions from colleagues sound nice but feel impractical. Where are they going to fit? A crucial conversation you have with those supporting you is about how you balance competing 'priorities'. If you have decided scripting and practising your explanation is your next step but can't figure out where it will fit, ask how. If you want to observe some teachers or book in some co-planning but can't find a time, ask for support to make it happen.

Work with your coach or mentor

A coach's job can feel like it is to critique your practice or tell you what to do, at least early on. These aren't really a coach's job. When we drill down into what a coach is doing, their role is to help you to create a set of mental models, rich in knowledge. Just shifting your view of those supporting you in this way can repurpose the relationship into something all the more powerful.

At times, you might be working with your coach on behaviour management, scripting and rehearsing phrases to use in the classroom. Or studying curriculum materials together to plan for the coming term. Specific actions are decided upon in these meetings: narrate the countdown, define relevant prior knowledge from previous lessons, practise the language of the behaviour policy, script and rehearse your initial explanation. Your job from these actions is to develop knowledge and automate process in order to master those things. But those things aren't ends in themselves.

To understand where current actions fit into a broader picture or your current model, ask questions as you talk through your next steps:

- How does what we're working on now build on what I've done before?
- What alternatives are we ignoring or leaving to focus on this?
- What problems will automating this/knowing this solve?
- What will success here enable me to do next?

Our aim is not the narrow view of an individual technique, another slice of granular development. Our aim is to understand how this task, here and now, fits into the broader mental model we're building, how this focus enables another step towards expertise to be taken.

Identify problems and solutions

Working with a coach early in your career should help you to identify where problems exist and possible ways to approach them. The types of knowledge we've looked at, the lenses we've been developing, should also help you to look at yourself or your classroom and consider the challenges you face and solutions available.

As you consider how to progressively problem solve, note down your thoughts in a notebook or document. You'll do a better job of capturing your thoughts and will make it easier to see how you've done. This process of capture and identification of problems and solutions is a process of using and expanding knowledge.

You begin with knowledge of your current practice. You identify gaps or weaknesses and seek out solutions. Your knowledge of how different solutions work in practice helps you to identify future problems and solutions.

1. Decide the area you want to work in.
   Write down every problem on your mind, every problem you can think of that you're facing currently. Think about every aspect of your current practice – planning, subject knowledge, teaching, assignments, behaviour management, other jobs.
   Your list might look something like this:

   ○ 7x are really slow to settle at the start of lessons.

   ○ Jo is really slow to do what I ask/influencing others.

   ○ Planning for 8 feels hard work/takes ages.

   ○ I don't know enough about Anglo Saxons.

   ○ My explanations all feel like a rambling mess, even the short ones.

   ○ End of lesson routines across classes don't feel tight/controlled.

   ○ Not sure where to start with reading for the next assignment.

   ○ I forget to give clear expectations for task (time/noise level) lots.

   ○ Not sure how to do whole class feedback for Year 10 – so many different errors in their books.

   Notice we're not trying to find solutions yet and we've not decided on an area to work on. Please don't stop here; that would leave you incredibly frustrated.
   How you decide what problem to prioritise from that list is up to you. Decisions about priorities should be driven by what is most time-sensitive but also what you can work on to save yourself time in the future. In our example above, the teacher might choose to focus on planning for Year 8 because that is draining their capacity to deal with anything else – it just takes too much time.

2. Define the problem specifically.
   Knowing there's a problem in the huge area of Year 8 planning doesn't help much. Break it down further:

   ○ Resources on the shared drive take a lot of work to adapt into something I can use.

   ○ I don't have good background knowledge of X.

   ○ I'm overthinking/spending too much time on my planning because behaviour can be difficult, particularly at the start of lessons.

Narrowing it down, the teacher decides they need to make planning more efficient by focusing on background knowledge. It seems to be taking too long because so much of the content needs to be revisited by the teacher before they feel happy to teach it.

Alternatively, behaviour is settled on as the problem, as it often is, but to narrow that down you need to break it into its component parts. There are difficult students in the class but they aren't currently the main issue. The class come into the room boisterously making the starts of lessons a constant battle. The problem is the entry routine.

At times you will proactively search out specificity from your problems; at others you might wait for the narrowest version of a problem to present itself to you as you plan and teach. Whatever you're doing, your job is to be on the lookout for what the *actual* problem is, not a broad category you're unhappy with.

3. Identify possible solutions.

To begin with solutions might mainly come from colleagues, from observation and conversation. Ask as many people as you can, *How would you deal with X?* Remember experts commonly suffer from a blind spot where they struggle to articulate embedded knowledge and automated process. Some answers might frustrate you. Other new teachers, a year or two ahead, often provide a more tangible solution than those with experience. The path you're taking is fresher in their minds.

Alternative questions to ask these colleagues are, *Why do you think I'm struggling with X? What could make X easier for me?* Note down the solutions you come across even if they feel counter-intuitive or unworkable to you. If there are several possible ways of dealing with a problem, order them in terms of how easy they are to implement right now.

4. Test the solutions.

You've selected the solution that seems fastest and easiest to implement. If time spent planning was the problem, perhaps background reading on the topic could help to make quicker decisions about what to leave in (and out) of lesson plans. Your mentor suggests some reading and diligently you go away and do it. Background reading helps you feel confident about the topic but planning still takes an age. Don't panic. Each solution that fails, or only partially succeeds, provides useful knowledge of what actually tackles the problems we're facing.

What's next? You decide to look at how other teachers use the shared resources. You arrange to meet with a colleague and ask them forensically about how these resources translate into their lessons. You watch this happen in their classroom. Slowly, the thinking behind the resources begins to make more sense to you. You trial their approach with a couple of adjustments of your own. Planning time reduces dramatically.

5. Identify what's next.

Planning time reduces. Great. You have a little more time and feel less stressed about those lessons. Progressive problem solving isn't about constantly trying to solve everything at once or about filling up every minute available to you. Instead, it's a recognition that there's another level to what you're facing. If planning has become easier, you could focus on tightening those rambling explanations. Alternatively, you might feel those can wait until you've sorted the classroom routines for this class.

6. Leave some problems for later.

As you develop a list of problems you want to solve, a parallel list of problems you are leaving until later is an important reminder that you can't do everything at once. Talk with your mentor about what can be left and what should be a priority.

Perfection is not possible

I've never been a perfectionist. The problem with problems and lists, with not settling for where you are, is that these things can drive you to feel that nothing is ever good enough. Problems don't exist in your classroom because you're a terrible teacher. Problems exist in every complex environment. The job of the teacher, then, is to cultivate a perspective of the problem solver whilst avoiding a negative fixation on everything that makes you uncomfortable or unhappy about your practice.

Although it's a cliché, it's true that teaching is a marathon not a sprint. You can't rush into the classroom and solve every problem you find there. The list you make to manage your time can and should include those next steps that are going to help you to improve. As you review that list each week, keep checking that you're still focused on finding solutions for problems rather than just clearing a bunch of tasks from a list. Don't settle for *doing the jobs*. Focus on improvement that will make a difference for your students. Manage your frustration with the slow rate of progress at times by keeping track of how you have improved and the problems you have solved.

Perfectionist teachers are often very good at what they do. They may teach thoughtful, engaging lessons. Perfectionists probably also manage behaviour well. They certainly know their students. Eager for the next thing, they devour reading on subject and pedagogy. Workdays for perfectionists extend beyond what might be considered reasonable or healthy. Burnout is a danger but so is a loss of enjoyment or lingering feelings of disappointment. Any road to expertise needs to be lined with stops to rest and refuel.

It's all very well saying that perfectionism can take us in the wrong direction but what can we actually do about it?

1. Stop.

Teaching is a job that we can never complete. Every aspect of it can be refined further. Knowing when we're ready – when a lesson is ready to teach, or when you're ready to give that explanation, or when we're ready to adapt in-lesson to student responses – knowing that with certainty is not always possible. We can feel uncomfortable with finishing a task when we know possible improvements are left. But something has to be left for another day, for another lesson, for another assignment, possibly for good.

Learning to say to yourself, *I could have probably done that better but I've done what I need to* is not easy but it is essential. Initially, it can be difficult to know if you're ready, and it's difficult to let go of preparation activities that make you feel safe and confident. And it is vital to prepare properly so, initially, a mentor, coach or colleague might have to work with you to discuss whether you're ready to stop and move on. Ask, *Am I done with this? Do you think I can stop there? Is this good enough for now?* Whilst others might help you consider these questions initially, their answers should push you on towards independence.

2. Switch off.

I am quite strange in that I will happily read about teaching or my subject in my spare time or on holiday. You don't need to be like this to be a good teacher. In fact, if long-term and sustained improvement is the goal, we need to be able to switch off at least for a time. Constant fixation on the next thing, the next problem, what we need to prep, what we need to get done – all of this is a recipe for burnout.

When I first started teaching, I didn't realise how stressed I was. I emptied Sunday of activity, trying – unconsciously, I think – to slow time before the start of another week. I didn't want to go out. I didn't really want to see or speak to anyone. Monday was this all-encompassing thing. Don't worry, that fear of Monday wasn't permanent. I've realised, over time, that I am happier when I have something, however insignificant, to do or someone to see. Distraction is the wrong way to see these activities that take you away from the worries and the problems and the unknown and the absence of solutions. It isn't distraction; it's just life. Don't give up the stuff of life just because you have to go to work on Monday. This may not be advice you need to hear but don't wait to feel settled before you switch off and do the activities you love and see the people you love. The problems will wait until Monday.

If the final challenge of teaching is accommodating your personal needs, we need to acknowledge, as Mary Kennedy does, that there are a 'variety of ways these challenges can be met'. Of greatest importance is 'finding strategies' to solve them which 'are consistent with [your] personal needs'.[2] How you solve the problems in front of you is up to you.

Notes

1 Kennedy, M. (2016). Parsing the practice of teaching. *Journal of Teacher Education*, 67(1), 6–17.

2 Ibid.

Conclusion

When you're writing a book about what teachers should know, everyone has something they think should be included. Generally, these titbits are about not microwaving fish in the staffroom as well as basic photocopier maintenance. Whilst not unimportant topics, these set the bar a little low for new teachers. You're embarking on a challenging, rewarding intellectual journey. Your knowledge will span from the debates within your subject area or phase to the minutiae of your students. Your understanding will reach back into the recesses of study as well, latching on to your rapid accumulation of current experience.

It would, however, be flippant or dishonest to claim this is a definitive guide of *all* new teachers should know. Specific areas of teaching have been dealt with briefly. Large policy areas have been ignored. This is not because they are unimportant. What to keep in and leave out has kept me up at night as I've chaired internal debates about the most vital knowledge for new teachers.

When such debates between me and myself reached unsatisfactory conclusions, I was comforted by a rather obvious realisation. It's not possible for a book to *give* you or *tell* you everything you need to know. Each part of this book, and each area of knowledge, is setting you off on a path that I can't join you on. These paths start out as little more than dirt tracks. Initial curriculum knowledge is a confusing wilderness that becomes a road that becomes a highway. Where the journey was arduous to begin with, increasing knowledge makes it effortless. Initial steps in behaviour management are steps in a city we don't recognise, one where we don't speak the language. Options overwhelm us. Knowledge gives direction until we can navigate with ease.

Any work we do to develop this knowledge is work to develop our understanding of the landscape of teaching. My hope is that, in reading this book, you have a rough guide, an initial blueprint or roadmap to overcome the first difficulties in navigation in your development as a new teacher. And that, as a new teacher, you recognise that you aren't powerless to find your own way because your development is a personal journey. Others will help, to be sure, but they can't do it for you. They can't turn your subject knowledge into pedagogical content knowledge for

 DOI: 10.4324/9781003281306-25

you. They can't automate processes. They can't get to know your students. But they will help. Their advice shouldn't be ignored.

The threads of our knowledge, if you'll forgive one more metaphor, start frayed and fragile but intertwine and, with time, become a single thick and powerful rope. Initially, like the parts of this book, the knowledge feels disconnected. With time, we see the connections between subject and pedagogy and student until the point where we can't unravel them.

Too often, teachers have to look back at a process they didn't quite understand and realise that progress *has* been made. *I have got better at this.* Development feels implicit and unconscious. My aim has been to clear the fog surrounding this development even just a little bit. I hope that, as you set out on your career-long journey towards expertise, your awareness of the route is a little clearer. I hope that, as it has been for me, teaching is an intellectually rewarding pursuit, enriched by knowledge.

Glossary

Antifragile – The quality of becoming stronger under pressure. From Nassim Nicholas Taleb's *Antifragile*.

Automaticity – A state where a person is able to complete a task automatically, with little strain on mental capacities.

Continuing professional development – A programme of activities, learning and coaching or mentoring focused on professional growth.

Cognitive Load Theory – A theory of learning based on the idea that our minds can only process a limited amount of new information in one go.

Completion Problem – A partially completed task which students are guided through before finishing the task independently.

Deliberate practice – A type of practice focused on a narrow skill, with clear success criteria and opportunities for feedback.

Disciplinary knowledge – Everything students learn about how knowledge is established and revised within a domain.

Element interactivity – The number of different new components or elements of a process a student has to think about during a task.

Exit ticket – A task completed at the end of a lesson to demonstrate what students can do to inform and adapt future teaching.

Extraneous load – The irrelevant, superfluous or unnecessary information to the learning process.

Formative assessment – Any assessment or task that provides the teacher with information that can then be used to adapt teaching.

Hinge question – A question asked at the point where the lesson should move on if, and only if, enough students demonstrate the required understanding.

Intrinsic load – In Cognitive Load Theory, the mental capacity taken up by thinking about the target information or skill to be learned.

Long-term memory – An effectively limitless store of memory that can be held for extended periods of time, even lifetimes.

Mental model – A representation or idea of how something works or how to do something in the real world.

Pedagogical content knowledge – An amalgamation of subject knowledge and pedagogy or the pedagogy of your subject.

Pedagogy – The theory, thinking or method behind our teaching behaviours.

Procedural knowledge – Skill or know-how within subject domain.

Progressive problem solving – The process of solving new and more complex problems in a complex environment (like the classroom). As we become more competent and reach automaticity, we are able to reinvest mental resources in new problems and more complex versions of problems we've already tackled.

Retrieval practice – A process that exploits the Testing Effect through attempting recall without prompts or aids.

Social norms – Standards, rules or common expectations that guide how a group behaves.

Spaced (or distributed) practice – The process of spreading out study or practice sessions in order to benefit retention long term.

The Split Attention Effect – Where students have to split attention between two sources of information (e.g. board and desk, reading a text whilst listening to the text being read).

Substantive knowledge – The content we teach made up of established fact, concept or idea.

The Testing Effect – The observable phenomenon where we remember more of what we are tested or quizzed on compared with other study methods.

The Worked Example Effect – Examples of completed or partially completed problems, questions or tasks, often used for discussion to demonstrate a process to students.

Working memory – The limited amount of information we can hold in our minds during a task.

Index

Printed in Great Britain
by Amazon